JOHN T. SHUMAN, Ph.B. Dickinson College; Ed.D. The
Pennsylvania State University, is Assistant to the Superintendent in charge of Vocational and Adult Education in
Allentown, Pennsylvania. He was formerly a Coordinator
of the Adult Retraining School and Williamsport Technical
Institute, and Assistant Director of the Williamsport Technical Institute.

English for Vocational and Technical Schools

By

JOHN T. SHUMAN

ASSISTANT TO THE SUPERINTENDENT IN CHARGE OF
VOCATIONAL AND ADULT EDUCATION, ALLENTOWN,
PENNSYLVANIA

SECOND EDITION

THE RONALD PRESS COMPANY ⋅ NEW YORK

PREFACE

The purpose of this book is to provide industrial and technical students with a brief but comprehensive survey of the essentials of good English in terms of practical use rather than theoretical mastery of abstract concepts. It is designed primarily as a textbook for a terminal course in applied English for students who are about to go out to work in industry. It is also well suited for use in industrial training programs for those already employed.

My own experience in teaching English to such students has convinced me of the overriding importance of correct motivation. Consequently, in this book skill in communication is developed through examples taken from real experiences in meaningful situations. The student is constantly shown that ability to write and speak good English can make a definite contribution to his vocational competence. The subject matter has been selected in accordance with the interests and needs of those engaged in industrial and technical occupations or in small businesses of their own. All illustrations have been taken from actual industrial and business situations. Names have been changed and identities concealed, but the materials are real. By means of such practical examples and carefully directed questions and problems the student is encouraged to express himself clearly and correctly in letters, reports, discussions, and conferences. Rapid improvement follows as soon as he has been led to put English to use for purposes which he clearly understands and appreciates.

Although the emphasis throughout is on writing and speaking in practical situations, the first section of the book gives a basic grounding in sentence structure, punctuation, vocabulary building, and the fundamentals of good usage. Reference to abstract grammatical concepts is kept to a minimum.

Here, as elsewhere in the book, correct English is absorbed in terms of use rather than learned as theory through rules. The organization of the book allows the greatest possible flexibility. Each chapter represents a complete unit. In motivation and value each lesson is essentially independent of those which precede or follow it. Thus the instructor can present different parts of the subject matter whenever he chooses and in any order which seems suitable for his purposes. At the same time, the cumulative effect of the successive chapters will assure the student a constant growth in his grasp of English as a tool subject.

The materials here presented have been used with a high degree of success in schools and industrial training courses throughout the nation. In preparing the book I have had the help of many people in industry and many teachers in different schools. Thus it reflects the judgment of competent persons in a large variety of fields who have wrestled with the problems of communication and curriculum-making in English. To all who have helped to make this book possible I express my sincere thanks.

JOHN T. SHUMAN

Allentown, Pennsylvania
    January, 1954

CONTENTS

PART I

Minimum Essentials of Good Writing and Speaking

PART II

Applying English to Your Job

PART III

Conducting Business by Correspondence

PART IV

English in Advertising and Selling

PART V

Report Writing

PART I

---

*Minimum Essentials of Good Writing and
Speaking*

HAVE YOU EVER WONDERED WHY YOU SHOULD LEARN TO SPEAK AND WRITE WELL?

You are about to begin the study of English for another school year. During this time you will try to improve yourself so that you can talk, read, and write much more effectively and easily.

Before you start to do even the first work, stop for a few moments and ask yourself: Why should I learn to speak correctly? Is the study of English actually profitable to me?

Then after looking at individuals you know, answer questions such as these for yourself: What successful men do I know? Can they express themselves forcefully and correctly? Would they hold the jobs they do if they could not present their ideas clearly to other men? Is their use of English a help or a hindrance?

Has it ever occurred to you that these successful persons had to learn to express themselves well, and that you can learn to do it also? No one is born with the ability to speak correctly and effectively, just as no one is born with the ability to swim or to operate a machine. Both are skills that must be learned through much practice.

The chapters in this book have been planned to help you learn to use better English. If you follow directions carefully, your English should improve and you should develop skills that will be very helpful. But it is not easy—success in the use of words and sentences and paragraphs comes only through real effort. Success in any undertaking never comes from just wishing; it comes only from regular and systematic work.

TO THE STUDENT

English—Your Basic Skill

Do you expect to live the rest of your life as a hermit in some forest or desert area? Certainly, you don't.

You will probably work with different groups of people and live in a community with many other persons. Since you will be working with and through people, your success will depend on your ability to communicate with them.

Your basic skill then is the ability to organize and express your thoughts and ideas in writing and in speaking so others will understand what you are driving at and can be persuaded. You must talk and write to all those persons with whom you work and live. The ability to speak and write well is important to you whether you work in industry, conduct your own business, or practice a profession.

What Good English Means to You

Recently a graduate of a technical school said to me: "You know, a man feels rather cheap when he suddenly realizes that he can't write a good letter and speak correctly."

Another graduate wrote this letter to his former English instructor:

One thing that I have learned since leaving the school is that as I advance on my job no subject is of more value to me than English. First, I had to use it in writing a number of application letters. Second, I have to use it daily here in the plant in my contacts with my superiors. Third, I have to use it in making short reports on equipment of which I have charge and in writing short messages to the various foremen.

Actually the last thing that I expected to see in a factory was a dictionary. But, believe it or not, my superintendent keeps one on his desk. And he uses it, too.

3

I want to take this opportunity to express to you my appreciation of your efforts to give us a course in English that was practical. I am now certain that any further promotions that I receive in the future will be due in a large measure to my ability to write and to speak well.

Since you use English constantly to interpret and to give instructions, you cannot do without it in your daily work. Sooner or later you will find yourself in a situation in which you will need to speak and to write well; and when the necessity actually arises, you will not have the time to acquire the information that you need. From a handbook you can get mathematical formulas or facts with which you can solve most shop problems easily, from fellow workmen you can secure assistance in doing an especially difficult job, but you cannot buy a book or hire another person to make a good impression for you on your employer or on customers. After all, you must regard your employer as a customer to whom you must constantly sell your services.

Start Now

As a far-sighted student you will want to prepare for the time when making a good impression on others through your speech and your writing will help you in your job. Consequently, toward the end of your technical course, you should study the practical applications of English for two reasons:

1. To learn to use English as a good tool which will help you to advance in your occupation.
2. To learn to express yourself clearly and effectively at work and in all your associations with other people for the personal satisfaction and confidence it gives you.

Remember that though two men may possess equal amounts of technical information and skill, the man who can organize and express his ideas effectively forges ahead while the other frequently remains where he is. With the help of this book, if you choose, you can improve your present writing and speaking.

Chapter I

GET THE MOST OUT OF WORDS

Learn To Use New Words

Persons who possess good vocabularies and who know how to use words correctly generally use good English. Persons with small vocabularies often have difficulty expressing their thoughts clearly. Merely knowing the meaning of a word is not enough; you must be able to use it correctly in a sentence to make your knowledge effective. Although the dictionary will help you do this, you must often go a step further. You must learn to use the word in sentences.

The two methods given here will help you learn to use many new words.

The First Method. Suppose that you wish to learn to use the word *dominant*. You can do this by following these steps:

1. Find a familiar synonym for the word.	*Dominant* Syn.—*principal, chief*
2. Use the synonym you know in a sentence.	Jim's love of money is his *principal* characteristic.
3. Substitute the unfamiliar word (dominant) for the synonym (principal or chief).	Jim's love of money is his *dominant* characteristic.

Thus when you can find a synonym that you know how to use, you can use it in a sentence and then substitute the unfamiliar word for it.

The Second Method. While reading books, magazines, or newspapers, all of us read words with which we are not familiar. One of the most effective methods of developing a larger vocabulary is the keeping of a list of these unfamiliar expressions which we encounter in our daily reading. A small notebook in which to keep such a list is invaluable. However, it is important that you make a list of **groups of words** rather than of single words; for example, instead of listing the word *subsequent* alone, list the expression *subsequent interviews*.

How many of the following words can you explain or use in good sentences?

alleviate	significant	filament
rigors	tedious	amplitude
anonymous	contemporary	transparent
pertinent	admirable	

Now how many of these expressions can you explain or use in sentences?

alleviate pain	contemporary world
rigors of the winter weather	admirable good humor
anonymous benefits	heating filament
pertinent questions	amplitude of the sound waves
significant questions	transparent membrane
tedious evening	

You have probably found that these groups of words are easier to understand and to use in sentences than are single words. Further, these complete expressions also give you more specific and more interesting ideas than do the words listed alone.

Exercise 1. Write ten of the following words in sentences of your own, using the first method:

design	agility	miniature	protracted
avert	obstacle	precise	contour
elicit	improvise	proficient	obscure
aperture	difference	data	memorandum
specific	comprehend	assimilate	technique
apropos	slovenly	invariably	enumerate

Exercise 2. From books, magazines, or newspapers that you read start a list of expressions which you do not understand thoroughly and which you are not in the habit of using. Write one such expression in your notebook each day. **Copy the expression or phrase, not just a word.**

Precision in the Use of Words

Words should be used just as carefully in writing and speaking as tools and instruments are used in the shop and laboratory. For example, a micrometer must be handled properly and accurately to be of any value. If it is not so employed, it is worthless as a precise measuring instrument. Exactly the same thing is true of words. They are of value only to the extent that we use them correctly.

One word is often misused for another. This sometimes happens because words sound or look alike. Confusion often arises because of careless pronunciation, or because the person using the word simply does not know its correct meaning. The activities in this chapter should help you improve your use of troublesome words.

Directions. On the following pages troublesome words are presented in pairs. Study carefully the spelling and the explanation of each word. Then try to supply the correct word in the practice sentence. You may need to change the form of the word slightly to fit it into the sentence correctly. For example, you may find it necessary to add an *s* or an *ed.*

Accept – Except

Accept: To receive a thing offered; to approve; to agree to. I can **accept** no money for this work.
Except: To omit; to exclude; to leave out. No one is **excepted** from these requirements. (*verb*) All may leave **except** Jim. (*preposition*)

Exercise

1. I will .... the contract if I may .... the third condition.
2. Are you taking all examinations .... English?
3. The draft board will not .... him from this draft call.
4. Charles may not .... this amount willingly.
5. This garage will not .... my check.

Affect – Effect

Affect:	To act upon or influence; to pretend. The new rule does not **affect** us.
Effect:	To complete or to accomplish. (*verb*) The police **effected** the capture. The result or consequence. (*noun*) The **effect** of the medicine was noticeable.

Exercise

1. Poor gasoline .... the operation of the engine.
2. The medicine did not .... his heart.
3. The .... of the storm was seen everywhere.
4. His living in a dry climate .... a complete cure.
5. What was the .... of using the new oil?

Among – Between

Among:	Used in connection with three or more things. He divided five dollars **among** them.
Between:	Refers to only two persons or things. He divided five dollars **between** the two boys.

Exercise

1. This strike is a struggle .... the AF of L and the CIO.

2. He found his wrench .... the other tools.
3. The airplane was found .... the trees.
4. The air hose broke .... the second and third cars.
5. You must choose .... these two.

Angry – Mad

Angry:	Indignant; resentful; provoked. He was **angry** with me for leaving.
Mad:	Mentally disordered; insane, as with disease. The little boy ran from the **mad** dog.

Exercise

1. He was .... because you did not wait.
2. The doctor saved the .... man from inflicting serious wounds on himself.
3. The dog has gone .... because of the intense heat.
4. Are you .... with us?
5. What are you .... about?

Beside – Besides

Beside:	By or at the side of. The calipers are **beside** the cloth.
Besides:	In addition to. **Besides** going for a swim, he went for a boat ride.

Exercise

1. She sat .... her mother.
2. .... going to the fair, he went to the city.
3. The dog walked quietly .... the boy.
4. A fine tree stood .... the fence.
5. Ten girls enrolled in the class, ... the twenty boys who were already there.

Fewer – Less

Fewer:	Answers the question **how many;** refers to a smaller number by counting. Each year there are **fewer** opportunities for untrained workers. (How many opportunities?)
Less:	Answers the question **how much;** refers to a smaller quantity by measuring. I am having **less** difficulty with English now. (How much difficulty?)

Exercise

1. .... men reported for work this morning.
2. You are making .... mistakes each day.
3. This problem will require .... effort to solve.
4. He needs .... money and more common sense.
5. .... men than women work in our plant.

Fix – Repair

Fix:	To fasten or attach to something. Can you **fix** this bracket on the wall?
Repair:	To put in good condition again after injury or damage; mend; renovate. I want to get my watch **repaired.**

Exercise

1. The committee failed to .... the responsibility on any other person.
2. We shall have our best mechanic .... your car.
3. That bridge approach should be .... before an accident occurs there.
4. Will you .... that loose strip of wallpaper?
5. John must .... his machine before he can continue his job.

Its – It's

Its:	The pronoun **its** is in the possessive case and must be used to show possession. The dog bumped **its** head on the loose board.
It's:	A contraction for the two words **it** and **is**. The apostrophe shows the omission of the letter **i**. **It's** not time to go home.

Exercise

1. The candy lost .... flavor after a time.
2. .... the poorest excuse that I have seen.
3. The tree is losing .... leaves.
4. James cut the tree before .... branches had died.
5. .... going to rain.

Principle – Principal

Principle:	A fundamental rule; a rule of conduct; a general truth. To be honest is always a good **principle** of conduct.
Principal:	Chief; leading, main; a sum of money. Market Street is the **principal** street in the town.

Exercise

1. Please give the three .... parts of these verbs.
2. James will invest the .... so he may realize 3 per cent interest.
3. Will you play the .... part in the class play?
4. You should observe the .... of the golden rule.
5. The .... will assign the class schedules at the beginning of the school term.

Real – Really

Real:	Actual or genuine. Is that a **real** diamond?
Really:	Actually; answers the question how. He is **really** interested in his work.

Exercise

1. Jim is .... in earnest.
2. Can you recognize a .... diamond when you see it?
3. The suggestion was .... helpful.
4. The clowns were .... funny, and it was a .... treat to watch them perform.
5. The movie was .... good; it was a pleasure to see it.

More Practice in Discrimination

The following is a list of some common words frequently confused.

Explain precisely the difference in meaning between the words in each of the following pairs. Write sentences which indicate the meaning of each.

1. addition edition	6. coarse course	11. formerly formally
2. advise advice	7. device devise	12. grate great
3. all ready already	8. dual duel	13. guess think
4. all together altogether	9. excess access	14. imminent eminent
5. biennial semi-annual	10. export import	15. irritate aggravate

16. lie
    lay

17. persecute
    prosecute

18. personal
    personnel

19. plane
    plain

20. proceed
    precede

21. recipe
    receipt

22. respectively
    respectfully

23. rise
    raise

24. sit
    set

25. stationary
    stationery

26. their
    there
    they're

27. to
    too

28. tool
    instrument

29. vise
    vice

30. your
    you're

Exercise
Develop Your Personal List

You will improve your use of these words if you will place in your personal notebook the words which you confuse. Arrange your information as is done in the boxes on pages 7 to 12 in this chapter.

Chapter 2

USING BETTER ENGLISH

A: AGREEMENT OF VERBS WITH SUBJECTS

1. How Many Do You Mean?

A verb agrees in number with its subject—not with any other word or group of words.

EXAMPLE:

An order for three dozen wrenches was received.

order————————————————→ was

The workmen, as well as the foreman, were injured.

workmen————————————————→ were

*Exercise 1.** In the following sentences select the correct form from the two words in parentheses. Write this form after the proper sentence number.

1. The train (is, are) ready to leave.
2. The string of cars (is, are) waiting on a siding.
3. Most railroad men (belongs, belong) to a union.
4. Train wrecks (was, were) more frequent thirty years ago.
5. Clouds of smoke (billows, billow) from the engine.
6. The United States (is, are) one of the largest countries in the world.
7. The number of automobiles in use (is, are) increasing every year.
8. A list of past employers (is, are) required on the application.
9. The men of the club (meet, meets) every Tuesday night.
10. The scales (was, were) out of balance.

* For each *Exercise* the student should number his answers carefully, the number in each case corresponding with the number of the sentence in the *Exercise*.

14

2. Talking About One or Two Things

Singular subjects joined by *and* take a plural verb.

EXAMPLE:

Jim *and* Bob were here.

Jim + Bob were here.

When *or* is used it refers only to acts the same as a + sign in mathematics; hence Jim *and* Bob means: Two boys were here.

Singular subjects joined by *or* or *nor* take a singular verb.

EXAMPLE:

Jim *or* Bob was here.

Jim was here.

or

Bob was here.

When *or* is used it refers only to the one or the other of the two items named; hence, Jim or Bob means only *one* boy was here, but not both.

When a sentence contains both singular and plural subjects connected by *or* or *nor*, the verb agrees in number with the nearer subject.

EXAMPLE:

Either the vernier caliper *or* the gauges **are** there.

Either the gauges *or* the vernier caliper is there.

Use *are* because the last subject, *gauges*, is plural.

Use *is* because the last subject, *caliper*, is singular.

Exercise 2. In the following sentences select the correct form from the two words in parentheses. Write this form after the proper sentence number.

1. The pitcher and catcher (was, were) talking together in front of home plate.
2. Bill and Joe (is, are) going hunting.
3. Either the end or the halfback (was, were) eligible to receive the pass.
4. Neither trains nor buses (is, are) arriving on schedule today.
5. Neither the cars nor the engine (was, were) derailed in the wreck.
6. (Is, are) John or Bill in line for promotion?

7. Neither the coach nor the players (expect, expects) to lose this game.

8. (Was, were) Harry and Jane at the dance last night?

9. The screens and shutters (was, were) all painted green.

10. Either he or his brothers (knows, know) the path to the hunter's cabin.

3. How Many After *There Is* and *There Are?*

There is should be followed by an expression meaning one thing.

EXAMPLE:

There is only **one reason** for making this trip.

There are should be followed by an expression meaning two or more.

EXAMPLE:

There are **several reasons** for making this trip.

Exercise 3. In the following sentences select the correct form from the two words in parentheses. Write this form after the proper sentence number.

1. There (is, are) too few policemen on the force.

2. Every year several good plays (come, comes) to our theatre.

3. (Was, were) there any good jokes told on the radio program?

4. To judge from what he said, there (occur, occurs) several periods of feeding activity by the fish every day.

5. In the old desk there (was, were) discovered many letters, a few comics, and some old legal papers.

6. There (was, were) some people who died in the flood of '89.

7. There (is, are) too many in the car.

8. There (is, are) many people who do not agree with what I say.

9. (Was, were) there many deer shot this year?

10. I hope there (is, are) a good chance for your son's recovery.

4. The *As Well As* Blunder

As well as, together with, including, in addition to, and similar expressions do not affect the number of the verb.

EXAMPLE:

The woman, as well as the men, **was** injured.

woman———————————→**was**

The expression *as well as the men* has nothing to do with the selection of the verb *was*. The subject is *woman* which is singular; hence, the singular verb *was* must be used.

Exercise 4. In the following sentences select the correct form from the two words in parentheses. Write this form after the proper sentence number.

1. Some valuable antique furniture, besides some old books and rare dishes, (were, was) found in the attic.
2. The three boys, as well as the old man, (is, are) coming this way.
3. The tools, including that wrench, (belong, belongs) to me.
4. The father, with his sons, (was, were) employed at the factory.
5. The engineer, together with the surveyors, (occupy, occupies) this office.
6. The foreman, no less than the men, (is, are) responsible.
7. The tracings, including the one on the table, (belong, belongs) to me.
8. The camera, as well as the flashlight bulbs, (are, is) in the case.
9. My brother, accompanied by some other men, (has, have) taken a fishing trip.
10. Jim, together with the other boys, (has, have) gone to the auditorium.

5. *Don't* or *Doesn't?*

Use *don't* when you mean *do not*; use *doesn't* when you mean *does not*.

EXAMPLES:

He **doesn't** (does not)	I **don't** (do not)
She **doesn't** (does not)	We **don't** (do not)
It **doesn't** (does not)	You **don't** (do not)
John **doesn't** (does not)	They **don't** (do not)

Notice that in each of the above expressions you can substitute *do not* for *don't* and *does not* for *doesn't*.

Exercise 5. Write the correct form (*don't* or *doesn't*) after the proper sentence number.

1. It (don't, doesn't) matter what you wish; we are going anyway.
2. He (don't doesn't) like football games.
3. Jim and I (don't, doesn't) care to go.
4. You and your brother (don't, doesn't) resemble each other.
5. You (don't, doesn't) know the way to our cabin.
6. The children (don't, doesn't) realize the danger from autos.
7. The auto's tires (don't, doesn't) have much tread left on them.
8. (Don't, doesn't) the owner's license have his address on it?
9. The tire and tube that (don't, doesn't) match in size are useless to me.
10. It seems almost a spring day in spite of the snow, (don't, doesn't) it?

6. They Refer to One Thing Only

Subjects such as *either, each, everybody, no one, nobody,* and *neither* are singular and refer to one thing only. Verbs and pronouns used with them must therefore be singular.

each	(one)	⎫
any	(one)	
every	(one)	
either	(one)	
neither	(one)	⎬ Mean one at a time and are singular
anyone		
anybody		
everybody		
somebody		⎭

EXAMPLES:

Each put on his oldest clothes.
Each (one)⟶his
Neither wanted to lose his place in line.
Neither (one)⟶his
Each of the men is an expert mechanic.
Each (one)⟶is

Exercise 6. Select the correct form from the two words in parentheses. Write this form after the proper sentence number.

1. Each of the players did (his, their) best for the team.
2. Everybody in the group volunteered to give (his, their) blood for the transfusion.
3. Each was told to bring (his, their) tools.
4. Anybody who works here (is, are) invited.
5. Either of the men (seem, seems) qualified for the job.
6. Neither of the men (like, likes) the work.
7. Each of the girls (play, plays) badminton well.
8. Anyone who fails to vote (are, is) not a good citizen.
9. Everybody in town (seem, seems) to be at the circus.
10. Neither of the boys (have, has) the ability to run (his, their) father's business.

Exercise 7. In each of the following sentences a personal pronoun has been omitted. Write in a column on your paper the correct forms for the following sentences.

1. Nobody wants to admit that .... has made a mistake.
2. Someone has left .... tools in my locker.
3. Has anybody lost .... micrometer?
4. Neither of them knew what .... wanted.
5. Everyone did as .... was told.
6. Everybody will pay .... own way.
7. Neither can say that .... is not fairly treated.
8. Each of the men must supply .... own tools.
9. Either of the children could help .... mother with her work.
10. This kind of dog sheds .... hair a great deal.

B: VERBS TO WATCH

7. *Lie* or *Lay*?

Lie means to recline or rest.

We **lie** down.

Principal Parts: *lie, lay, (have) lain*

EXAMPLES:

I think that I shall **lie** down.
Last week I **lay** down for an hour each day.
Every day this week I **have lain** down for an hour.

Lay means to place or put some object down. It must be followed by the name of the object put down.

Principal Parts: *lay, laid, (have) laid*

EXAMPLES:

Please **lay** the chart on the desk.
He *laid* the chart on the desk.
He **had laid** the chart on the desk before you called.

Exercise 8. In the following sentences select the correct form from the two words in parentheses. Write this form after the proper sentence number.

1. (Lie, lay) down and rest because you are tired.
2. The book has (laid, lain) on my table all day.
3. I wonder how long it would take to (lie, lay) a mile of railroad track.
4. While my brother (lay, laid) down, I went to the store.
5. If the boards are properly (laid, lain), they will not warp.
6. I (lay, laid) here all day and watched the clouds.
7. In the evening I (lay, lie) aside all cares.
8. The children have (laid, lain) in bed since seven o'clock.
9. The tree (lay, laid) where it had fallen.
10. How long have these tools (laid, lain) here in the rain?

8. *Sit* or *Set?*

Sit means to take a seat, to rest in an upright, sitting position.

Principal Parts: *sit, sat, (have) sat.*

EXAMPLES:

He usually **sits** on a stool.
He **sat** there for an hour.
The dog **has sat** there all day.

Set means to place something, to put it down. We *lay* or *set* things down.

Principal Parts: *set, set, (have) set.*

EXAMPLES:

I **set** the bucket on the rack.
He **set** the hen last week.
They have **set** the box on the truck.

Exercise 9. In the following sentences select the correct form from the two words in parentheses. Write this form after the proper sentence number.

1. Jack (sat, set) the box on the floor.
2. Four people are (sitting, setting) at the table.
3. Who usually (sits, sets) here to rest?
4. I often (sit, set) up late.
5. Jim (sat, set) the box on the floor. Then he (sat, set) on the box.
6. The lad (set, sat) the pitcher outside the door.
7. I must (sit, set) the alarm clock.
8. The house (sits, sets) far back from the street.
9. Please (sit, set) down.
10. Where were you (sitting, setting)?

9. *Rise* or *Raise?*

Rise **means to ascend or get up on its own power.**

Principal Parts: *rise, rose, (have) risen.*

EXAMPLES:

Prices may **rise** rapidly.
The sun **rose** an hour ago.
The sun **has risen** already.

Raise **means to lift or to make move from a lower position.**

Principal Parts: *raise, raised, (have) raised.*

EXAMPLES:

Please **raise** the window.
The men **raised** the beam to the top of the barn.
The maintenance crew **has raised** the engine three inches.

Exercise 10. Number from 1 to 10 on your paper. In the following sentences select the correct form from the two words in parentheses. Write this form after the proper sentence number.

1. The sun has (risen, raised) above the horizon.
2. He quickly (raises, rises) his head.
3. They (raised, rose) the heavy weight from the floor.
4. The river (rises, raises) every spring when the ice melts.
5. His salary has been (raised, risen) twice during the year.
6. Dick (raised, rose) to the opportunity.
7. The invalid slowly (raised, rose) himself in his bed.
8. The plane (raised, rose) slowly.
9. The creeks (raised, rose) until they overflowed.
10. The mercury was (raising, rising) rapidly.

10. *Let* or *Leave*

Let means to allow or to permit.

Principal Parts: *let, let, let.*

EXAMPLES:

I often **let** my dog run on the lawn.
He has **let** Jim take a trip.

Leave means to go away from or to allow to remain.

Principal Parts: *leave, left, left.*

EXAMPLES:

He could not **leave** his sick partner.
He **left** his books in the shop.

Exercise 11. In the following sentences select the correct form from the two words in parentheses. Write this form after the proper sentence number.

1. Please (leave, let) me go early.
2. The teacher (left, let) us go at two o'clock.
3. If you will (leave, let) us alone for five minutes, we shall finish.
4. It is dangerous to (leave, let) loaded firearms around the cabin.
5. Will your foreman (let, leave) you go?

11. When To Use *Have, Has,* and *Had*

Always use *have, has,* or *had* with the third principal part of a verb.

EXAMPLES:

They **have** eaten *or* **had** eaten
She **has** seen   *or* **had** seen
I **have** gone   *or* **had** gone
He **has** done   *or* **had** done

Exercise 12. Select the correct verb form for each sentence.

1. Has John .... to town for the axe?
2. He has .... three oranges during the lunch hour.
3. James has .... his work very well.
4. Fred had .... his dinner before the accident.
5. Have you .... for a drink since noon?
6. He has .... the last movie at the theater.
7. Henry had .... before the bell rang.
8. The cow has .... all the grass in the pasture.
9. Has the mechanic .... his work well?
10. John has .... all the books in the library.

Exercise 13. Write ten sentences using *have, has,* or *had* in front of the past participle of ten verbs from the following list.

12. Principal Parts of Verbs You Should Know

Present	Past	Past Participle
am	was	been
begin	began	begun
blow	blew	blown
burn	burned	burned
come	came	come
choose	chose	chosen
dive	dived	dived
do	did	done
drag	dragged	dragged
drink	drank	drunk
drive	drove	driven
eat	ate	eaten
fall	fell	fallen
fly	flew	flown
forget	forgot	forgotten
go	went	gone

Present	Past	Past Participle
give	gave	given
grow	grew	grown
hang	hung	hung
hang	hanged	hanged
know	knew	known
lie	lay	lain
ride	rode	ridden
ring	rang	rung
rise	rose	risen
run	ran	run
see	saw	seen
shrink	shrank	shrunk
sing	sang	sung
sink	sank	sunk
speak	spoke	spoken
spring	sprang	sprung
steal	stole	stolen
swim	swam	swum
take	took	taken
throw	threw	thrown
tear	tore	torn
wear	wore	worn
write	wrote	written

C: PROBLEMS WITH ADJECTIVES AND ADVERBS

13. Words Ending in -ly

Words that answer the question *how* usually end in -ly.

EXAMPLE:

He has been acting **queerly.**

The word *queerly*, which ends in -*ly*, answers the question: *How* has he been acting?

Exercise 14. In the following sentences select the correct form from the two words in parentheses. Write this form after the proper sentence number.

1. Your watch must be running (slow, slowly).
2. Your watch must be (slow, slowly).

3. We worked (steadily, steady) all morning.
4. The car was traveling very (rapid, rapidly).
5. He spoke (distinct, distinctly).
6. The workers became (quiet, quietly) very (quickly, quick).
7. This report does not seem (correct, correctly) to me.
8. He made the repairs (quick, quickly).
9. It was (real, really) hard for him to get that much money together.
10. He lifted the table (easy, easily).

14. Words That Describe *Taste, Feel, Smell, Sound,* and the Like

Words that describe *taste, feel, smell, sound, appearance,* and the like do not end in *-ly.* These are adjectives and follow verbs which do not indicate action.

EXAMPLES:

The peach tastes **bitter**.	*Bitter* describes peach. It is a *bitter* peach.
He looked **angry**.	*Angry* describes man. The sentence really means: He has an *angry* appearance.
He looked **angrily** at us.	Here *angrily* is used because it answers the question **how** he did something.

Exercise 15. In the following sentences select the correct form from the two words in parentheses. Write this form after the proper sentence number.

1. This board feels [is] (smooth, smoothly).
2. The engine is running (smooth, smoothly).
3. The flower smells (sweet, sweetly).
4. That salad tastes (good, well).
5. Delivery men usually sound their horns (loud, loudly) at this intersection.
6. Bill felt (bad, badly) about the incident last night.
7. You look (hungry, hungrily).
8. They looked (hungry, hungrily) toward the table.
9. He felt the oil (suspiciously, suspicious).
10. He tasted the hot coffee (careful, carefully).

D: PROBLEMS WITH PRONOUNS

15. Choosing Between *I* and *Me, We* and *Us, He* and *Him,* etc., Using the Pronoun as Subject

Two forms of these pronouns are frequently confused:
"*I*" Family (Nominative), *I, we, he, she, they*
"*Me*" Family (Objective), *me, us, him, her, them*

Members of the "*I*" Family are used as subjects. Members of the "*Me*" Family are never used as subjects.

If you keep in mind what you know to be correct, you can easily train yourself to use these various forms correctly.

A simple procedure which you apply to determine the correct form is:

1. Write each noun or pronoun in a separate sentence.

He returned to work. I returned to work.

2. Combine them into one sentence, using the same pronoun forms.

He and I returned to work.

Now let us determine the correct form in the following sentences:

1. Write as two separate sentences.

Jim and (she, her) are going to the dance.
Jim is going to the dance. She is going to the dance.

2. Combine into one sentence using the same forms.

Jim and she are going to the dance.

Using the Pronoun as Object of a Verb

We seem never to make mistakes in such sentences as the following where only one pronoun is used:

The suit fits **me**.   The showers soaked **us**.

But when two pronouns, or a noun and a pronoun, are objects of the same verb, many persons carelessly use the incorrect form of the pronoun.

EXAMPLE:

Wrong The foreman hired Jim and **I.**
Right The foreman hired Jim and **me.**

1. Write the original sentence as two sentences.

The foreman hired **Jim.** The foreman hired **me.**

2. Combine these two sentences into one, using the same forms of the pronouns.

The foreman hired **Jim** and **me.**

EXAMPLE:

Wrong The headlights revealed **we** and **they.**
Right The headlights revealed **us** and **them.**

If you wish to be certain about the correct form in these situations, follow the simple procedure given above:

1. Written as two sentences.

The headlights revealed **us.** The headlights revealed **them.**

2. Written as one sentence.

The headlights revealed **us** and **them.**

Exercise 16. Supply the correct form of a personal pronoun in the blank space in each of the following sentences:

1. In a few minutes Jim and .... are going swimming.
2. Dad says that you and .... may go to the game.
3. He and .... went to work.
4. Jack and .... came home.
5. The foreman and .... quit early.
6. No one knows better than ....
7. .... and .... traveled together.
8. Harry, Jane, and .... went together.
9. That seems strange to you and ....
10. Neither the superintendent nor .... was able to find the mistake.
11. George hit .... and .... accidentally.

12. The flying glass struck .... and ....
13. Will you show .... how to install the battery?
14. The wind was so strong that it blew .... across the street.
15. Tell .... and .... to get their tickets at the office.

Exercise 17. In each of the following sentences there are two words in parentheses. Only one of the words is correct. Select the correct pronoun form in each sentence.

1. The police caught (they, them).
2. We want (she, her) and you to come to the meeting.
3. The rain soaked (him, he) and (I, me).
4. You must be a good toolmaker to satisfy the superintendent and (me, I).
5. The teacher gave Jim and (we, us) these problems to solve.
6. The manager decided that (she, her) and (he, him) should do the work after quitting time tonight.
7. Mary and (I, me) are going to see Sarah and (he, him).
8. As soon as Joe arrives, I shall invite (he, him) and his father to eat with us.
9. Will you go with Martha and (I, me) to the football game?
10. They have invited Dick and (she, her) to the party.

16. Choosing Between *I* and *Me*, *We* and *Us*, *He* and *Him*, etc.

Using the Pronoun as Object of a Preposition

Members of the "*Me*" Family (objective case) are used as objects of prepositions.

	Prepositions		"*Me*" Family (*Objective Case*)
After such words as	to toward from about except of between in for	**Use**	me him her us them

EXAMPLES:

Every one was there **except** you and (he, him)
Every one was there **except** you.
Every one was there **except** him.
Every one was there **except** you and him.

When you omit one of the pronouns, you will use the correct form of the other practically every time. Follow the steps given in the example when you do the exercise given below.

Exercise 18. Which words in parentheses would you use in each of the following sentences?

1. The package was addressed to (he, him) and (I, me).
2. I saw both (she, her) and (he, him) at the dance last night.
3. Will you please pay the money to (he, him) and (I, me)?
4. It makes little difference to either (she, her) or (we, us).
5. Charles went to the game with father and (I, me).
6. Nothing whatsoever was done to keep the property in good condition until you and (I, me) bought it.
7. Boys like Howard and (he, him) are well suited for outdoor work.
8. Every one looked at him except Carol and (we, us).
9. Between you and (I, me) the whole interview was unsatisfactory.
10. Gregory sent a telegram for (they, them) to meet him.

17. What Is Used After *Is, Are, Was, Were,* etc.?

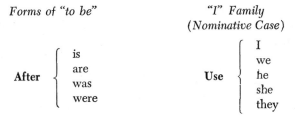

Forms of "to be"		*"I" Family* (*Nominative Case*)
After {	is are was were	**Use** {	I we he she they

Many persons today say *It was me, It was her,* etc. Although these expressions are accepted "on the street corner," they are not accepted as standard by educated people. If you will memorize the above outline, you will find that it will help you to use these forms correctly.

Memorize the following examples:

It is I.	It is she.	It is we.
It was I.	It was he.	It was they.

Exercise 19. In the following sentences select the better form from the two words in parentheses. Write this form after the proper sentence number.

1. Did you think that it was Joe? No, it wasn't (he, him).
2. It was (he, him) without a doubt, who cut his initials in the tree.
3. Bill, is that you? Yes, it is (I, me).
4. Would you buy more insurance if you were (I, me)?
5. Does the manager think the last girl was (she, her)?
6. Among the persons present were (he, him) and (she, her).
7. It was (I, me).
8. Evidently it was (she, her) instead of her sister.
9. When I asked, "Who is there?" she replied, "It's only (me, I)."
10. Is it (he, him)?

18. What After *Than* and *As?*

After *than* or *as* supply the missing or omitted words to determine what pronoun forms to use.

You are taller **than** (I, me).
You are taller **than** I am.
You are taller **than** I.

"You are taller *than* I am" is the complete sentence.

"You are taller *than* I" is a shortened form of the complete sentence. Merely shortening a sentence is no reason for changing the form of the word (pronoun) at the end of the sentence. For example, would you say, "You are taller *than* me am"? Certainly you wouldn't, but you would say, "You are taller *than* I am"; and this is the correct form even though the word *am* is omitted at the end.

Exercise 20. In the following sentences select the correct form from the two words in parentheses. Write this form after the proper sentence number.

1. They were just as fortunate as you and (I, me).
2. You were promoted sooner than (he, him).
3. I thought that you were as old as (she, her).
4. We were more willing than (they, them) to make the trip.
5. Betty says that you helped her much more than (they, them).
6. I played during the entire game also, but the captain complimented Fred more highly than (I, me).
7. I played during the entire game also, but Fred deserves more credit than (I, me).
8. They called the girls sooner than they called (we, us) boys.
9. You are as good a student as (he, him).
10. He likes this kind of work better than (I, me).

19. When To Use *Who* or *Whom*

Many persons do not know when to use *who* or *whom* correctly. If you will study carefully the explanation given here, you will soon learn when to use each of these forms.

"I" Family	"Me" Family
Nominative Forms	*Objective Forms*

I
we
he   } = **who**
she
they

me
us
him   } = **whom**
her
them

Look closely at the diagram above. Remember that *who* corresponds to *I, we, he, she, they*; that is, when one of these forms can be used *who* can be used there also.

Whom corresponds to *me, us, him, her, them*; that is, *whom* can be substituted for any one of these forms in a sentence.

That is a very easy method for selecting either *who* or *whom*, isn't it? Now let us see how it works in actual practice.

EXAMPLE:

Should **who** or **whom** be used? .... was at the dance?
Use **he** or **him** instead. **He** is   **He** was at the dance.
selected since we know that is
correct.

Since **who** corresponds to **he,** substitute **who** for **he.**	**Who** was at the dance?

A MORE DIFFICULT EXAMPLE:

Who or **whom?**	(**Who-Whom**) do you wish to see?
Reverse the sentence and use one of the forms of the "I" or the "Me" Family.	Do you wish to see **her?**
Since **whom** corresponds to **her,** substitute whom for her.	Do you wish to see **whom?**
Place **whom** at the beginning to improve the sound of the sentence.	**Whom** do you wish to see?

Exercise 21. Use *who* or *whom* in each of the following sentences:

1. I want to see the clerk .... sold me this radio.
2. McDonald is a man .... I wouldn't trust.
3. Jim Smith is a man .... can be trusted.
4. The man .... was my partner has failed.
5. The man .... I worked with last year has failed.
6. This pie is a credit to the woman .... made it.
7. It was Harry .... I met at the convention.
8. Don't invite some one .... I do not know.
9. This is the mechanic about .... I spoke.
10. .... shall I ask about his bill?
11. .... do you wish to see?
12. May I ask for .... you are waiting?
13. Mr. Gregory, ... is head of the service department now?
14. I didn't know .... you talked to.
15. May I ask .... got the job?

Chapter 3

WRITING GOOD SENTENCES

What a Sentence Is

A sentence is a group of words that makes a complete statement or that asks a question. The following sentence makes a complete statement: *We dislike sending you letters about your overdue account.* The next sentence asks a question: *Do they have a course in developing the sense of humor?*

Sometimes sentences are spoken and written in shortened forms. This is done when words are dropped and the speaker and the listener understand clearly the shortened form. For example, you do not say, *You come in,* but instead, *Come in.* Here the word *you* is omitted, yet the sentence is perfectly clear because the person to whom you speak knows exactly what is meant.

Exercise 1. Determine which of the following groups of words do not make complete statements and which groups make complete statements. Those which do make complete statements are sentences. Those which do not make complete statements are not sentences. Try to add something to each incomplete sentence to make it complete.

1. Referring to your letter of February 9.
2. I shall be glad to hear from you.
3. Will you please let us hear from you?
4. We assure you that we dislike sending you letters about overdue bills as much as you dislike receiving them.
5. If, however, the account is correct.
6. I am enclosing an outline of the service.
7. Very interesting.
8. One study which was made.

9. Should I borrow fifty dollars to pay the bill?
10. As soon as you have time.

Recognizing a Sentence

Many persons have not learned to divide sentences in the proper places. The examples and practice exercises that follow are intended to show how poor that kind of writing is and to give you some experience in writing sentences that say or ask only one thing.

Two sentences run together:

I do not know why the paper bill is so large Shade's work was finished some time ago.

Two different ideas are expressed here. First: *I do not know why the paper bill is so large.* Second: *Shade's work was finished some time ago.* Since these two ideas have nothing to do with each other, they should be written as two separate sentences.

I do not know why the paper bill is so large.
Shade's work was finished some time ago.

Exercise 2. Write the following expressions as sentences, using the words exactly as they are written here:

1. Not a cent has been collected should I borrow fifty dollars to pay the bill?
2. I do not know whether Jack sent you five dollars Monday evening he borrowed some money from me so he must be broke.
3. I recommend that you avail yourself of our special school shop membership service I am enclosing an outline of this service.
4. According to the records we have, you have not paid for the books if there is anything wrong with this record, will you please sit down right now and write us.
5. I feel sure that you will agree that our suggestions are constructive as soon as you have had time to consider them, I shall be glad to have you write me your frank reactions to them.
6. The foreman, in all fairness to the worker, should try to give him the opportunity to qualify for a better job once he has become skilled on his present job and is still ambitious to advance it is certainly to

the company's advantage to have every competent worker advance to the best job he can hold.

7. A capable foreman can easily develop his ability as a teacher however there are a few fundamental principles which he must master and apply automatically when he instructs men on the job.

8. Have you ever seen a "shooting star" those bright objects which shoot across the night sky are not stars at all they are actually meteors which are too small to be seen by astronomers and are visible only after they drop into the earth's amosphere at a terrific speed.

9. The human brain operates something like an electronic computing machine it contains millions of short nerve-lengths comparable to wires and millions of nerve connections comparable to switches the workings of this complex system are not fully understood but we do know that electrical impulses pass through it at a very regular speed of four hundred feet per second it is the passage of these impulses that constitutes our thinking.

10. My family lived in grandfather's house when I was a boy he impressed us early with the importance of learning to do things for ourselves he told my brother and me that he would help us acquire tools or materials to make things with but would never give us money to buy ready-made playthings he engaged a professional carpenter-mechanic to teach us how to make things properly he insisted too that we keep our tools in good shape for he felt that one who would neglect his tools was likely to neglect other important things as well.

Grandfather himself had always had a knack with his hands when he was a small boy in Peekskill, N. Y. his family was so poor that they were unable to afford shoes for their children one day young Peter brought home an old shoe he had found and took it apart to see how it was made then he ran errands and did chores until he had enough pennies to buy some leather needles and thread he succeeded in making himself a pair of shoes—not good ones but far better than nothing after a few more attempts he was making shoes for the whole family.*

Saying Two Things in One Sentence

Sometimes two statements are made about the same thing so that the person who reads the sentence will think of the two statements together. In cases of this kind the two statements are connected with such words as *and, but, or,* and *nor.* A

* Condensed from Edward R. Hewitt, *Those Were the Days* (New York: Duell, Sloan & Pearce, Inc., 1943).

comma is placed before the connecting word when two complete statements are so combined. In the following example, the sentence contains two statements, but each statement refers to the same unpaid bill.

We have now called your attention to your unpaid account several times without result, *and* we are wondering whether there is some mistake on our part.

NOTE: *Either-or* and *neither-nor* may also combine related ideas into one sentence. Example:

Either a liquid wood filler can be used, *or* a coat of shellac can be applied.
Neither a coat of liquid wood filler can be used, *nor* can a coat of shellac be applied.

Things you have learned thus far about combining two ideas in one sentence:

1. It is possible to combine in one sentence two statements when they apply to the same thing.
2. Words used to combine statements into one sentence are: *and, but, for, yet, or, nor, either-or, neither-nor.*
3. The comma is placed before these connecting words when they connect two complete statements.

Exercise 3. Write a sentence for each of the following, each one containing two complete statements:

1. A sentence with *and.*
2. A sentence with *but.*
3. A sentence with *or.*
4. A sentence with *either-or.*
5. A sentence with *neither-nor.*

Emphasizing the Important Idea

Jim threw down his tools and walked out of the shop.

In the above sentence the word *and* may be compared with the equals sign in mathematics; that is, when *and* connects two complete statements it makes both of the statements of equal importance.

Jim threw down his tools = (Jim) walked out of the shop.

Actually, Jim's walking out of the shop and quitting his job is more important than his throwing down the tools, but in the sentence above both ideas are expressed as if they were of equal importance. That Jim's walking out of the shop is the more important idea can be shown by making the unimportant idea an incomplete statement and the important idea a complete statement.

Original	Revised
ɹım threw down his tools and walked out of the shop.	*After* Jim threw down his tools, he walked out of the shop.
	Throwing down his tools, Jim walked out of the shop.

Notice that emphasizing the main idea also tends to make the thought of the sentence more direct and clear. Three methods by which you may be able to emphasize the main idea are:

1. Begin the unimportant idea with a word ending in *-ing*.
2. Begin the unimportant idea with words such as *who, which, that,* etc.
3. Begin the unimportant idea with words such as *since, because, as soon as, as, until, if, although, while, unless, provided,* etc.

Exercise 4. Change the following sentences so that the important idea is emphasized in each.

1. Walter read your letter and decided that he ought to do what you suggested.
2. As you know, I am new at supervisory work, and what you said was very helpful to me.
3. We have called your attention several times to your unpaid account without result, and we are beginning to wonder whether there is some mistake on our part.

4. This is the best buy that we have ever seen and we urge you to take advantage of this opportunity and inform us by return mail if you care to secure the machine.

5. We would like to know if you can help us with our electric welding problem and lend us a generator for a short time.

6. I lifted myself and the camera on an awning and I crawled gingerly along the sagging canvas until I was able to lean right over the sidewalk.

7. Our team made a tremendous effort, crossing the goal line just as the whistle blew.

8. I began to increase the speed when the turning tool broke.

9. Business is increasing. We will need three new clerks.

10. Mr. DeWald is an expert mechanic and he is foreman in the toolroom.

Combining Short Sentences

It is poor practice to write several short sentences when the thought of all of them can be expressed as one complete thought in a single sentence. When this is the situation, it is best to combine them into one sentence. Here again the important idea should be given as a complete statement and the less important ideas as incomplete statements which explain the main idea.

Childish	*Better*
The boy who is assigned to toolroom duty should report for work at 8:35. If he can't do this, he should report as soon as possible after this time. He should do this so that he is ready to hand out checks and tools to those who may want to start work early.	The boy who is assigned to toolroom duty should report for work as near 8:35 as possible, so that he is ready to hand out checks and tools to those who want to start work early.

Exercise 5. Combine the sentences of each of the following groups into a single sentence. You may omit or rearrange words, but do not omit any ideas.

1. We accepted the job for two reasons: First, we did not have much work in the shop. Then, we would like to get more work from the same company.

2. This is a good typewriter. And since that's so, I can't understand why it doesn't work better.

3. There are many bad accounts on our books. Some can be collected and others cannot be. This is the case because a number of small business men were extended credit and they didn't have any capital.

4. The offices are in a small building. This building is in front of the main factory building. The factory building is a brick structure, five stories high. The manufacturing is done on the four upper floors of this building, and the packing and shipping are done on the first floor.

5. Requisitions for material or stock must be filled out properly by the workman. Each requisition must be approved and initialed by the foreman. It must then be presented to the clerk in charge of supplies. After the requisition is filled, the clerk will file the application.

Misplaced Words

Sometimes a sentence is not clear because a word which explains another is not close enough to the word it explains.

Poor: I *only* heard about the accident yesterday.
Better: I heard about the accident *only yesterday.*

Since *only* explains *yesterday, only* should be placed as close to *yesterday* as possible.

Exercise 6. Change the order of words in the following sentences so that each word or expression is as close as possible to the word it explains:

1. As we only had fifty cents, we sat in the balcony.

2. Just then I saw a man standing in front of the lathe wearing a pair of clean blue overalls.

3. The superintendent decided to give a bonus to the man doing the most accurate work, amounting to ten dollars.

4. I couldn't even lift the beam six inches.

5. A man should not be allowed to operate this machine, who cannot read blueprints.

6. The fire started in a pile of oil-soaked rags which had been used for cleaning under the locker.

7. I enjoyed the fishing as much as any feature of the trip for my part.

8. He drove along the street in an old car eating an ice cream cone.

9. The farmer who drove us to father's cabin hid a fishing rod with which he expected to fish in one of the boxes at the lake.

10. We started the foundation for the new house which will have a length of forty feet on June 1.

Exercise 7. Explain how the meaning of each of the following sentences may be changed by inserting the word in parentheses in either blank.

1. The wind .... blew .... all the telephone poles down. (almost)

2. Jim .... lost .... all his money. (nearly).

3. I .... looked at .... one tool. (just).

4. The girl .... nodded .... to Charles. (only)

5. I've .... finished .... the last job. (just)

Dangling Expressions

Frequently a sentence is not clear because it contains words which do not explain anything in the sentence. Example:

While standing on the scaffold, a loose brick fell and struck him.

Was the loose brick standing on the scaffold? Certainly not. What the writer means is:

While the bricklayer was standing on the scaffold, he was struck by a falling brick.

Exercise 8. Rewrite the following sentences, making them as clear as possible.

1. On entering the shop a large airplane engine is seen.

2. The blueprints should be followed exactly, checking each operation carefully.

3. Jumping across the boards, his foot caught in a bent nail.

4. While finishing the job last night, the telephone suddenly rang.

5. While riding to work on his bicycle, a truck hit him.

6. After slicing the bacon, the coffee was put on to boil.

7. Walking up the road a dense smoke was seen above the trees.

8. By flying over the water, submarines can easily be located.

9. The car ran better after adjusting the carburetor.

10. While sleeping in the tent the mosquitoes bit me badly.

Uncertain Reference

Sometimes a sentence is not clear because certain words do not refer definitely and clearly enough to the proper words in the sentence.

Original	*Revised*
John then told his father that his tools were lost.	John then said, "Father, your tools are lost."
A night watchman should never sleep while on duty; that is very dangerous.	A night watchman should never sleep while on duty; such negligence is very dangerous.

Exercise 9. Rewrite the following sentences so that they are clear:

1. Walter went to the store with his brother where he bought a micrometer.

2. Ed met Gerald on the way home. He offered to pay him for his trouble.

3. He dropped all our food in the mud which he was bringing to camp.

4. John spoke to the foreman, and he was very angry.

5. A box stood near the machine which served as a seat.

6. After riding with my brother in the airplane, I decided that I wanted to be one.

7. The shop sections are so large that the instructors can hardly learn their names.

8. He returned the magazine to the library which he had read.

9. The foreman changed the adjustment on the machine. It was very satisfactory.

10. Jim has poor health. He is ambitious and industrious, and his intelligence is above the average. This makes him a poor apprentice.

Shift in Construction

Similar sections of the same building always have the same type of construction. In a sentence two parts that have the same relation to the rest of the sentence should have the same form. Remember that *and* and *or* really have the force of equality signs and the expressions on either side of these words should have the same construction. This is known as parallel construction. Example:

The mechanic began *to work* and *grumbling* loudly.

On the one side of *and* is the verb form *to work*, but on the other side is a word ending in *-ing*. The expressions on both sides of *and* should be formed alike, as in the revised sentences.

The mechanic began *to work* and *to grumble* loudly.
The mechanic began *working* and *grumbling* loudly.

Original	*Revised*
I decided *to attend* evening school and *on learning* to read blueprints.	I decided *to attend* evening school and *to learn* to read blueprints.

Exercise 10. Rewrite the following sentences, making similar parts of the same sentence the same construction.

1. I saw the demonstrations last year and have gone again this year.

2. I can't decide whether to take machine shop practice or if drafting is better.

3. My boss insists on our visiting the plant and to go immediately.

4. It was very interesting to see how carefully they worked and their speed.

5. He seemed interested in his job and to have skill in doing it.

6. You have three duties:

    1. Issuing tools.
    2. To collect the tools.
    3. Check attendance.

7. Transport planes carry passengers and mail is carried also.

8. Charles wants to be a toolmaker and specializing on lathe work.

9. Make us a box ten inches long, six inches wide, and eight inches in depth.

10. Please help us by signing the card and then mail it.

Building Sentences by Adding Definite and Interesting Details

Sounds, colors, smells, smiles, an angry word by somebody, twenty-five cents in your pocket, missing a home run or a touchdown by a few seconds or inches, a new suit of clothes—your life and my life are made up of little things such as these. It is these details that make life colorful. Yet when you talk, do you talk about the little things that are interesting? When you write a letter, do you tell about the unusual details of your trip? You should, because it is the details, the specific things that make stories and letters interesting. Let us see what a big difference a few interesting details make in a sentence.

EXAMPLES:

An uninteresting sentence:	We finally reached our camp. (This sentence is uninteresting because it doesn't tell us such things as When? How? Under what circumstances?)
The same sentence with details added:	After a long, hot paddle in the leaking canoe, we finally reached our camp at the mouth of the river.
An uninteresting sentence:	Smoke came from the blaze.
Questions about details:	What kind of smoke? What kind of blaze? How much smoke?
An interesting sentence with these details added:	Clouds of black, sooty smoke poured from the high building and settled on the streets below while orange-red flames and sparks shot toward the sky.

Exercise 11. Here are some rather short uninteresting sentences. Try to rewrite each so that it is more interesting.

1. Then Buxton stole second base.
2. The building burned this morning.
3. Jim made a table.
4. We just bought a new radio (or TV).
5. We were camping this summer.
6. The pilot had to make a landing with his plane.
7. The union is on strike.
8. My brother bought a bat.
9. We decorated the Christmas tree.
10. The soldier wore several decorations.

Exercise 12. Write five sentences about things you have seen, done, or experienced. Try to include some interesting and descriptive details in each sentence.

Variety of Expression Is the Goal

If writing is to be interesting as well as clear and correct, the writer must achieve variety of expression. Sentences in a paragraph should be different: that is, sentences should vary in length; they should begin with different kinds of words, etc. These hints may aid you to secure variety:

1. Do not begin two successive sentences with the same word or words having the same sound.
2. Avoid the same construction in two successive sentences except to show contrast.
3. Vary the length of sentences.
4. Do not repeat the same word too often. Use a synonym.

Chapter 4

BUILDING A GOOD PARAGRAPH

The main thing generally observed about a paragraph is that it is indented. The indention is merely a device to attract attention. It is a signal to the reader that a new topic begins at that point.

What a Paragraph Is

A paragraph, however, is more than an indention. A paragraph consists of a group of sentences all explaining a single topic or idea. Each paragraph contains all that the writer wants to say about one idea. This idea, of course, is only one small part of a much larger topic which is the subject of the paper or the letter. The following selection may help you understand better just what a paragraph is:

SENTENCES, THEN, LIKE BANANAS, GROW IN BUNCHES. THESE BUNCHES ARE PARAGRAPHS. As the shape of each banana is partly determined by its place in the bunch, so the build of each sentence will depend upon what it has to do in the paragraph. And this is true of the paragraph that narrates as well as of the paragraph that explains. Each has a unity of its own, but each is part of a larger unity, the unity of the whole essay or of the whole story. To study any sort of paragraph we must catch it by its stem, its subject, and hold it up. As we look at it thus hanging down, we can judge of the fitness of its parts and learn how to make our own paragraphs hang together.*

In the above paragraph Smith tells us that a paragraph is not just a bunch of sentences, but rather a group of related sentences all dealing with the same subject. Each sentence

---

* C. Alphonso Smith, *What Can Literature Do for Me?* (New York: Doubleday, Doran & Co., Inc.).

presents some detail that is closely related to the topic and helps to explain it just as each banana hanging to its stem helps round out and complete the bunch.

The Topic Sentence

Notice that the author stated the subject of his paragraph in the first two sentences. By so doing he found it easier to write other thoughts closely related to the central idea given at the very beginning. *The sentence which states the main idea of a paragraph is called the topic sentence.* The topic sentence can be placed at the beginning, at the end, or within the paragraph. However, it is usually easier to write a good paragraph if the topic sentence is placed first and is as short as possible.

In other words, the topic sentence tells the reader at the beginning of a piece of writing what he will read about in the following sentences. For example, a topic sentence for a paragraph in a paper on fuels might say to him: "In this paragraph we will discuss the (effect of heat on petroleum) . . ."

Here is an example of a topic sentence:

The microphone changes sound into electrical impulses.

The paragraph can then go on to explain how this is done.

Exercises. In each of the following paragraphs find the topic sentence and copy it:

(1)

Heat acts upon petroleum exactly as a hammer acts upon stone. It breaks it up. The pieces are called benzine, gasoline, kerosene, etc. These pieces are very large and complex, chemically speaking. It was found that by applying heat under pressure, petroleum could be "cracked up" into much smaller pieces. As far back as 1860, chemists were trying to devise ways to apply heat to petroleum under pressure, but it was not until the automobile demand for gasoline created a real crisis that any serious industrial effort was made to "crack up" kerosene and similar heavy oils into lighter gasoline. William M. Burton, a noted chemist of the Standard Oil Company, worked for years on the cracking idea to obtain more gasoline and in 1913 secured a patent for a cracking process which is used extensively at the present time by the Standard Oil Company. It marks one of the milestones in the history of petroleum-refining.—Ernest Greenwood, *Prometheus U. S. A.*, Harper & Bros.

(2)

If two surfaces could be held apart by some material which permitted both surfaces to slide past it much more readily than the two surfaces under consideration, the friction would be much reduced. That is the function of lubricating oil. A steel shaft could not easily revolve in a bearing because of the friction between the steel and the bearing. By inserting a film of oil between the bearing and the steel shaft, the two metals are held apart and the shaft revolves freely. The oil fills a clearance space of several thousandths of an inch between the shaft and the bearings and the particles of oil serve much as the balls in a ball bearing, they slide easily past each other and past the two metal surfaces and thus lubricate the bearing.—*The Shop Review.*

(3)

At this point I wish to correct the general impression that aviation engines are delicate, sensitive pieces of machinery. They are designed with infinite care and with every attention to saving weight. Aviation engines are wonderful examples of engineering design. Every thought possible has been included to make them "fool-proof" and reliable. The point to be remembered about aviation engines, particularly when they run into hundreds of horsepower, is that they are delivering a tremendous amount of work at fairly high speeds. Consequently all parts must operate in perfect unison, if the engine is to function efficiently and for a long period. If anything happens while parts are under these terrific stresses, motor failures can be swift and serious. Any mechanical contrivance put under severe stress and operated near its maximum capacity at considerable speeds can suffer serious injury before it can be stopped if one of its vital parts fails; aviation engines are working under these conditions.

Let us take the analogy of an automobile engine by way of illustration. If an automobile engine is operated carefully and seldom driven at high speeds, it will last indefinitely. But if the car is run at very high speeds, and the engine made to turn out at least 80 per cent of its full power at all times, how long will that engine last? Or, again, the oil system of an automobile engine might not be functioning perfectly but still be operating well enough for ordinary driving speeds. As long as the speeds are kept down, no trouble develops and the engine will keep functioning. But if the engine is run full out, with a defect in the oil system, how long will the engine stand up?

This is the operating condition to which aviation engines are subjected. They are working practically all the time, delivering 80 per cent or more of their maximum power. Therefore, if anything does go wrong, trouble develops very quickly, and at times so quickly that a failure takes place even before the engine can be throttled down. This is what actually happens sometimes when the lubricating system suddenly fails. As stated above, the area of the wearing parts is so great and the lubrication is used so rapidly that, if the oil pressure suddenly drops, the heat generated by friction develops so fast that before the pilot is aware of it, the engine may become seriously damaged.—Byron Q. Jones, *Practical Flying*, The Ronald Press Company.

(4)

The moon is the earth's nearest neighbor. It is only about a quarter of a million miles away. That distance is about ten times as great as the distance around the earth at the Equator, but it is very short compared with other "sky distances." The sun is more than 90 million miles away from the earth. It is, you see, more than three hundred times as far away as the moon. Many of the stars are thousands of millions of millions of miles away. The distance to the moon is a mere step toward the nearest star.*

A Summary of Important Points on the Paragraph

1. Paragraphing is a device used to separate one topic from another. It helps the reader follow the different steps in the development of a letter or other written paper.

2. A paragraph consists of a group of related sentences all explaining a single topic which is a part of the main subject.

3. The main thought of a good paragraph can be summarized in one sentence.

4. The main idea of a paragraph is stated in the topic sentence.

* From Bertha Morris Parker, "The Earth's Nearest Neighbor," p. 3, *The Basic Science Education Series*. With special permission of the publishers, Row, Peterson & Co., Evanston, Illinois.

5. Some principles helpful in developing effective paragraphs are:

   a) Discuss only one main idea in a paragraph.

   b) Emphasize the most important ideas by placing them at the beginning or at the end of the paragraph. The topic sentence, therefore, is usually placed at the beginning of the paragraph.

   c) Connect each paragraph with what has gone before and to that which comes after. A good paragraph helps the reader to carry the thought from one paragraph to another. This can be done in the following ways:

      1) In the beginning of the paragraph make a reference to the preceding paragraph.

      2) At the end of the paragraph place a reference to what is to follow.

   d) Make a plan of your paragraph before writing it.

Developing the Paragraph

You will find the writing of a paragraph much easier if you first make an outline. Just as a blueprint guides the mechanic or the carpenter a paragraph outline will guide you in writing. Further, planning your paragraph by making an outline will help you organize your material and select only the ideas that are related to your topic sentence. The following is a student's paragraph outline:

Topic sentence	A man should be loyal to the one who is responsible for his work.
Developing thoughts	Superior picks you for certain jobs—teaches you the job —try to be loyal even though he doesn't seem always to be doing the right thing—can recommend you for advancement or keep you back—he will be loyal to you if he is a good supervisor—your job is to help him.
Thoughts arranged in order	1. Your job is to help him. 2. He picks you for specific jobs. 3. He teaches you the job.

4. Be loyal even though he doesn't seem always to be doing the right thing.
5. He will be loyal to you in turn.
6. He can recommend you for advancement.

From the above outline the student wrote this paragraph:

Topic sentence　　A man should try to be loyal to the person who is responsible for his work. Your job is to help him get the work done. Often this superior is the one who actually picks you for specific jobs. He is also the one who teaches you your job as it should be done; and in teaching you, he gives you the benefit of the knowledge and skill he has gained through years of intensive work and experience. On your part then there is an obligation to support him. Even though you may sometimes think that he is not doing the right thing, try your best to be loyal to him. A good supervisor, on the other hand, will be loyal to you and will approve your work and support you if your work conforms to good standards. Remember that your supervisor or superior can recommend you for advancement if he has an opportunity, but he is most likely to recommend the man who has proved his loyalty as well as his ability.

Developing thoughts written as sentences

Applying Your Knowledge

HELPFUL QUESTIONS:

1. What sentences in the paragraphs that you have studied seem to summarize the thought of the paragraph?
2. How many main ideas are there in each paragraph?
3. In what positions may a topic sentence be placed? Which positions seem to emphasize the paragraph thought most?
4. What is a paragraph?
5. Why is a composition made up of different paragraphs? Why not write a composition using just one long paragraph?
6. What is the value of a paragraph outline? Why is it a good thing to write a concluding sentence in the paragraph outline?
7. Tell how to develop a paragraph outline.
8. Why is it a good procedure to arrange your ideas in the order in which you want them to appear in the paragraph?

PROBLEMS:

1. Select one of the following statements and write it on your paper. This sentence is to be the topic sentence for a paragraph. Make a paragraph outline using this sentence as the key idea. After you have completed the outline, expand it into a paragraph by expanding the ideas in the outline to sentences.

a) The average man talks too much, especially in making a business deal.

b) Study the job ahead of you and prepare to fill it.

c) Every citizen should vote.

d) It is best to read all instructions before starting work on any job.

e) A foundry is a great chemical and physical laboratory.

f) There is not likely to be any happy morning when the American wakes up and finds that his world-wide problems have gone away.

g) Every person needs both liberal and vocational education.

h) This is a wonderful age in which to be alive.

i) "Learning drawing is much more than simply learning how to draw; it is learning to read and write a new language such as English or French."

j) The fundamental principles of oxyacetylene welding are simple and easily understood.

k) There has been a large increase in the application of electrical power in industry.

l) Every high school senior should learn to use the slide rule.

m) While in school every boy, if he possibly can do it, should buy some tools that he can use in his trade.

n) We did a very interesting job in our shop last week.

o) The most interesting play of the game was made. . . .

p) The hobby I like best is. . . .

2. Write ten good topic sentences. The following titles may suggest ideas for topic sentences:

Fishing for Trout	Saving Time With the Slide Rule
What I Want To Be	The Care of Tools
A Visit to a Factory	Getting a Job
Why I Am Studying My Trade	The Importance of Voting
Direct and Alternating Current	What Is the UN?
Using a Plane	Radar
Filing a Saw	Atomic Energy
Splicing a Belt	Changes in Our Country

Some Work I Have Done in the
School Shop

An Interesting Experiment in
Science

The Value of Science in a Technical Course

The Books I Like To Read

Our Football Team

The Student Council

Different Kinds of Soil

Erosion

TV Programs

School Spirit

Democracy

Conservation

3. Select one of your topic statements from Problem 2 and develop it into a paragraph of not less than 100 words. Use the method outlined earlier in this chapter. You will find that probably seven to twelve sentences are needed to develop a good paragraph.

Chapter 5

LEARN TO PUNCTUATE CORRECTLY

Correct punctuation helps make written matter clear, so that the reader can see readily the relations of the various word groups. Many persons punctuate carelessly and thoughtlessly; very few punctuate correctly.

The business and technical man should be especially careful in his use of punctuation. A misplaced comma in a bid, a contract, a set of specifications, or in an order for equipment may result in serious mistakes and a consequent loss. Hence, the technical man should use punctuation just as accurately as he uses mathematical formulas and tools.

Do not use too much punctuation. Short sentences usually need very little or no punctuation. Long sentences, on the other hand, are made clearer by the use of the comma, the semicolon, or other marks. However, too much punctuation tends to make the sentence difficult to read, confuses the reader, and does more harm than good.

All the rules of punctuation are not presented here, but your application of those that are will help make your writing clear. It is not necessary that you memorize all the following rules. Instead, try to understand them and to think about them and to apply them in the exercises on the following pages.

Use these lessons on punctuation constantly for reference. Whenever you are confused about a certain point, refer to the explanations and the illustrations given here, so that you gradually learn to punctuate accurately the kinds of expressions with which you have difficulty. Further, compare the sentence with which you have trouble with similar sentences that are correctly punctuated.

1. When To Use the Comma Before *But*

Use the comma before *but* when it connects two complete statements.

EXAMPLE:

The contract calls for completion of the house by September 1, *but* that is now impossible.

OUTLINE:

　　　　　　　　　　(A complete statement)　　　　　　　　　, *but*
(a complete statement).

In the above example you will see that the two contrasted ideas are connected by *but* and that the interruption in the thought of the sentence is marked by the comma before *but*. Note also that if the word *but* were removed there would be two sentences in place of one.

But is also used to connect other contrasted ideas that are not complete statements. No matter how short these groups of words are, a comma can be used before the word *but* when it is used to connect ideas.

EXAMPLE:

You are to make shipments beginning next week, but not before that.

OUTLINE:

　　　　　　　　　　(Complete statement)　　　　　　　, *but* (contrasted idea).

CAUTION: Do not use the comma in front of *but* when it means *except*.

EXAMPLE:

Everyone has gone *but* the watchman.
Everyone has gone *except* the watchman.

In this sentence the word *but* means *except*, so that you should not use the comma before the word *but* here. Whenever you can substitute the word *except* for the word *but,* no comma is necessary. (In this case the word *but* is a preposition and not a conjunction.)

Exercise 1. Study the punctuation in the following sentences. Write them from dictation, then correct your mistakes.

1. My radio is small and inexpensive, but I get considerable pleasure from it.

2. The car is getting rather old, but so far it has given us no trouble.

3. We were going to come to see you next week, but circumstances have arisen that make it impossible.

4. Everybody has gone but Dick.

5. We could not get Columbus, but got approximate checks for position on Elmira and Erie.

2. When To Use the Comma Before *For*

Use the comma before *for* when it connects two complete statements.

The word *for* is used much the same way as the word *but,* and when *for* connects two complete statements a comma should be placed before it. For example, the sentence given below can be written as two separate sentences by omitting the word *for,* which joins the two statements.

We won the game easily, *for* our team was in excellent condition.

   (Complete statement) *, for*   (complete statement)   .

We won the game easily.   Our team was in excellent condition.

In the next example no comma is needed in front of *for* because it does not connect two different ideas or statements. In this sentence *for a good mechanic* is not a complete statement because it does not make a complete sentence when placed by itself.

EXAMPLE:

We are advertising *for a good mechanic.*

   (Only one complete statement)   .

Exercise 2. Study the punctuation in the following sentences. Write them from dictation, then correct your mistakes.

1. There was no movement anywhere except for the rushing water.
2. We will stop at your cottage for you, for we must pass near it on our way to the lake.
3. He boxed very well for the first ten rounds, for he had trained faithfully.
4. We are looking for first-class mechanics.
5. I thought that I was hooked on some weeds, for the bass pulled just like a dead weight.

3. When To Use the Comma Before *And, Or, Nor*

Place a comma before *and, or, nor* whenever they connect two complete statements unless both statements are very short.*

EXAMPLE:

The carpenters reached the building at 8 o'clock, *and* the lumber arrived at 8:15.

<u>   (A complete statement)   </u> , *and* <u>(Another</u>
<u>complete statement)</u>.

To prove that these are complete statements we can omit the *and* to determine whether each statement will make a complete sentence.

The carpenters reached the building at 8 o'clock. The lumber arrived at 8:15.

When you can omit the words *and, or, nor,* and write each statement as a separate sentence, you should use a comma before them.

Exercise 3. Study the punctuation in the following sentences. Write them from dictation, then correct your mistakes.

1. It is liable to rain before we finish painting, and the job is supposed to be finished on Friday.
2. I'll play or you can sing.

* This same rule applies also to *so, yet, though,* and *while.*

3. I do not know whose tool box it is, nor do I know who brought it here.

4. Do you want me to paint the walls or repair the screens?

5. This is one of the best buys that we have seen, and we urge you to take advantage of this opportunity.

Exercise 4. Review Sections 1 to 3, then copy and punctuate the following sentences:

1. A small perch flopped around on the bottom of the boat and tangled my line.

2. Every motorist should carry a first-aid kit and he should know how to use it.

3. We had planned to visit you at the cottage but you know what happens to a lot of our plans.

4. Why should a man be anything but a good workman?

5. We shall ask Mr. Rolker to write directly to you or we shall send you the information ourselves.

6. Will you please do a favor for me the next time you go into the city?

7. I want to take your job very much but I must give my present employer two weeks' notice.

8. Ralph arrived with the bait so we all went fishing.

9. I am familiar with your record and what you have done and know you would be a valuable asset to some organization.

10. We walk into town for the mail for it is only a mile away.

11. We do not know of any company seeking a man of Mr. Gilmore's qualities nor do we know to whom to refer him for employment.

12. The ground wire on the battery may be loose or the fuse under the dashboard may have fallen out of the holder.

13. Am I to report to the Oliver Street plant or to the foundry?

14. We regret the inconvenience caused you in the matter but are glad you wrote us in order that we could make a prompt adjustment so you would not be further inconvenienced or delayed in your work.

15. The complete unit will be rebuilt at our factory and will carry the same guarantee as a new one.

4. Use the Comma To Separate a Series of Items

Use a comma to separate words or groups of words used in a series; that is, used to name a succession of things.

NOTE: If a conjunction (*and, or, nor*) is used before the last item, it is best to place a comma before this conjunction.

EXAMPLE:

He secured *brushes*, *paint*, and *turpentine* from the stockroom.

<u>   First item   </u> , <u>second item</u>, *and* <u>third item   </u> .

Exercise 5. Study the following sentences carefully. Have some one dictate them to you, then correct your sentences to see whether you have punctuated them correctly.

1. During the confusion Charles dropped his paddle, seized the life preserver, and threw it to Jim.

2. He started the engine, ran it until it was warm, and then adjusted the carburetor.

3. A long, narrow, tall-masted sailboat won the race.

4. The three courses offered are auto mechanics, printing, and carpentry and cabinetmaking.

5. The outside of the house has been painted, the inside has been papered, and the cellar has been whitewashed.

Exercise 6. Copy and punctuate the following sentences:

1. Twenty thirty forty minutes passed while I sat in the car waiting.

2. The color of the paper can be blue yellow or white.

3. I met Mr. Cottrell yesterday talked to him and gave him my application blank.

4. You will find a small thin blue book in the top bureau drawer.

5. I am nineteen years old five feet six inches tall and weigh one hundred forty pounds.

6. The colors were blue red green and yellow.

7. Jim was ambitious honest and kind.

8. For the second time that day we ate beans potatoes and apples.

9. Newspapers magazines radio and television are our most used advertising mediums.

10. She was wearing a beautiful white dress.

5. Use the Comma in Dates and Addresses

EXAMPLE:

Robert Black was born at 1753 Second Street, St. Louis 4, Missouri, on March 1, 1915.

CAUTION:

Be sure to use the comma after the state or year when it is not the last word in the sentence, as Missouri in the preceding example.

Exercise 7. Study the punctuation in the following sentences. Write them from dictation, then correct your mistakes.

1. You will remember that a severe flood on the Chenango River, New York, occurred about July 8, 1935.
2. On June 5, 1954, I went to work for the Atlas Chain Company.
3. John lives near Rockville. Ohio.
4. I worked for six weeks in the repair shop of the Andrews Radio Company, 4115 West Jefferson Boulevard, Los Angeles 16, California.
5. Bob has $150 in the First National Bank, Danbury.

Exercise 8. Copy and punctuate the following sentences:

1. He said that he graduated from Contra Costa Jr College Martinez California in June 1954.
2. During the last two summer vacations I have worked as a shipping clerk for the Reed-Prentice Corporation 677 Cambridge Street Worcester 4 Massachusetts.
3. I suggest that you write to Portland Cement Association 33 West Grand Avenue Chicago 10 Illinois.
4. Our old home at 19 Locust Street Waterbury Vermont was torn down during September 1953.
5. If you experience any difficulty in obtaining such information our representative Mr. J. W. Ward 32 North Sixth Street Philadelphia 7 Pennsylvania will be pleased to serve you.

6. Commas Around Extra Words

Put commas around words or groups of words that are not needed and that can be omitted without changing the meaning of the sentence.

In many sentences there are words or groups of words that add merely an extra thought or a descriptive detail to the sentence. If these words can be taken out of the sentence without changing in any way the meaning of the main idea, commas should be placed around them. The commas help the reader to see what expression is an extra detail. In the following example notice how the commas point off the extra words that merely interrupt the main thought of the sentence.

EXAMPLE:

    Exposed wires, *I suppose,* caused the short circuit.
    Exposed wires, (extra words), caused the short circuit.

TEST: If these words are removed from the sentence, will the meaning of the sentence be changed? Let us try this test and see what happens.

    Exposed wires   caused the short circuit.

Leaving these words out of the sentence does not change the meaning; consequently, they are just extra words which interrupt the thought and they should have commas around them.

Sometimes it is more difficult to decide whether a group of words is necessary in a sentence. The next example may illustrate such a group of words for you.

EXAMPLE:

    The stationery *which I bought at Plankenhorn's* does not absorb ink.

The question is: Are commas needed around the words *which I bought at Plankenhorn's?* To determine this, let us remove them from the sentence and note whether the meaning of the main idea is the same without them.

    The stationery does not absorb ink.

When the words are left out of the sentence, the meaning of the sentence is changed because we do not know what stationery is meant. Since the meaning of the sentence is not clear without these words, no commas should be placed around them.

CAUTION:

    Place no commas around the necessary words. Place commas around the unnecessary words.

Exercise 9. Study the punctuation in the following sentences. Write them from dictation, then correct your mistakes.

1. Robert Metzger, who lives next door to us, won the tennis tournament.
2. The boys, however, did not get seasick.
3. The lake which is near New Milford, Connecticut, is Lake Candlewood.
4. We could, with very little difficulty, take more supplies with us.
5. Roy Durling, the boy who spoke to me, is a good student.

Exercise 10. Copy and punctuate the following sentences:

1. The bill for any service in connection with the settlement of an estate even for a friend should be at least fifty dollars.
2. Lake Candlewood which is near New Milford Connecticut is an artificial lake.
3. The signature however is not mine.
4. A citizen who is loyal to his community will support the various civic organizations.
5. The fuselage or body was made of aluminum.
6. Jane Green one of your old friends has moved out of town.
7. *Gone with the Wind* a novel by Margaret Mitchell is one of the best novels ever written about the Civil War Period.
8. *The Inland Printer* a magazine for printers usually contains information on punctuation.
9. The rest of course is to be shipped to Plant No. 2.
10. We have just sent you for examination a sample of our new waterproof glue.

7. A Comma After the Extra Words at the Beginning of a Sentence

Place a comma after the extra or the introductory words at the beginning of a sentence if they would be enclosed by commas within the sentence.

EXAMPLE:

For example, the boat must be able to sail in three feet of water.

OUTLINE:

(Extra words), _____ (main and necessary statement) _____ .

TEST:

The boat, for example, must be able to sail in three feet of water.

Exercise 11. Study the following sentences carefully. Have some one dictate them to you, then correct your sentences to see whether you have punctuated them correctly.

1. Frankly, I believe that you can do the job.
2. However, we have issued our credit memorandum S-5353 to cover the cost of the thermostats.
3. Yes, we shall be glad to go next week.
4. In the first place, we have thought about buying a rowboat instead of a canoe.
5. In short, a rowboat is safer for children.

Exercise 12. Copy and punctuate the following sentences:

1. However we have not yet received your acknowledgment of our last order.
2. Finally no boat is safe unless it is properly handled.
3. In spite of all that you have said I still believe that the boy is honest.
4. First we built the tent platforms and erected the tents. Next we went into town to buy some food.
5. Well we shall see what happens when Mike learns about it.

8. A Comma Before an Added Thought

When an additional thought is added to the end of a sentence, place a comma before the added expression when it is not needed to complete the meaning of the sentence.

EXAMPLE:

I walk to work every morning, a distance of three miles.

OUTLINE:

<u>I walk to work every morning,</u> extra statement can be omitted.

Exercise 13. Study the punctuation in the following sentences. Write them from dictation, then correct your mistakes.

1. The round-trip week-end ticket will be five dollars, a saving of three dollars.

2. His body was found in the river three days later, lodged behind a large rock in the rapids.

3. Just now I'm trying to concentrate on each stroke, keeping my eye on the ball until I hit it.

4. At present I am taking a course in economics, which I enjoy very much.

5. He assured me that he would keep my application before him, and I believe that he will call me if an opening occurs, but I won't depend too much on it.

Exercise 14. Copy and punctuate the following sentences:

1. I studied for six full weeks while taking the course later forgetting everything that I had learned.

2. He was not at home though his car was in the garage.

3. I am willing to contribute to the Crippled Children's Fund especially since it is carefully administered.

4. We have changed our purchase order #5251 to read 6000 feet instead of 4000 feet 2000 feet of which has already been received.

5. He is not a good student as he never takes time to study.

9. A Comma for Direct Address

When you address or speak directly to a person, set off the name or title by commas.

EXAMPLE:

Frankly, Jim, I cannot accept your invitation to the party.

OUTLINE:

>   addressing
> _____ , Jim, _____ .
>   directly

Exercise 15. Study the punctuation in the following sentences. Write them from dictation, then correct your mistakes.

1. Try to come out to the cabin, Bob, and help us catch some of these large bass.

2. The truth is, boys, that I must work until ten o'clock tomorrow night.

3. Really, Jane, we want you to come to the dance tonight.

4. Do you think, Paul, that this job is still open?

5. Do you think Paul will want to come with us?

Exercise 16. Copy and punctuate the following sentences:

1. Robert said that Jane is an excellent dancer.

2. A letter from you Jane will be welcome any time.

3. In your letter Dick will you write out for me the story that you used in your after-dinner speech a week ago?

4. The first point Jim is this.

5. Jack may I borrow your rifle for the first week of hunting season?

10. The Comma and the Sentence Order

The comma is used to set off groups of words out of their natural order in a sentence.

EXAMPLE OF NATURAL ORDER:

A man is little more than a walking workshop if he has only a technical education.

OUTLINE:

_____(Statement of main idea first)_____   if   (reason for statement second).

EXAMPLE OF SENTENCE OUT OF NATURAL ORDER:

If he has only a technical education, a man is little more than a walking workshop.

OUTLINE:

If . . (reason first) . . education, a   (statement of idea after reason for it).

NATURAL ORDER:

Statement first   Reason second (no comma)

UNNATURAL ORDER:

Reason first,   Statement second (comma used)

Sometimes the reason or less important idea is found within the sentence, splitting the statement into two parts. In this case commas are placed before and after the reason for the statement. Study carefully the next example.

The foreman, *after he saw the accident,* decided to discharge the man.

(First part of statement), (reason for statement), (rest of statement).

If you study the above example carefully you will notice that there is a comma before and after the words, *after he saw the accident,* because these words are out of their natural order in the sentence and they interrupt the statement of the main idea.

Exercise 17. Study the punctuation in the following sentences. Write them from dictation, then correct your mistakes.

1. My radio did not prove to be expensive since I was allowed a 20 per cent discount at the store where I work.

2. If you saw the accident, you should be willing to serve as a witness.

3. A few days ago, when I was driving to Cleveland, I passed very few cars on the road.

4. Since the sunset is red tonight, we can expect clear weather for tomorrow.

5. We shall file this information for reference when we again need a quantity of these gaskets.

Exercise 18. Copy and punctuate the following sentences:

1. When you have finished the job please notify us immediately.

2. Trout fishing will not be good because the water will be too high.

3. After some thought he said that he would take a chance.

4. I shall try since you asked for a frank answer to give you one in this letter.

5. If you wish to purchase this equipment immediately we shall be glad to allow you a discount of 5 per cent for cash with the order.

If you have found the explanation at the beginning of this lesson difficult perhaps the following directions will help you:

When such words as *when, if, since, because,* **etc., begin a sentence, put a comma at the end of the idea which they introduce.**

EXAMPLE:

When he became eighteen, he joined the navy.
When   (idea)   ,   (main idea)   .

If the main idea comes first in the sentence and the *when* idea last, the sentence has natural order and no comma is needed unless the sentence is very long.

EXAMPLE:

He joined the navy *when* he was eighteen.
(Main idea followed by *when*   idea)   .

Exercise 19. Study the following sentences carefully. Have some one dictate them to you, then correct your sentences to see whether you have punctuated them correctly.

1. Before he had been there two weeks, he completed the job.
2. When the time for the contest finally arrived, he forgot his nervousness and made an excellent speech.
3. He crammed the note hastily into his pocket because he did not want her to see it.
4. As soon as the storm had passed, we backed the car out of the barn and continued the trip.
5. He does excellent work as a mechanic whenever he feels like working.

The following words introduce ideas that should be followed by commas when they begin sentences.

as soon as	even though	if	even if
as	as if, as though	since	unless
while	although	when	because
until	in order that	after	before

Exercise 20. Copy and punctuate the following sentences:

1. I am mailing this letter at this time because I shall leave for my vacation in a few days and I am very eager that your material reach me ultimately.
2. I shall be glad to send you a copy of the report of our study if our own survey materializes.
3. Perhaps it may have been misdirected if you mailed it a week ago.

4. Since I have had complete charge and had to direct every step of the work myself I feel that it represents my own effort almost as much as if I had actually done every bit of the work myself.

5. Mr. Schuyler entered our employ December 2 1954 as a machinist and served in this capacity until he was promoted to the position of safety supervisor.

6. Since we must do the work anyway let us do the best we possibly can.

7. Although Jim left Sunday afternoon the rest of us stayed at the cottage until Monday morning.

8. Even though it rained for two days we had a lot of fun playing bridge before the fire.

9. On Saturday evening Dick danced as if he had taken some lessons since the last dance.

10. Although what you say may be true I still believe that Jane didn't do that.

Exercise 21. Write and punctuate ten sentences beginning with the introductory words (subordinating conjunctions) named below:

1. When ...., ...
2. While ...., ...
3. If ...., ...
4. Unless ...., ...
5. Although ...., ...
6. Since ...., ...
7. After ...., ...
8. Because ...., ...
9. In order that................, ...
10. Until ...., ...

11A. *He Said* Followed by the Exact Words of the Speaker

When *he said* or a similar expression is followed by the exact words of the speaker, place a comma after the word *said*.

EXAMPLE:

Father said, "Don't take the river road because it is too muddy."

OUTLINE:

Father said, "_____(exact words that father said)_____."

NOTE:

A direct quotation (the exact words of the speaker) must always begin with a capital letter and be enclosed by quotation marks.

Exercise 22. Study the punctuation in the following sentences. Write them from dictation, then correct your mistakes.

1. He said, "I arrived at two o'clock. Where were you at that time?"
2. The guide replied, "Shooting those rapids will be exciting enough."
3. Tom yelled, "Get off my toe."
4. The mechanic shouted, "Don't run that engine."
5. The mechanic shouted that he shouldn't run the engine.

Exercise 23. Copy and punctuate the following sentences:

1. Bob called bring an extra baseball with you.
2. The coach said the wrestling team is to report to me in the gym at 3 P. M.
3. John replied I'm sorry I can't give you a ride today.
4. The principal announced that tickets could be bought in the office.
5. Dick asked Bob will you carry my newspapers tomorrow

11B. The Exact Words of the Speaker Followed by *Said He*

When *said he* or a similar expression follows the exact words of the speaker, place a comma before the word *said.*

EXAMPLE:

"That is a poor job," *said the foreman.*

" (Direct quotation) ," *said the foreman.*

NOTE:

An exclamation mark or a question mark takes the place of a comma.

EXAMPLES:

"What do you want now?" *asked the foreman.*
"What a job!" *exclaimed one of the men.*

Exercise 24. Study the punctuation in following sentences. Write them from dictation, then correct your mistakes.

1. "Where were you at two o'clock?" he asked.
2. "A guide boat will be best," advised the guide.
3. "Get off my toe," yelled Tom.
4. "Don't race that engine," shouted the mechanic.
5. "We are unable to ship you any grinding wheel stubs at the present time because we just recently sold the entire quantity which we had on hand," are the exact words in his letter.

Exercise 25. Copy and punctuate the following sentences:

1. Give me an apple please said Johnny.
2. I had a flat tire today reported the driver.
3. Where is the newspaper asked my father.
4. The game was close right up to the end my brother told me
5. Please pass the bread Jim said.

11C. A Direct Quotation Divided by *He said*

When *he said* or a similar expression occurs in the middle of a quotation, place a comma before and after the expression unless it begins or ends a sentence.

EXAMPLE:

"If you can find a man to do the job," *wired the foreman,* "hire him immediately."

" (Exact words of the speaker) ," *wired the foreman,* " (rest of exact words)."

A comma is placed in front of and after the words *wired the foreman* because they merely interrupt the direct quotation and neither end nor begin a sentence.

A quotation may consist of more than one sentence. When it does, simply use a period where the sentence should end and a capital letter where the new sentence begins.

EXAMPLE:

"That looks much better," *he said.* "The next time tell me when you get into difficulty."

OUTLINE:

"   (First sentence)   ," *he said.* "   (Second sentence)   ."

Exercise 26. Study the punctuation in the following sentences. Write them from dictation, then correct your mistakes.

1. "Did you get the problem?" Jim asked. "I had some trouble with it."
2. "But," said Mr. Smith, "we have selected another patrol leader."
3. "Yes," he agreed, "Budd Lake is sixty feet deep in some places. However, there are no lake trout in it."
4. "I'll repair the car," said Tom, "but how about paying me for the last work I did? I don't like to mention it, but I can't afford to work for nothing."
5. "Well," continued the workman, "then we found the tool room locked."

Exercise 27. Punctuate the sentences in this exercise, supplying all necessary marks of punctuation. Remember that the exact words of the speaker are always enclosed in quotation marks.

1. Ralph boasted that he could run the hundred-yard dash in ten seconds.
2. The stranger just grunted I don't know.
3. As usual the letter began we have just caught a large lake trout weighing about thirteen pounds.
4. Just then the boys yelled beat it here he comes.
5. Your exact words were I'll meet you at three o'clock.
6. That machine replied the doctor produces an artificial fever in your body.
7. Why not asked Philip I can do the job as well as anyone else.
8. Henry then wanted to know where we had left his tools.
9. When Mr. Kennedy asked me abruptly did you quit your last job.
10. Try eating some glue then you might be able to stick to one job for a while my uncle grumbled at me.

12. A Comma Plus a Conjunction Equals a Semicolon

Use a semicolon between two complete statements when they are not separated by *and, but, or, for,* or *nor.*

EXAMPLE:

We form the habit of work, *and* we become restless when we cannot work.

OUTLINE:

___(Complete statement)___ **,** *and* ___(second complete___ statement).

If the *and* is omitted, then the semicolon must be used as in the following sentence:

We form the habit of work; we become restless when we cannot work.

___(Complete statement)___ **;** ___(second complete statement).

Perhaps the outline given below will help you to remember that the semicolon is used when the connecting word is omitted.

$$, + and = ;$$
$$, + but = ;$$
$$, + for = ;$$
$$, + or = ;$$
$$, + nor = ;$$

Exercise 28. Copy and punctuate the following sentences:

1. Amateur radio operators are valuable to the industry for they often become discoverers or inventors.
2. I saw Mr. McFarland about work but he was not very encouraging.
3. John went to work in the silk mill and Francis went to work in the tannery.
4. The magnet picks up the scrap iron but it doesn't pick up the other waste.

5. We may stay at the farm or we may go to Canada on a fishing trip.

Copy and punctuate the sentences in Exercise 28, omitting the words *and, but, for, nor,* and *or* when they connect complete statements.

13. A Semicolon Plus a Conjunction Equals a Period

When a sentence contains two complete statements which are long or which contain commas, use a semicolon between the statements.

Two complete statements written as two sentences.	When we arrived at the abandoned camp, we tried to get a good photograph of it. When the film was finally developed, nothing whatever showed on the negative.
Written as one sentence, the two statements connected by "; + but"	When we arrived at the abandoned camp, we tried to get a good photograph of it; but when the film was finally developed, nothing whatever showed on the negative.

Diagram of sentence

(First complete			,
	statement)		; *but*
(Second	,	complete	
statement)	.		

The diagram of the example shows clearly the two complete statements and the commas within them. Here the semi-colon is needed to separate the two main ideas of the complete sentence because the commas are needed to separate the smaller parts of each idea.

The outline given below may help you to remember that the semicolon and a conjunction or connective are used to join two rather long statements containing commas.

; + *and* = .	; + *then* = .
; + *but* = .	; + *consequently* = .
; + *for* = .	; + *hence* = .

Exercise 29. Copy the following pairs of statements. In each case omit the period and add a semicolon and a conjunction.

1. We expect to have our mechanic in St. Louis in two weeks. If that is not too late, please write us so that we can have him stop at your plant.

2. Under the federal procedure I doubt whether we can permit any-one who is not under the Federal Oath to examine our files. However, if you will call at my office in the near future, I shall be glad to discuss this further with you. (Since *however* acts as a conjunction or con-necting word, you need only substitute the semicolon for the period.)

3. The new physics instructor proved to be an expert at tennis, for he won the city championship in the tournament. He also proved to be a sportsman when one of his own pupils defeated him in a later match.

Exercise 30. Study the punctuation in the following sentences. Write them from dictation, then correct your mistakes.

1. When you do not think from where it is coming, you can always find a reason for spending money; but Frank, it seems that you can never think of a good reason for saving any.

2. We are looking for a reliable source of supply for this part; and if you are in a position to furnish fittings of this type, please inform us as soon as possible.

3. The V-belts which drive from the motor to the wheel spindle are in need of replacement; but before placing an order for these, we shall appreciate your informing us definitely as to the size and price of the belts required.

Make diagrams of the above sentences to get a picture of them thus:

_____ , _____ ; *however,* _____ , _____ .
_____ , _____ ; *then* _____ , _____ .

Exercise 31. Copy and punctuate the following sentences:

1. Since I am leaving today I cannot let your remarks pass without telling you that you are correct he is the best all-round mechanic in town.

2. If I had heard about your job before I would not have applied for the other one but not knowing about your changing jobs I secured the other.

3. We are disappointed to find that you did not send in this check and as there is $31.20 overdue on your account we expect that you will let us have a remittance at this time without fail.

4. We have not as yet received the last order and as it was sent to you over a month ago we are wondering why shipment has not been made.

5. If it is more convenient to you I shall be glad to accept part of this balance in some sort of service that you can give me but I shall be frank to tell you that I need the money badly to help finance my sister's expenses at college.

14. *That Is, Namely,* and *For Example*

When these words and their abbreviations are used to introduce examples or illustrations of something that you have been saying, place a semicolon in front of the expression and a comma after it. Perhaps the list given below will help you to remember them.

; *namely,*	; *viz.,*
; *that is,*	; *i. e.,*
; *for example,*	; *e. g.,*
; *for instance,*	

EXAMPLE:

The magazine has improved steadily; *that is,* the articles have continued to become more and more interesting.

OUTLINE:

<u>   (Main statement)   </u> ; *that is,*<u>   </u> (explana-
<u>   tion of main statement)   </u> .

Exercise 32. Study the punctuation in the following sentences. Write them from dictation, then correct your mistakes.

1. The club has never had a better treasurer than Fred; *that is,* no one has ever placed the club in such good financial condition.

2. Remember especially the books I mentioned first; viz., *George Washington, The Old Man and the Sea,* and *The Course of Empire.*

3. He has done many things to improve the town; *for example,* he has had all the main streets paved and the playgrounds placed in good condition.

4. Dave has always been very polite and courteous; *for example,* he has always been very careful to escort to their partners the girls with whom he has danced.

5. I must commend Edwin for two things; *namely,* his truthfulness and honesty.

For example is often used at the beginning of a sentence. When this occurs, place a comma after it.

Exercise 33. Copy and punctuate the following sentences:

1. The price of land is going up for example building lots are now selling at $30 a front foot.
2. The house is attractive and would be rented now but for a serious drawback namely the incessant piano playing next door.
3. You had better bring some clothes for cold days namely a sweater some warm socks flannel pajamas and a heavy bathrobe.
4. The engine has continued to become worse that is the compression has become poorer.
5. The foundation of a house is often faulty for example the footing is sometimes too small to support properly the foundation walls and the building.

15. *However, Therefore, Hence,* etc.

Place a semicolon before such words as *therefore, however, nevertheless, hence, thus,* and *consequently* when they connect two complete statements. *

EXAMPLE:

The last two pages are smeared; *therefore,* they must be retyped.

OUTLINE:

<u>   (Complete statement)   </u> ; *therefore,* (complete statement) .

You may find the list of words given below helpful. Remember, however, that the semicolon is not used in front of these expressions unless they connect two complete statements.

; *accordingly,*	; *however,*
; *besides,*	; *hence,*
; *consequently,*	; *moreover,*
; *furthermore,*	; *nevertheless,*

* Other words often requiring the same punctuation are: *accordingly, finally, besides, also, thus, still, perhaps, otherwise, likewise.*

Note: The comma is frequently omitted after some of the above words when the sentence reads smoothly.

Exercise 34. Study the punctuation in the following sentences. Write them from dictation, then correct your mistakes.

1. John thought that there was something wrong with the motor; *consequently,* he drove off the road and stopped.
2. We have failed to win the football championship; *therefore,* let us win the basketball title.
3. We saw no reason for moving; *hence,* we rented the same house.
4. The Zenith refrigerator operates on the same principle as the Federal; *moreover,* it has three inches of insulation.
5. It requires, *therefore,* considerable patience to learn this.

Exercise 35. Copy and punctuate the following sentences:

1. I saw no good reason for refusing his invitation besides I enjoy his company very much.
2. The boys in the other clubs refused to cooperate hence he became discouraged and resigned.
3. I didn't want to go fishing however since he was so eager to go I went along.
4. His clothes were torn and muddy besides he looked sick.
5. The men without a trade were hired as unskilled laborers consequently they were frequently unemployed.

16. Using the Colon

Use a colon after such expressions as *the following, as follows, thus, these,* and other expression introducing something, such as a question, a statement, or a list of things.

EXAMPLE:

The following subjects will be taught: English, mathematics, economics, mechanical drawing, and machine shop practice.

OUTLINE:

The following _____ : (1) , (2) , __
(3) , (4) , _____ (5) .

Exercise 36. Study the punctuation in the following sentences. Write them from dictation, then correct your mistakes.

1. The difficulties are these: first, the garage is too small; second, we do not have enough money to get the proper equipment; third, we do not know where we can borrow the money.

2. We are rushed on the following days: Monday, Wednesday, Friday, and Saturday.

3. The officers of the club are as follows: Bill Morrison, president; Paul Florey, vice-president; and Paul Seitzer, secretary-treasurer.

4. I would believe that you are telling the truth except for one thing: You were seen at the movies last night.

5. The problem now is: How are we to dispose of all the bass?

Capitalize the first word after a colon when it begins a new sentence. (See sentences 4 and 5 above.)

Exercise 37. Copy and punctuate the following sentences:

1. Our company has offices in the following cities new york chicago new orleans and detroit.

2. You will have better success with your painting if you will proceed in this way first use enough linseed oil . . .

3. The difficulty is simply this where can I borrow enough money to meet expenses?

4. I want to do three things this year study hard and make a good record participate in some student activities and learn to dance well.

5. Please send these boys to me at 3:15 on the football field sharp brown donley baier and peterson.

17. Other Uses for the Colon

Use the colon:

To follow the salutation in a business letter.

EXAMPLE:

Dear Sir:
Gentlemen:

To designate time.

EXAMPLE:

We arose at 7:15 this morning.
They arrived at 9:00 A. M.

To precede a long formal quotation.

EXAMPLE:

James A. Michener describes Australia as follows: "It is a land of untold capacities! Its deserts are more cruel than the Sahara, yet they abound in mineral wealth. Its people are courageous, yet more than two thirds of them huddle within twenty miles of the sea, while the dead heart of their continent lies barren." °

18. Using the Hyphen

Hyphenate an adjective consisting of two or more words when they are used immediately before a noun.

EXAMPLE:

A *cast-iron* stove	*but*	The stove is made of *cast iron*.
A *well-known* author	*but*	As an author he is *well known*.
A *well-built* house	*but*	The house is *well built*.

NOTE:

Do not use the hyphen after a word ending in *ly* (as, *A carefully designed machine*).

Exercise 38. Study the punctuation in the following sentences. Write them from dictation, then correct your mistakes.

1. Unemployed men show much clear-cut resentment toward employed women.
2. They're old-fashioned coal burners.
3. The baseball game turned into a knock-down and drag-out fight on the part of some rowdies.
4. My trip after the job turned out to be just another wild-goose chase.
5. The length and the pitch of the trombone can be altered by means of a U-shaped tube.

Use the hyphen to connect numbers between twenty-one and ninety-nine.

EXAMPLE:

fifty-five   sixty-three   twenty-first
Ninety-eight boys attended the meeting.

° Reprinted by courtesy of Random House from *Return to Paradise.*

Use a hyphen to connect a number or a letter and another word used together.

EXAMPLE:

2-in. board   60-hp. motor   *three-foot* stick
This is a *four-ply* tire.   This tire has *four plies* of fabric.
X-ray (*modifier*)   T-square   U-shaped

Exercise 39. Study the punctuation in the following sentences. Write them from dictation, then correct your mistakes.

1. The pole is ten feet long.
2. We sold ten three-bladed knives.
3. There were twenty-four couples at the dance.
4. I paid only thirty-five dollars for our new radio set.
5. Give me thirty five-dollar bills.
6. We need a 36-inch length of 1-inch pipe.

Exercise 40. Copy and punctuate the following sentences:

1. The engine develops one hundred twenty five horsepower.
2. You can buy typewriters having ten or twelve point type.
3. A ten foot pole will be long enough.
4. Dan is the roller on a 22 inch rolling mill.
5. A self addressed envelope is enclosed.
6. Jim plays a B flat saxophone.
7. Did you buy a first class passage?
8. He was flying a new low wing single engined monoplane.
9. To the rear of this seat is a 12 inch shelf.
10. Dad caught a twelve pound salmon yesterday.

19. The Apostrophe in Place of Missing Letters

Insert an apostrophe wherever a letter or group of letters is omitted from a word.

Complete Expressions	Contractions	Letters Omitted
do not	don't	o
are not	aren't	o
you are	you're	a
I shall	I'll	sha
you have	you've	ha

Notice that the contracted form of the expression is written as a single word.

Exercise 41. Write the proper contractions for the following expressions: *does not, cannot, would not, it has, she shall, we shall, I will, have not, were not, you are, had not.*

20. The Apostrophe Indicates Possession

The apostrophe is used with nouns and pronouns to indicate possession.

The apostrophe comes sometimes before the *s* and sometimes after it. To determine the position of the apostrophe follow these steps:

1. Write the simple word.

man   men   women   ladies   George

2. Add an apostrophe to the simple word.

man'   men'   women'   ladies'   George'

3. If the simple word does not end in *s* add an *s* after the apostrophe.

man's   men's   women's   George's

If the simple word ends in *s* add nothing after the apostrophe.

ladies'

NOTE:

Except for the possessive pronouns, such as *my, our, her, their,* etc., most possessives end in *s*.

By using the three steps given above we can make the following words indicate possession:

1	2	3
boy	boy'	boy's
boys	boys'	boys'
everybody	everybody'	everybody's
Jones	Jones'	Jones'

NOTE:

A one-syllable word ending in *s* may be written as Jones's, Charles's, etc.

Exercise 42. Copy and punctuate the following sentences:

1. I have had over seven years experience as a toolmaker.
2. You will find Charles fishing rod in the corner cupboard.
3. At Mr. Boltons suggestion we are sending you additional expense money.
4. Our proposal is probably in Mr. Kellys files.
5. A passing automobile splattered the ladies dresses with mud.

21. Capitalization

Every sentence should begin with a capital letter.

EXAMPLES:

All this is for defense.
Where did Jim go?
The subject for discussion is this: Mathematics is an important subject for apprentices. (Notice that a second sentence is introduced by the colon after *this*.)

Every direct quotation should begin with a capital letter.

EXAMPLES:

Mr. Winkler said, "There are 5,497 parts in the Wright Cyclone G-200 engine."
The captain said, "Tell John to report at once."

All important words in the titles of books, plays, stories, articles, poems, etc., should be capitalized. Unimportant words, *and, of, the, a, with,* etc., are not capitalized when they are within the title.

EXAMPLES:

"The Ransom of Red Chief" is one of O. Henry's best stories.
"The Man with the Hoe" is the title of both a poem and a picture.

All proper names should be capitalized.

EXAMPLES:

churches:	Presbyterian Church, Catholic Church
cities:	New York, Atlanta, Chicago
clubs:	Susquehanna Canoe Club, University Club
firms:	Union Pacific Railroad
holidays:	Armistice Day, Christmas
parties:	Republican Party, Democratic Party
races:	English, Norwegian, Finnish
streets:	Fourth Avenue, Second Street
schools:	Mechanics Institute

Capitalize

Definite sections of the country

the South, the East, the Middle West

Definite events or times

Civil War, Thanksgiving Day

Titles before names

Major Andrews, Dr. Smith

Words part of a proper name

South Side High School
Hudson River Parkway
Taylor-Winfield Corporation

Do Not Capitalize

Directions

an eastern state, a north wind, traveling westward.

Seasons

spring, summer, fall, winter

Titles alone or after words

the major, a doctor, my aunt

Words not part of a proper name

a high school on the south side of the river, a corporation

Exercise 43. Rewrite the following sentences, supplying capital letters where necessary:

1. the local union elected as president a new worker whose name is charles hoffman.

2. do you belong to the kiwanis club or to the rotary club?

3. the trees leaned toward the north after the hurricane.

4. i think main street needs a good bus system.

5. the baldwins just returned from toledo.

6. have you read captain horatio hornblower by forester or the little history of the united states by mabel pyne?

7. henry said, "will you go with us, or must we go to the city alone?"

8. my grandfather, aaron smith, fought in the civil war because he believed in freedom for the slaves.

9. frank always buys the sunday edition of the grit and the new york times.

10. charles is an accountant for the california light and power company.

Exercise 44. Applying Your Knowledge of Punctuation. The following exercises consist of actual letters similar to those you may reasonably expect to write. These letters are already punctuated for you. Study the punctuation carefully. Take the letter from dictation, then compare your letter with the one in the book to see what mistakes you might have made.

The numbers at the left are section references. If you make a mistake at any point, study the section for that line.

5	Saranac Inn, N. Y.
5	August 15, 19—

Dear Walt,

 This catching of big fish is beginning to get chronic again. Yesterday morning I was rowing Dad when he
18 caught an eleven-pounder. Bad luck arrived soon though when he caught his lucky spoon on the bottom. The lake
3 was very rough, and I had to hold that boat in the same
7 place for an hour and a quarter. Finally, we caught
20 & 3 Stark's attention, and he brought us a dry log on which to fasten the line until calmer weather arrived. Either
2 the log sank, or the waves helped pull the line loose, for now we can't find it anywhere.

7, 19, 8 However, I'll go on with the story. Stark, while
10 & 18 coming home with a load of wood, pulled in a fourteen-
16 pounder. The problem now is: How to dispose of all the trout?

 In a few minutes Peg and I are going swimming at the
20 Harveys'. I believe that they have our old raft and spring-
8 board, which we built the last time you were camping with us.

10 Since you can't be with us, write and tell us what is happening in the old home town.

          Sincerely yours,
            Tom

42 Maple Avenue

5 Morristown, New Jersey

5 July 8, 19—

Dear George,

We are looking forward eagerly to your visit with us
16 in two weeks. Now the question is: How to make the
7, 19 time pass more quickly? In the meantime, I'll try to
4 get some work done on the car, get some correspondence
4 written, swim, and play some tennis.

Freddie had his tonsils taken out today. He was operated on at the Roosevelt Hospital in Newark. A local
8 anesthetic was used. Mother, who is staying there,
phoned that he is coming along nicely. Either tomorrow
19 or Wednesday I'll drive the Dodge into the city and
bring him home.

This evening after supper I played tennis with Henry
and Allen Burns until about ten minutes of nine. My
6 game, it seems, was only slightly better. Just now
19 & 8 I'm trying to concentrate on each stroke a little more,
keeping my eye on the ball until I hit it.

You ought to send Gregory a couple of quarters. To-
3 day he took his nap in my room, and on the dresser was
19 your picture. The little imp didn't feel much like sleep-
13 ing; so every now and then he would appear out on the
8 sleeping porch where we were, only to be chased back
to bed by his mother. The conversation on one trip ran
16 something like this:

9, 20 Gregory. "Mama, is that picture of Jane's George?"
Betty. "Yes."
Gregory. "Is he going to camp with us?"
Betty. "Yes."
Gregory. "I think he is beautiful."
Loud laughs from everyone but me.
6 Gregory. "I mean his face, you know."
9 Betty. "You make tracks for your bed, young man."

19 I hope that it hasn't been so hot in Elmira today as it
has been here. This afternoon has been just like a steam
7 furnace. Well, here goes for a good cold shower.

Sincerely yours,

Can you give the reason for each mark of punctuation used in the next letter?

On board the D. L. & W.
6:30 P.M.
October 10, 19—

Dear Slim:

So you are filling your think-tank at an out-of-town gas station? Just think of learning so much that one has to go away to get more. What, if it's a fair question, are you going to do with it after you've loaded on all you can carry—jam in the cork and seal it?

Do they have a course in developing the sense of humor, and another in unsettling some of the accepted values of life? If they do, I hope your program includes them. Mind you, not that you need them especially; but rather that you come so near to not needing them that if you took the above "specials" you might run a chance of attaining happiness in this moth-eaten, gold-plated, soulless, sordid, but enormously interesting civilization in which we find ourselves immersed, and in the words of any Rotarian "of which we are so justly proud."

My oldest unmarried daughter is having the time of her young life, although as yet she is not quite at home in the new consciousness that there is a difference 'twixt he-ones and she-ones of the well-known genus Homo Sapiens. It's great to have a boy friend at school to write to, make fudge for, etc. But there are so many other nice boys, too, you know. It just seems a pity to waste 'em, now doesn't it? She doesn't say this, but it's only a few years ago since I was "teen age" and had an omnivorous yearning for everything that wore dresses.

Try to borrow *The Sea Around Us* by Rachel Carson. This is some of the most interesting and best scientific writing which I have read. It is a delightful book—vastly entertaining and informative.

The train is pulling into Summit, and the paper is all covered with scrawls. Write me; tell me what you think about, if anything.

Sincerely,
Arthur Rushmore

The next two letters have not been punctuated. Punctuate them, then have some one correct your punctuation.

August 20 19—

Mr Ernest W Gehr
1040 State Street
Spokane 3 Washington

Dear Mr Gehr

in accordance with your request we have measured the floor space required for the feet of the simplex master speed press and find that the distance between the legs from center to center is twenty four inches the length is thirty four inches if in making a concrete foundation you make each side of the foundation eight inches wide it will be ample to support this machine

incidentally this same width is required for the new kluge automatic press and if you will build the supports forty eight inches long instead of thirty four you will have a foundation of adequate size for a kluge automatic press in case you ever decide to install one

we hope that this information will enable you to go ahead with your plans and permit your order to come forward to us the other arrangements in regard to delivery and terms will be satisfactory and since you have now overcome all obstacles that stood in the way we suggest that you send in the order as soon as possible because we have only this one simplex press of the latest model

Cordially yours

1014 Fourth Avenue
Williamsport Pa
November 5 19—

Mr J W Lundy
Ralston Pa

Dear Mr Lundy

we understand that you are the tax collector for cascade township and we are wondering whether you might be able to give us some information concerning certain land in the township

mrs brown and i are interested in buying a seventeen acre plot of ground back of the robert evans property on rock run near lycoming creek we shall appreciate very much your giving us correct information concerning the following

1. who now owns the land immediately in back of this seventeen acre plot now owned by the lycoming lumber company this i suppose would be in a southerly direction on the mountain

2. does george hamiltons land extend along the west side of this said plot for its entire length

3. has the 800 acre plot formerly owned by the pennsylvania lumber company been sold to the state or does the pennsylvania lumber company still own it

4. what are taxes on the plot in question

we shall certainly appreciate very much any courtesy that you can extend us in this matter.

very truly yours

22. The Punctuation of Typical Sentences *

Rules are given students to use as guides in punctuation. But like everything else, there is frequently more than only one right way to punctuate certain sentences. This section of the chapter will show you the different ways in which typical sentences can be punctuated.

Punctuate to Separate Statements of Equal Value

1. I have no money, and I anticipate receiving none.
I have no money and I anticipate receiving none.

The comma is optional in this sentence. Since the two statements are short, the break is a slight one, and the sentence is easily understood without any punctuation. The comma may be used or it may be omitted.

2. My books and papers had been taken from the desk, and all my work had been scattered over the floor.

The comma is preferred in front of *and* when it connects long unpunctuated statements. However, a semicolon instead of a comma can be used here if the writer wishes.

3. The result of this long delay in making shipments, as we had expected, was a number of cancellations of large orders; *and* the

* The methods of punctuating given here have for the most part been adapted from Sterling A. Leonard, *Current English Usage* (Chicago: National Council of Teachers of English).

shipping clerks, expecting each hour to receive additional help, worked all night to get the orders filled and shipped.

Here the semicolon is preferred before *and* because it connects two long statements each of which contains commas. It is possible to use the comma before *and* as long as the break between the thoughts of the statements is not too great.

4. I didn't like the contract which they offered us, but there was nothing that we could do about it.

In sentence 1 the comma before *and* was optional. In Sentence 4 the comma before *but* is preferred.

5. The men had cleaned the shop thoroughly, for they expected the inspector that day.

The comma is always preferred in front of *for* when it connects two complete statements.

Summary of *And, But,* and *For*

When *and* connects short statements the comma may or may not be used before it. When *but* and *for* connect short statements, it is best to use the comma before them.

When *and, but,* and *for* join complete statements containing commas within themselves, it is better to use the semicolon than the comma.

Punctuation of *So, Yet, Hence,* and *However*

6. Ralph arrived with the bait, so we all went fishing.
   Ralph arrived with the bait; so we all went fishing.

Here the comma is preferred; the semicolon is permissible. When *so* connects two complete statements of equal value, it is best to use the comma before the connecting word *so*. However, the semicolon can be used here if the writer wishes. The punctuation before *so* is very much like that before *but* and *for*.

7. The weather had been getting colder. It had been raining, then it began to snow.

The weather had been getting colder. It had been raining; then it began to snow.

In a sentence of this kind either the comma or the semicolon may be used before *then* when it connects two complete statements.

8. I believe that he will come, yet he has never promised me that he would come.

I believe that he will come; yet he has never promised me that he would come.

As with *so* and *then*, either a comma or a semicolon may be used before *yet*.

9. Your letter arrived too late; hence we could not change our plans.
Your letter arrived too late, hence we could not change our plans.

The semicolon is preferred here in front of *hence*, but the comma may be used. The sentence may also be punctuated this way:

Your letter arrived too late; hence, we could . . .

10. We have spent several days cleaning the office; however, we have not yet been able to move our desks into it.

The semicolon is preferred before *however* when it connects two complete statements. The word *therefore* would probably require much the same punctuation as *however*. Notice that the comma is used after *however*.

11. Our advertising program has been a success; our research program a failure.

Our advertising program has been a success, our research program a failure.

Either the comma or the semicolon may be used between complete statements having closely related meanings. In this sentence both statements are about the success of programs within the same company. Perhaps it is usually better to use the semicolon in sentences of this kind.

12. The grape industry has been ruined, the fields have been reduced to masses of mud, the people living here are utterly discouraged —for a flood respects no man's property.

The grape industry has been ruined; the fields have been reduced to masses of mud; the people living here are utterly discouraged —for a flood respects no man's property.

Either the comma or the semicolon can be used here. Probably the comma is sufficient in this sentence because the entire sentence reads easily and smoothly. The last statement *for a flood respects no man's property* applies with equal force to each of the three preceding statements; consequently, the dash is used before this expression.

13. We must increase our sales; we must reduce our overhead expense; and we must do more experimental work.

The semicolon is preferred here. As a general rule it is safer to use the semicolon between statements not joined by a conjunction, but there are some situations, such as in Sentences 11 and 12, where the comma may be sufficient.

14. We ordered red, white, and yellow paper for the different forms.
We ordered red, white and yellow paper for the different forms.

Although the comma may not be absolutely necessary between the last two elements in a series, it is perhaps best to use it.

15. The three courses offered are printing, cabinetmaking and patternmaking, and machine shop practice.

Here both commas are needed so that the reader need not stop to figure out just what the three courses are.

Divided Quotations

16. "Charles is right," we insisted, "there is nothing seriously wrong."

"Charles is right," we insisted; "there is nothing seriously wrong."

In divided quotations (the exact words of the speaker), where the interrupting element separates two statements of equal importance, either the comma or the semicolon may be used. Perhaps the comma is sufficient here because the words *we insisted* mark a division in themselves.

17. "What's the matter, anyway?" asked George. "We haven't even touched the engine."

Here the distinction between the two statements is much sharper than it is in Sentence 16; hence the period is preferred. The first part of the example asks a question and the second part states a fact. For this reason it is best to consider the two ideas as two complete sentences.

18. "What do I care, anyway," retorted George, "especially since you haven't done anything about it?"

Since the second part of the quotation is necessary to complete the question, the question mark is placed at the end of the quotation, and the interruping element *retorted George* is set off by commas.

Subordinate Ideas—Statements Beginning with *When, If, Since, Because, Which,* etc.

19. When John spoke we always listened.
When John spoke, we always listened.

Because the sentence is short and easily understood without punctuation, the sentence can be punctuated either way as shown above. A short subordinate idea coming first in the sentence need not be set off by commas.

20. While we were collecting our tools to go out and do what we could to start the car, somebody phoned to tell us that the engine was ruined.

The comma is advisable at the end of the *while* idea beause both it and the sentence are rather long and a break is desirable.

21. On my way to work I talked to Jim about your suggestion.

Short groups of words even though out of natural order in a sentence need no comma after them when they begin a sentence.

Expletives—Additional Unnecessary Words

22. I dislike to work at night, don't you?
   I dislike to work at night—don't you?

The comma is preferred; the dash can also be used because of the break in thought.

23. I repeat, he certainly has my permission to do it.
   I repeat: He certainly has my permission to do it.

The comma is preferred in this sentence, but the colon can also be used. *I repeat* like *don't you* is felt to be less important than the rest of the sentence.

If *I repeat* is for emphasis, then the colon is best; if it is only introductory or an interrupter, then the comma is enough.

Punctuation of *Oh, Yes,* and *No*

24. Oh, John, why did you do it?

When used with words in direct address, the *oh* is usually followed by a comma.

25. Yes, I shall go along. No, I shall not be able to go.

Yes and *no* are usually followed by the comma.

Punctuation of Extra Words and Expressions, Such as *Finally, Of course,* and *On the other hand*

26. Finally, the school was closed for the holidays.

When such words as *finally, however,* and *of course* merely interrupt the idea or the thought of the sentence, they are usually separated from the rest of the sentence by commas.

27. He can, of course, go ahead with the job if he wishes.

Of course interrupts the thought or flow of the sentence and is set off by commas.

28. Of course he can go ahead with the job if he wishes.
Of course, he can go ahead with the job if he wishes.

In this case the comma is probably not necessary after *of course*, because the emphasis is such that the sentence reads smoothly and is easily understood without punctuation. There is a possibility that the comma can be used here for more emphasis.

29. Of course, if you think it's worth the risk, we shall be glad to back you in the enterprise.

It is probably best to use the comma after the introductory words *of course* and again after the subordinate idea introduced by *if* and ending with *risk*.

30. On the other hand, we cannot afford to take the trip.

Here the comma is used to set apart the introductory words *on the other hand*.

31. It began to rain, however, before we could get started.

In this sentence *however* is set off by commas as an interrupter of the thought. *However* is not a part of the idea expressed.

Necessary and Unnecessary Groups of Words

32. My friend Bill Smith will go with us.
My friend, Bill Smith, will go with us.

The commas are preferred here, but they are not necessary.

33. His words, though harmless in themselves, created a bad impression.

Here the words *though harmless in themselves* add merely a descriptive detail not necessary to the main thought of the sentence; hence they are enclosed by commas. These commas apply also to the following example:

The piano, an excellent piece of workmanship, was sold at a very low price.

34. The sounding board in the piano was badly cracked, so that he had to fasten the ribs together.

The statement introduced by *so that* is not necessary to the main thought and adds an additional idea to the sentence; consequently, the comma is used before *so that*.

35. Jim's new Ford, which we drove, is much different from my old one.

Here commas are placed around *which we drove* because these words add merely a descriptive detail and can be omitted without changing the meaning of the sentence in any way.

36. Most persons who have had anything to do with the civic theater want it to be permanent.

The group of words *who have anything to do with the civic theater* is necessary to the complete meaning of the sentence. Since they cannot be omitted, no punctuation is used.

37. He worked all day, not even stopping to eat.

Not even stopping to eat is an additional idea which can be omitted because it is not necessary to the main idea; hence, a comma is used before it.

Indicating Possession with the Apostrophe

38. Charles' bicycle was stolen.
    Charles's bicycle was stolen.

Either form is permissible.

39. The Jones' party was a success.
    The Jones's party was a success.

Either form is permissible.

40. We had several dollars' worth of fun.
    We had several dollars worth of fun.

Either form can be used, but the possessive with the apostrophe is preferred.

41. We took a two weeks' vacation.
    We took a two weeks vacation.

The apostrophe is preferred, but the other form is sometimes used.

42. The salesmen's convention was well attended. (*Correct*)
    The salesmens convention was well attended. (*Incorrect*)

Geographical Names

43. Our company ships goods to New England and the Middle West.

New England and *Middle West* are capitalized because each term refers to a definite area.

44. Our company ships goods farther west than that.

Here *farther west* is not capitalized because it does not refer to any definite area.

Schools, Grades, etc.

45. Our junior high school was built in 1954.
    Our Junior High School was built in 1954.

The form *junior high school* is preferred, but the capitals can be used if the writer wishes.

46. I am taking courses in history, mathematics, chemistry, mechanical drawing, and English.

Capitals are not needed when writing the names of courses except with such words as *English*.

47. John is in the seventh grade and Sarah is a junior.

Capitals are not necessary in writing the school grade.

48. We go to Sunday school regularly.

Sunday requires the capital, but *school* does not.

49. We expect mother and father to visit us.
    We expect Mother and Father to visit us.

Either form may be used. When used in place of names, however, the capitalized form is probably better.

50. I have not seen my father for a long time.

Here the small *f* is preferred to the capital.

51. Our dictaphone is in constant use.

In popular usage the trade name "Dictaphone" has been widely applied to any recording and reproducing instrument used in business offices, particularly in handling correspondence; when the word is so used, no capital is required. Similar words are *simoniz* and *kodak*.

Titles of Books and Magazine Articles

52. The magazine article was called "Father Forgets."

Use quotation marks around the title of a magazine article.

53. I have just finished reading "The Adventures of Sherlock Holmes."

Use quotation marks around the titles of books. When printed, italics may be used.

Miscellaneous Forms

54.	6:00	*preferred*	P. M.
	6.00	*permissible*	p. m.

PART II

Applying English to Your Job

FIGURE 1.* Your English Must Fit the Occasion—and the Audience.

Different Kinds of English *

There is a story about a plumber who wrote to the Bureau of Standards in Washington that he had found hydrochloric acid good for cleaning out clogged drains. He got the following answer: "The efficacy of hydrochloric acid is indisputable, but the corrosive residue is incompatible with metallic permanence."

So the plumber wrote back that he was glad the Bureau agreed with him. The Bureau tried again: "We cannot assume responsibility for the production of toxic and noxious residue with hydrochloric acid and suggest you use an alternative procedure."

The plumber wrote again that he was pleased the Bureau agreed with him.

Finally, the Bureau realized they had to use a different kind of language. The next letter read:

"Don't use hydrochloric acid. It eats the devil out of the pipes."

* Rudolf Flesch, *How to Write Better.* Life Adjustment Series (Chicago: Science Research Associates). Reprinted by permission.

Then there's another story about a lady who approached the elevator in a Philadelphia department store and asked: "Are you ascending or descending?"

The elevator man stared at her and said: "Sorry, lady, you'll have to ask Information about that." Then he stuck his head out of the door and called:

"Going up!"

Use the Right Kind of Language

Do you see at what these stories are driving? Always make certain that your language fits the case and the persons to whom you are speaking or writing.

If you are writing or speaking to persons like yourself about ordinary everyday things stay away from the unusual and the technical words.

If, on the other hand, you are explaining a technical subject to a group who understand it, then go ahead and use the technical words that best express your thoughts.

But whatever you do, be sure to use the kind of English suited to the occasion and the listener.

Chapter 6

A RELATED INFORMATION SCRAPBOOK AND NOTEBOOK

It is not always the thing that you make in your school shop that counts so much as what you learn while you are making it. As you spend day after day or evening after evening in the shop constructing various articles, you should learn as much as possible about some of the following things:

1. The material used.
2. The different methods employed.
3. The advantages or disadvantages of certain methods.
4. The proper method of operating the machines.
5. The information needed to do certain jobs.
6. Safety precautions and safe working practices.

Technical Knowledge Makes a Difference Between Men

Other things being equal, the thing that makes one workman stand head and shoulders above another is the extent of his technical knowledge or information. Such information cannot be accumulated overnight; for that matter, it cannot be acquired over a period of several months. You can become a master of your occupation only after years of effort and work.

Frequently, up-to-date trade information is not available in books just when you want it because much of the best and latest information comes directly from trade and technical magazines and from manufacturers in sheet, booklet, and pamphlet form. Much of this information cannot be found elsewhere and many of the papers are difficult to preserve.

101

Because of these difficulties, many wide-awake men save items of value on a particular subject. Why then would it not be a good idea for us, as we study these various occupations over a period of time, to save articles or notes containing worth-while trade and technical information?

Collect and Organize Information

As a part of your English work, you should collect and arrange such material as is interesting and valuable to you in your field. You can do this in one of several ways, namely:

1. Use a loose-leaf notebook. Collect magazine articles, newspaper articles, or small pamphlets. Paste them on notebook sheets and insert them in the notebook as you would any other sheet of paper. If you cannot secure the articles themselves, you can take and preserve notes on the articles.

2. Make a cardboard folder to hold your material and then use the folder much the same as a loose-leaf notebook. You might fasten together two pieces of cardboard with adhesive.

3. Get a large envelope measuring 8½ x 11 inches or larger and merely save your material by placing it in the envelope.

Collecting Materials or Information About Your Jobs

You should collect material which applies to jobs that you do in the shop from time to time; for example, if you spend a week constructing a table from oak, you should locate information concerning oak lumber, its properties and uses, its advantages and disadvantages, and place the information in your scrapbook or notebook. When you are finishing the table, you should secure material for the scrapbook giving information on the different types of finishes and their costs, methods of application, advantages and disadvantages, etc.

Another excellent idea is to place in your scrapbook any compositions or papers that you write for your shop teacher. Usually these papers are required by your shop instructor because he feels that a certain subject is important for you, and you generally write the paper only after studying that particular subject.

Arrange Material in an Orderly Way

Material that is arranged in an orderly way is much more valuable to you than is unorganized material. There is little

```
                    Subject or Topic

Name of Author ......................................

Title of Book or Magazine Article (and Magazine).....

.....................................................

Name of Publisher...................................

Date Published .....................................


                         Notes
```

FIGURE 2. Follow a Simple but Systematic Arrangement When Taking Notes. The Above Arrangement Is a Good One.

use in collecting material if you cannot find the particular items that you have saved. At the end of each month or semester, as your instructor directs, you should arrange your material under a series of headings and then make a short index or table of contents showing under what headings information on the different subjects can be found. For example, students in printing and cabinet-making can arrange their notes under headings such as the following:

Printing	*Cabinet-Making*
Binding	Finishing
Composition	Fillers
English	Stains
Imposition	etc.

Printing	*Cabinet-Making*
Layout and design	Glue
Paper cutting	Joinery
Presswork	Miscellaneous materials
Proofreading	Nails
Style	Screws
	etc.
	Tools
	Woods and their properties

Definite Suggestions for Conducting Your Project

1. Secure a folder or notebook sufficiently large to use as a scrapbook.

2. Place in your notebook all papers written for your shop instructor and returned to you.

3. Collect any material containing trade or technical information in which you are interested or which is worth while for you to have.

4. Place only one subject on a page.

5. Arrange your material in an orderly manner.

6. Make a table of contents or a short index of your material.

Chapter 7

USING TRADE AND TECHNICAL MAGAZINES

Three Kinds of Magazines

Most magazines which you read can be placed in one of three groups; namely, the popular magazine, the general-scientific magazine, and the trade or technical journal. The popular magazine is so named because it is edited to appeal in a general way to the large mass of people. The popular magazine contains a variety of material such as short stories, accounts of travel, political and economic discussions, and other articles of general interest.

The second group of magazines, the general broadly scientific magazine, appeals to a more limited class of people who are interested in science and mechanics. This group includes such magazines as *Popular Mechanics, Scientific American, Popular Science, Science and Mechanics,* etc.

The trade or technical journal is issued for the benefit of a limited group which is interested in one particular field. This type of magazine is of most value to the trade and technical student. The articles usually apply to some phase of the trade or profession or to some related subject and are as carefully written as books. The advertisements appearing in the trade journal are also of considerable value to the alert student because they usually contain important news about recent machine and technical developments.

Some of the trade and technical magazines to which the student usually has access are the *American Builder, The Inland Printer, Architectural Record, Automotive Service Digest, Aero Digest, Machinery, American Machinist, Radio News, Welding Journal, Electric Light & Power, Modern Plastics,* etc.

Why Read Technical Magazines?

Magazines are one of the best and most reliable sources of up-to-date trade and technical information. Because of research with its consequent discoveries and improvements, books are soon out of date on many technical topics. On the other hand, newspapers are printed too hastily to supply either adequate or accurate information on most subjects. Magazines should, therefore, usually contain the most up-to-date and accurate technical information.

How to Read Trade and Technical Journals

After you have selected the magazine in which you are interested, you must select the articles that you wish to read. For almost the same reason that you do not read everything that a newspaper contains, you would be unwise to try to read everything that a magazine contains.

First. Look through the table of contents. You can select the articles that you wish to read by looking through the table of contents. If you are not certain what the article is about, read a little in the different articles that attract your attention. In this way you can skip the ones that do not interest you.

Second. Have a purpose for reading each article. If you ask yourself, "Why am I reading this article?" or "What do I want to learn from it?" you will remember more and you will understand more of what you read.

Third. Skim through the article, then go back and read it thoroughly. Skimming first will give you a general idea of what the article is all about, and you will know how it is organized. In other words, you will have in your mind a "rough blueprint" that will help you to get meanings and see the relationships between the different ideas.

Fourth. Read the article carefully. As a result of your skimming, you will already be familiar with the central thought of the article. You may think that reading it twice will take too long. But you will find instead that if you skim it first you will be able to read it much more rapidly, and also that you will understand it better.

Fifth. Think it over or talk it over. Have you found the answer to your questions? Have you found any new ideas?

Sixth. If the information is important, place it in your file or notebook.

Applying Your Knowledge

HELPFUL QUESTIONS AND PROBLEMS:

1. Name three general types of magazines. Give the distinguishing characteristics of each.

2. Why should you not expect to secure reliable trade or technical information from newspapers?

3. Why is the material printed in technical and trade journals usually more reliable than the same type of material printed in books?

4. Make a list of suggestions for reading trade periodicals.

5. Make a list of the general scientific magazines that are available through the library.

6. Make a list of the trade and technical magazines that deal with your trade.

7. Read a trade magazine according to the suggestions given in the chapter. Write a short report on what you read. Explain how you decided what to omit. Be prepared to give an oral report in class on this same material.

8. Carefully examine several trade journals. School, city, or factory libraries will probably be adequate. Prepare a report for class on each magazine examined. Point out the differences between magazines. Some points that you might consider are:

a) Kind of articles published.

b) Is the magazine more interesting to the mechanic, the engineer, or the owner of a business?

c) Are the articles difficult or easy for you to understand?

d) Do the articles deal with problems that you meet on the job or in the operation of a business?

e) What kind of advertising does the magazine contain? Does the advertising tell you about new developments in your trade? Does the advertising give you any new ideas?

9. Of what value to a technical man or to a journeyman are the advertisements in a trade magazine?

10. Locate in some periodical several advertisements worth reading. Write out briefly why you think that each advertisement selected merited your attention. Make for your notebook or scrapbook a copy of the advertisements. If you can secure a copy of the advertisement, place the advertisement itself in your collection.

Chapter 8

DESCRIPTION OF TOOLS AND INSTRUMENTS

How to Describe Tools

Technical description attempts merely to make clear the appearance of an object and sometimes its method of operation. The chief aim is to reproduce in the reader's mind a mental picture of the object, not to make him feel any certain way about it. In order to accomplish this, you must assume that the reader is not familiar with the object to be described. The main problems then confronting you are: (1) how best to create a picture of the object in the reader's mind, (2) how much to include, and (3) how to arrange the details of the description.

Helping the Reader Visualize the Object

Three common methods of painting a picture in the mind of the reader are:

1. By using a photograph, sketch, or drawing.
2. By showing how the object is like or unlike another object already familiar to the reader.
3. By taking the object apart; that is, by naming and describing the parts in order.

Using Photographs or Drawings to Help the Reader. It is natural for any one who is attempting to describe something to say, "This is the way it looks," and then to make a drawing of the object. However, six rules that you should follow when using drawings or photographs to help make descriptions clear are:

1. The illustration should be placed as near as possible to that part of the description with which it belongs.

2. The illustration should show clearly the essential parts of the object described.

3. The illustration should be neat. A messy drawing is always displeasing and it is usually inaccurate.

4. The drawing should be accurate.

5. A good-sized margin looks much better than a narrow one.

6. When the drawing illustrates a complicated object, it is well to label the essential parts with symbols or figures. Such symbols should be orderly in arrangement and easy to find.

Comparing the Tool with a Common Object. The second method of assisting the reader to visualize something is that of comparing the tool or object to something with which the reader is already familiar. We do this when we mention the T-square of the draftsman or the S-hook of the machinist. If you cannot make a comparison in this way, you can sometimes compare a new tool or machine with an older one of the same type. For example, you might compare a current model Chevrolet with an earlier model Chevrolet, with which the reader would probably be familiar.

It is usually better to give first some idea of the appearance of the whole object before giving a separate description of each of the parts. For example, if a teacher of geography were to attempt to describe the United States by drawing the Hudson River and the Catskill Mountains and a few chief cities without first drawing the general outlines of the entire country, he would fail to show his pupils how these sections are related to the other sections of the country.

Describing the Different Parts in Order. Sometimes it is easier to visualize the machine if it is described one part or section at a time. In other words, the machine is taken apart and the parts are described separately. The outline which appears on page 111 may help you understand just how this plan is used.

A Description of a Machine or Tool

I. The general appearance of the machine.

II. The parts of the machine.
   A. The first part.
      1. Its general appearance.
      2. The way it fits into the second part.
      3. Its use.

   B. The second part.
      1. Its general appearance.
      2. The way it fits into the first or the third part.
      3. Its use.

   C. (Same as above.)
   D. (Same as above.)

III. How the parts work together.

IV. The uses and the importance of the machine.

Arrangement of the Description

To be effective a description must be arranged in an orderly manner. The arrangement of a description frequently determines whether or not it presents a clear picture of the object. Although every description might be arranged in one of several different ways, there are certain principles and rules which you should know and which you should follow when describing a tool or machine.

Usually the following order or arrangement of a description will prove satisfactory:

1. Define the object and give its general appearance.

2. Describe the details such as the shape, size, weight, color, materials, etc.

3. Give the uses of the object or its principle of operation.

4. Make a sketch of the object if helpful. Sometimes it is easier to make a sketch first and to keep it in front of you while writing the description.

Student Descriptions for Class Analysis

The Miter Box

Definition and General Appearance   A miter box is like a short shallow trough, about 15 inches long and 4 inches deep. It is formed by a bottom and two side pieces of wood or metal fastened together and having saw cuts through the sides at angles of 45 degrees and 90 degrees. *Use* This device is used to guide the saw in cutting work to form miters.

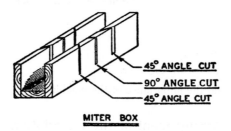

45° ANGLE CUT
90° ANGLE CUT
45° ANGLE CUT

MITER BOX

The Level

Definition and General Appearance   The level consists of a long rectangular piece of wood or metal cut away on its side and near the ends to receive glass tubes which are almost filled with a non-freezing liquid. Since each tube is not quite filled with the liquid, a small bubble is formed which is free to move when the level is raised at one end.

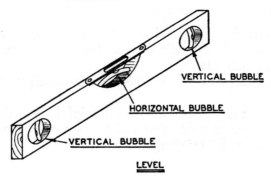

VERTICAL BUBBLE

HORIZONTAL BUBBLE

VERTICAL BUBBLE

LEVEL

Details   The side and end tubes are at right angles so that when the bubble of the side tube is at the center of the tube, the level is exactly horizontal; when the bubble of the end tube is at the center, the level is vertical. Consequently, when held on a surface, the level indicates whether the surface is horizontal or vertical.

Use   The level is used to guide and test work in bringing it to a horizontal or vertical position, and to determine whether or not completed construction is truly horizontal or vertical.

The Hand Hacksaw

Definition and General Appearance   The hand hacksaw is a metal-cutting saw consisting of three parts: a handle, a frame that resembles a very large, broad and inverted U, and a thin narrow blade fastened to the two open ends of the frame.

Details   The handle which is just large enough to be grasped by only one hand is fastened at right angles to the one leg of the inverted ∩-shaped frame. The frame is made either in fixed or adjustable lengths to take the more common 8, 10, or 12-inch blades. The blade is fastened to the two open ends of the frame and is so attached that it cuts on only the forward stroke. The blades used for hand sawing are thin and narrow, averaging about .5 inch wide, .025 of an inch thick, and 8, 10, or 12 inches long. The blades are made from a high grade of steel scientifically hardened and tempered; consequently, they are very hard and very brittle.

Use   The hand hacksaw is used to cut metal when the piece is not too large or too hard.

Applying Your Knowledge

HELPFUL QUESTIONS:

1. What is the object of technical description?

2. In what ways does technical description differ from other types of description?

3. What problems confront the writer of a technical description?

4. When describing a tool should you give first the details and last the general appearance, or give first the general appearance and then the details of the object?

PROBLEMS:

1. Write a description of some tool with which you are familiar. By means of notes in the left-hand margin show what order or arrangement you have used in the description.

2. Write a description of some tool, machine, or instrument used in your school shop. After you have finished with the description, explain the method or methods that you have used to create a clear picture in the mind of the reader.

3. Write a description of one more object with which you are familiar. Be prepared to explain to the class your arrangement of the description and the methods that you have used to help the reader secure a clear picture.

4. Bring a tool or instrument to class or draw an illustration on the blackboard. Describe the tool orally to the class, using either the actual tool or the blackboard drawing for reference.

SUGGESTED SUBJECTS FOR DESCRIPTION:

ball-peen hammer	keyhole saw
block and tackle	magnet
blowtorch	mallet
blueprint	marking gauge
brace	micrometer
bodkin	pipe wrench
camera	pliers
carpenter's square	plumb bob
charcoal furnace	pocket knife
composing stick	protractor
cone pulley	quoins
dowel plate	radio tube
file	rip saw
galley float	socket wrench
galley	soldering iron
hand-screw clamp	spalling hammer

S-wrench
thermostat
trowel
T-square

vernier caliper
vise
voltmeter
wheelbarrow

Chapter 9*

DESCRIPTION OF MATERIALS

Describing Materials Used in the Shop and in Industry

Our minds are similar to sensitive camera film in that they are constantly receiving and recording impressions through our senses of sight, hearing, touch, taste, and smell. When we pick up a piece of copper, for example, we note that it is a reddish-brown color, that it is softer than many other metals with which we are acquainted, that it is rather heavy, and that it tarnishes slightly after it has been exposed to air. When we try to reproduce in words these impressions, we make use of description.

Use Nontechnical Terms

Any material commonly used in the trades can ordinarily be described in terms understood by the average person. Although such description does not require the use of technical terms, it does require that one notice and record carefully the characteristics of the material. For example, every one studying the electrical trades should be able to write a description of copper somewhat as follows:

Copper

Copper is a very soft, pliable metal, reddish brown in color. It has a tendency to tear when it is machined, but it can readily be rolled, stamped, drawn, brazed, or cast. It can be hardened by hammering, and softened by quenching. It is usually furnished in the form of sheets, wire, rods, or bars. It melts at 1950 degrees Fahrenheit. Al-

* Material in this chapter adapted from "How to Describe Materials Used in Shop Subjects," by Merritt W. Haynes, *Industrial Education Magazine*. By permission of The Charles A. Bennett Co., Inc., Peoria, Ill.

though it is only slightly corrosive in air, it is readily corrosive in acids. Finally, it is an excellent conductor of electricity.

This description is not a dictionary definition; it contains no technical terms or unusual words. Yet all that the average electrician needs to know about copper is mentioned. At the end of a year in the electrical shop the pupil has learned all this about copper, but he can seldom state it in such orderly, simple, concise language without considerable practice.

Planning a Description of a Material

The average mechanic almost unconsciously recognizes the materials with which he works, but rarely can he describe these same materials in words. A woodworker may say that a certain board is white or yellow pine and that he recognizes it as such because of its color and grain. This is quite true, but all kinds of lumber have color and grain and many kinds of lumber are very much alike. Even though the woodworker can distinguish between the different kinds of wood, it is often difficult for him to describe readily and accurately all the exact features of any material that he commonly uses.

In all descriptions the names of the features or characteristics of any material are nouns, such as color, fiber, pore. Each of these nouns must in turn be described by adjectives, as *yellowish-white in faint streaks* to describe the color; *straight* fibers to describe the fibers; *small* pores or *inconspicuous* pores to describe the pores. These adjectives really paint the word picture of the material. Without them no distinguishing features would be given.

Many Ways to Identify Materials

Usually materials can be distinguished by sight alone. For example, a machinist can usually tell the difference between a piece of cast iron and a piece of machine steel by noticing the difference in color and surface. It is also frequently possible to distinguish between materials by feeling them. The weight of a piece of metal helps us determine whether it is tin or aluminum. The dressmaker can easily feel the difference in texture between a piece of linen and a piece of cotton. Sometimes the woodworker depends upon his sense of smell to distinguish between two pieces of wood that appear very much alike; the fruit grower likewise often distinguishes apples by their odor.

Sometimes the skilled workman uses various tests to determine just what the material is. Several kinds of steel that look very much alike can be distinguished readily by applying the specimens to a grinding wheel and noting the kind of spark given off, since each kind of steel produces a different kind of spark.

All these various sources of identification must be used to describe a material accurately. To assist the student in learning to describe materials, several keys giving the terms describing the ordinary properties of the common classes of materials are printed later in this chapter. The name of the general quality is printed at the left, and to its right are printed the possible degrees, forms, or descriptive terms. If the proper term for each property is selected, an adequate description of the material can be made. To describe cast iron, for example, the list helps you to write out the following description:

Step 1: List qualities of the material, using the key as a guide.

Gray Cast Iron

chip—sandy
color—gray
content—carbon, sulphur, phosphorus, silicon
density—450 pounds per cubic foot
finish—rough
flexibility—rigid
grinding spark—dull
hardness—medium
luster—dull
oxidation—does not rust easily on the cast surface
       rusts on the machined surface

stock shapes—castings
strength—tensile strength, weak; compression strength, high
structure—finely crystalline
temperability—can be tempered
treatment—can be case-hardened
         can be machined easily

Step 2: Combine these ideas into a paragraph.

Cast iron is a gray, dull, rough-surfaced metal of medium hardness. It is usually weak in tensile strength, but rigid. On the other hand, it has a high degree of compressive strength. Because it is finely crystalline, it gives off a sandy chip and a dull grinding spark. Contrary to the beliefs of many people, it can be tempered. It can also be case-hardened, and it machines easily. Although it rusts very little on the cast surface, it rusts rather easily on the machined surface.

Two Kinds of Properties

If you will read again the description of copper and that of cast iron, you will notice that the appearance, the feel, and the hardness of the metals are given at the very beginning of the description. These characteristics are known as recognition properties because it is through them that you can recognize a substance by sight, touch, or smell. These senses enable you to recognize and determine color, form, distance, surface, texture, and odor.

Following the recognition properties you will find described the working properties. These properties describe how the material behaves when it is subjected to various operations. Answers to such questions as the following give the descriptions of the working properties of a substance: How well does the material conduct electricity? Does it tear easily? Does it rust when exposed to air? Does it machine easily?

Read again the description of cast iron, noticing particularly the two kinds of properties used in writing the description.

Recognition   Cast iron is a gray, dull, rough-surfaced metal of medium
Properties   hardness. It is usually weak in tensile strength, but rigid.

On the other hand, it has a high degree of compressive strength. Because it is finely crystalline, it gives off a sandy chip and a dull grinding spark. Contrary to the beliefs of many people, it can be tempered. It can also be case-hardened, and it machines easily. Although it rusts very little on the cast surface, it rusts rather easily on the machined surface.

Working Properties

Using the Keys

The keys printed in this chapter give a more extended list of properties than will interest workers in any one particular trade. For example the electrical conductivity of copper is of no interest to a machinist, but it is of considerable importance and interest to an electrician. In using one of the keys, therefore, it is necessary to consider only the properties that pertain to the use of the particular material in your trade or for a definite industrial application.

These keys are suggestive, not exhaustive. They can be revised and enlarged considerably; they may also serve as models for the construction of keys for other classes of materials in addition to those given here.

Properties of Lumber

Bending Power	Brittle, elastic, pliable, stiff.
Cleavability	Splits evenly, crooked, ragged, easily, moderately, with difficulty.
Color	Red, dull red, brown, dull brown, reddish brown, chocolate, yellow, greenish yellow, straw, cream, white, blue, gray.
Cost	Cheap, moderate, expensive, very expensive.
Defects	Knots, checks, shakes, wormholes.
Fibers	Fine, medium, coarse, straight, wavy, twisted, curly, gnarly, crooked.
Finish	Stain, filler, dull polish, high polish, varnish, paint.
Grain	*See* Fibers and Pores.
Hardness	Spongy, very soft, soft, medium, hard, very hard.

Medullary Rays	Obscure, visible, prominent, pronounced, small flakes, large flakes, few, many, very numerous.
Odor	Pitchy, swampy, fragrant, characteristic.
Pores	Invisible, fine, medium, large, very large.
Resistance to Weather	Decays readily, decays moderately, decays slowly, lasts many years.
Resin or Pitch	Nonresinous, slightly resinous, moderately resinous, very resinous, gummy, very gummy.
Retention of Shape	Springs, winds, twists, warps, retains shape.
Shapes	Logs, bolts, timbers, planks, boards, veneer.
Strength	Very weak, weak, moderate, strong, very strong.
Suitability	Framing, sheathing, flooring, trim, furniture, patterns, carving, turning, molding, boats, poles, posts, veneer, crating, implements, barrels, baskets.
Weight	Very light, light, medium, heavy, very heavy.
Workability	Easy, moderate, difficult.

Properties of Metal

Chip	Sandy, short, long, curly, spiral.
Color	White, gray, yellow, blue, brown, black.
Content	Pure, alloy (give ingredients).
Density	Weight per cubic foot.
Electrical Conductivity	Excellent, good, fair, poor, nonconductor, insulator.
Finish	Polish, lacquer, chemical.
Flexibility	Rigid, bends, springs.
Fusibility or Melting Point	Give degrees in Fahrenheit scale.
Grinding spark	Dull, bright, starry, profuse, moderate, sparse, none.
Hardness	Very soft, soft, medium, hard, very hard.
Luster	Dull, bright, very bright.
Oxidation	Rusts or corrodes readily, moderately, noncorrosive or rustless in air, in moisture, in acid, in alkali.
Stock Shapes	Sheets, bars, rods, wire, castings, ingots.
Strength	Fragile, brittle, weak, moderate, strong, tough.

Structure	Porous, compact, fibrous, granular, crystalline with fine, small, medium, or large facets.
Temperability	Hardens or softens with hammering, heating, quenching.
Treatment	Can be welded, brazed, soldered, cast, rolled, drawn, stamped, forged, annealed, hardened, case-hardened, machined easily, moderately, with difficulty, not at all.
Weight	Light, medium, heavy.

Applying Your Knowledge

HELPFUL QUESTIONS:

1. What is the difference between the right and the left columns in the keys?

2. Why does a description of a material require especially the use of nouns with modifying adjectives rather than the use of verbs with modifying adverbs?

3. What is the difference between the recognition properties and the working properties of a substance?

PROBLEMS:

1. Construct a key of properties relating to some class of materials used in your field. (The following lists of properties for oil and paper may help you with either of these two materials:

Oil: viscosity, fluidity, specific gravity, flash test, flame test, volatility, color, film strength, purity, durability, base—paraffin or asphalt, or mixed.

Paper: thickness, color, content, cost, durability, erasure, finish, folding qualities, pliability, stock sizes, special qualities, strength, weight, watermark, uses.

2. Describe accurately some material with which you are familiar and which is used in your trade or occupation.

3. Copy from an unabridged dictionary a description of the same material which you described under Problem 2, and compare the two descriptions. What differences can you find?

Chapter 10

WRITING WITH IMAGINATION ABOUT YOUR WORK

Painting Pictures With Words

Description is the painting of pictures with words. In a previous chapter you learned that technical or practical description attempts only to make clear the appearance of an object. Artistic description, which you will study in this chapter, attempts to present a vivid picture of the object *plus the way the writer feels about it.*

Technical description is concerned with exact measurements, degrees of hardness, pounds of weight; it expresses no feeling or emotion. Artistic description expresses emotion and tries to picture these qualities so that you feel a certain way about them. Technical description appeals only to your mind; artistic description appeals not only to your mind but also your feelings.

Good artistic description not only conveys the feelings of the writer toward the object, but it presents one main picture or impression. To one who observes closely, a person, place, or thing will present one main impression of beauty or of ugliness, of strength or of weakness, of slowness or of speed, of neatness or of disorder. This central impression may present itself in the form of a comparison; for example, the sight of a steam locomotive with its single gleaming eye may call to mind *Cyclops,* the giant who had only one eye in the middle of his forehead; a hook may resemble the letter S; or a machine, an *iron man.* On the other hand, the chief impression may be one of sound, as the *drone* of an electric motor or generator, the *clanking* of a chain, the *chatter* of a loom, or the *shriek* of automobile tires as they skid over concrete.

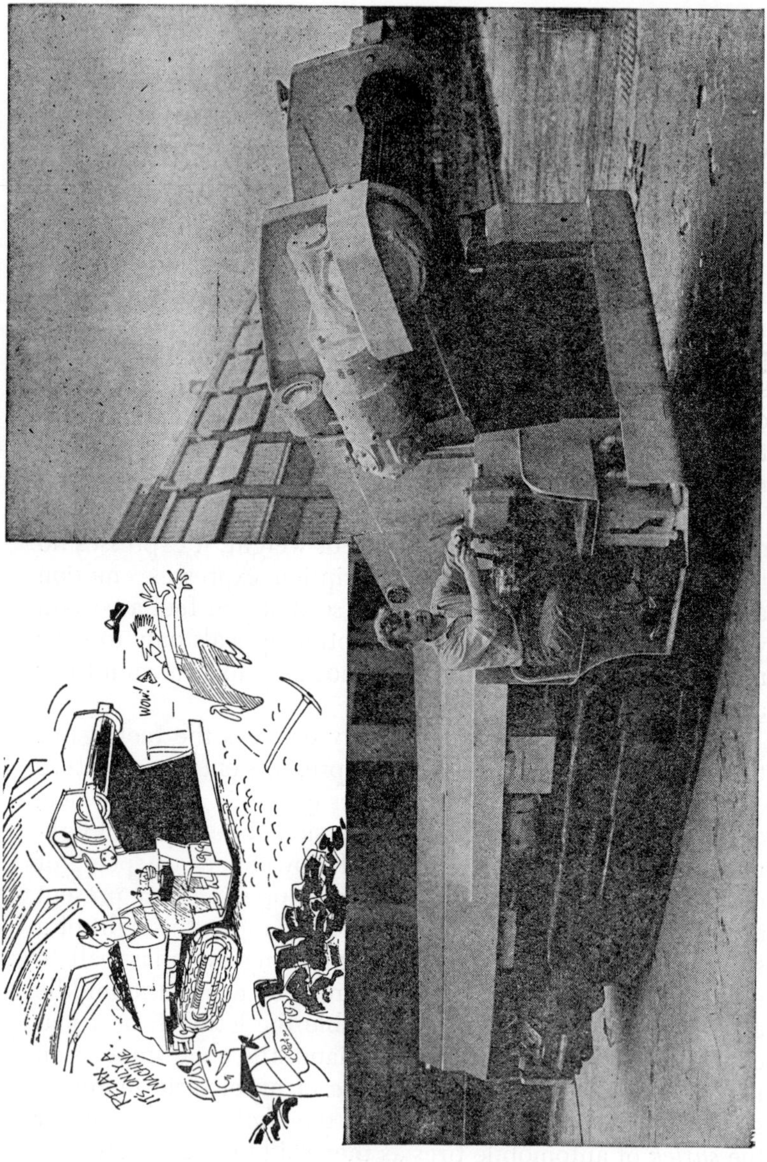

FIGURE 3. Mechanical Hippo (Courtesy General Electric Company)

What the cartoonist sees. Can you describe things as a cartoonist would draw them? This is Imaginative Description.

"This was the result when General Electric Company pitted a cartoonist's pen against a photographer's lens. Their subject was a strange vehicle which operates like an Army tank and looks like a yawning hippopotamus. Developed by G.E., it will be used in shuttling coal from veins to cars far beneath the earth's surface. The shuttle car is powered electrically; its 600 feet of extension cable plugs into an outlet in much the same way as a household appliance. A distinctive feature of the car is its conveyor-belt snout, which can be raised or lowered, enabling the machine to disgorge its load into waiting cars for the journey to the surface."

Point of View

Usually photographs of the same object do not look alike because the pictures have been taken from different positions. Similarly, if you stand in one place to describe an object or a scene, you will see only a part of it. Should you change your position to get another point of view, you will see other parts that you did not previously see. Point of view, therefore, refers to your relation to the thing you are describing.

In describing an object or a scene, you should include in your description only those things which you can see from that point, and you should clearly state from what position you are looking. If you walk about and describe something from different angles, you should show that you are changing your position by the use of such expressions as the following: *to the right, on that side, above, below, across*, etc. By using such terms as these, you can lead the person about in your description rather easily.

Outline for Any Description

You will find the writing or the presentation of a description much easier if you will attempt to follow some such outline as the one given here.

I. Point of View (your relation to the thing you are describing—where you are standing)
II. General Appearance
   A. Size

B. Shape (or build in describing a person)
C. Color
III. Details (give these in the order of their importance)
A.
B.
C.

Examples of Technical and Imaginative Description

The two examples following illustrate the difference between technical and imaginative writing.

Technical description of a factory taken from the beginning of a report. Notice that this description is concerned with the size and shape of objects, the methods of doing things, etc.

All the buildings are of one story; this allows easy transportation of materials, either by conveyers or trucks.

The buildings have sawtooth roof construction with skylights facing the southwest. This gives excellent daylight illumination and also provides for proper ventilation.

It is interesting to note that practically all heating is accomplished by using unit heaters which . . .

Imaginative description of a scene in the Milwaukee plant of the Globe Steel Tube Company. (Note how this description appeals to your feelings through your senses of hearing and sight.)

The siren screech of overhead cranes; the orange-red lights of the controls; a man with his mouth to another's ear yelling at the top of his voice and the result only a whisper; the whir and drone of generator and motors; and the ceaseless staccato of metal clanging metal. . . .

Read the following examples of description before you write any of the exercises yourself. While you are working on descriptions of your own, it will be a good idea to refer frequently to these examples. Try to determine whether the impression in each is one of sight, sound, feeling, smell, or any combination of these sense impressions.

A Scene in a Steel Mill

Here are my thanks to be through with this job and still intact, though I expect to locate in one or two more mills before I go back to assume the white (collared) man's burden. I'm only sorry that I can't stop for a go at the blast furnace or the Bessemer. But I will say that it doesn't take many twelve-hour nights of uninteresting hand labor to seem like a mighty long time.

It would seem longer were it not for the flaming panoramas and the monster noises always on hand. To be close to all the mammoth power they spell gives somehow a subtle pleasure—as though it were somehow in the process of becoming part of your own personal equipment. As you stand on the rim of the pickling-tank waiting to guide the crane-load of billets into the acid for taking off the scale, you suddenly feel warmth at your back, and turn to marvel at the wondrous orange-colored ingots following the dinky through the yard as silently as if they were the iridescent oil jars of Ali Baba. Then over in the open-hearth the building's outlines are in an instant thrown out black against the sky by the dazzling silver whiteness of the tapping—as if the devil himself had suddenly switched on the lights of Hell's General Head-quarters. A moment later the crane bell in the nearby building sounds its urgent warning, and the soaking pit opens to throw out a lemon-yellow glow on the great room's black steel rafters. Then the crane's huge and sinister multilated hand of finger and thumb reaches down into the fiery abyss under the guidance of the unseen man above and then relentlessly soars up and over with its dripping yellow ingot to the receiving tables of the blooming-mill. Too-oot! goes the whistle of the bar roller from his bridge, and looking like some dumb helpless beast, the ingot is rushed onto the roller tables, clankety-clank, up to and through the huge, sputtering rolls that shower hot, fiery scale every-where, only to be stopped suddenly with a colossal bang. After an instant's pause of silence the rolls are reversed, the yellow beast, now turning red, is pushed back through and, clankety-clank, again, stopped, bang!—till it is become lean and thin and comparatively cold, ready to be cut and hustled again into other furnaces for later heating and further rolling into the finished beams of the new skyscraper. Too-oot! goes the whistle again, and on the instant the soaking-pit craneman has deposited his dripping burden and another ingot Beast is on his way to the slaughter of the tirelessly grumbling and ceaselessly sputtering rolls, for these are tonnage-men, and every instant means money. Marvelous, too, are the deeds and doings of the crane-men who reach into the furnace to clasp one of these elongated blooms, lift it off the tables, and then by a sort of swing-your-partner movement, which is too complex to try to describe, contrive to place it into other furnaces, and then put the reheated steel back again onto the "tables" which carry it to the smaller rolls. These give it its final form and leave it to cool until it is put into the cars for shipment or use.—Whiting Williams, *What's on the Worker's Mind,* Charles Scribner's Sons.

The next selection describes a steam railroad train and its engine. Notice how Edward Yeomans has used his imagination to compare them with living things. The last selection is a description of the launching of an experimental rocket.

Pacific 4–6–2

Pacific 4–6–2 stands boring out into the rain-streaked night with its Cyclopean eye. It has before it the familiar pattern of tracks and colored lights, low and high. Behind stretch the long heavy cars, four baggage and express and ten Pullman, diminishing in perspective and dotted with yellow lights from warm interiors steadily populated by insectean humans such as fill train after train without knowing or caring to know what is involved in getting them to their destination.

. . . But this beast which stands here in the rain-streaked night on its 4–6–2 chassis, weighing three hundred and sixty thousand pounds this amazing simulacrum of life, breathing gently with its duplex air pumps, humming slightly at the safety valve, gleaming faintly on its polished sinews, a huge demonic figure condensed from the darkness, a djinni of the Arabian Nights tied to a string of fourteen cars which it is prepared to drag in a furious rush to New Haven en route to New York and Washington—this beast, I say, is the most impressive symbol of the courage and craftsmanship of man since the clipper-ship era.—Edward Yeomans, "Pacific 4–6–2" (*Atlantic Monthly*).

Rocket Shoot at White Sands

A rocket shoot at White Sands Proving Ground is more than interesting, more than beautiful, more than exciting. It is inspiring in a way that is equaled by few sights on earth.

Behind the austere buildings of the military post rise the spectacular Organ Mountains of New Mexico, with a fringe of dark pine trees climbing to their highest ridges. An uninhabited wilderness presses from all sides upon this isolated outpost of technological man. Jack rabbits bounce among the cactus and yucca. Deer dance down from the mountains at night and . . .

In front, for forty miles, sweeps the gray-green desert of the Tularosa Basin. . . .

The works of man seen from a distance look small in this setting, but some of them are startling when seen from close by. On a steep mountain slope perches a massive concrete structure that has the soaring aloofness of a Tibetan monastery. This is a test-stand where the biggest rocket motors are put through their flaming paces. It really looks like an adjunct for a flight to the moon.

Far out on the desert stands an even weirder structure—a peaked concrete igloo with walls and roof as solid as the stone of a pyramid. The "blockhouse" has . . .

Inside the massive blockhouse on a long control panel under a slit window glows a line of little red lights. When one of them goes out, it means that some circuit is completed, some instrument far away has declared itself alert and ready. . . .

The little red lights on the control panel wink out one by one. Voices report trouble, then trouble overcome. "Zero minus twenty minutes," chants the loud speaker.

Trucks and jeeps loaded with men dart away from the danger area. Gates are being closed; chains are being drawn taut across distant highways. The men at the framework around the rocket are administering to it a kind of extreme unction. They check its intricate instruments for the last time and close the flush-fitting doors that cover access ports. They climb down reluctantly, and the steel framework is wheeled away, revealing the graceful shape of the doomed rocket. At this moment of unveiling, it looks like the most beautiful thing that has ever been built by man . . .

"Zero minus one minute," chants the loud speaker. . . .

Now a solemn hush spreads across the desert. No men are in sight. They have all fled away or gone inside the blockhouse like ants going underground ahead of an approaching shower. Only a few red lights still show on the control panel. . . .

"Zero minus one minute," chants the loud speaker.

Now the impersonal voice at the unseen microphone shares the growing excitement. "Zero minus forty-five seconds," it chants in a higher key. Then "Zero minus thirty seconds."

The last of the little red lights is gone from the control panel, leaving nothing between the rocket and its moment of glory. It stands naked and alone like a human sacrifice watched by a thousand priests. A plume of brilliant red smoke spurts from the ground beside it and drifts across the desert. This is a final visual warning to men, instruments, and airplanes with no electronic ears.

"Zero minus five seconds," chants the loud speaker. Now its words come faster. "Four—three—two—one—ZERO!"

In the tense, hushed blockhouse, the firing officer throws the switch. A stab of yellow flame and a dense white cloud of smoke bursts from the tail of the rocket, and a screaming roar rolls across the desert. The rocket rises slowly at first as if an invisible hoist were drawing it upward. It wobbles a little, standing on its tail of flame. Then it gains confidence, gathers speed, and shoots up toward space like a bellowing arrow. In a few seconds it is gone, leaving only a trail of smoke like a chalk mark against the blue sky.—From *Flight into Space*. Reprinted by permission of Random House, Inc. Copyright 1953 by Jonathan Norton Leonard.

Applying Your Knowledge

HELPFUL QUESTIONS:

1. What are the differences between technical writing and imaginative writing? What are the uses of each?

2. What is meant by point of view? What is its importance in description?

3. Why is it best, at least in practice, to follow some form of outline when you are making a description?

4. Of what value is the ability to make an artistic or imaginative description?

PROBLEMS:

1. Copy one of the descriptions given on the preceding pages. Underline the words that describe.

2. What is the best starting point from which to begin a description of the following:

a) the exterior of a house
b) the inside of a house
c) armature
d) micrometer
e) a table
f) a rowboat
g) an automobile
h) your school shop
i) the place you work
j) some machine with which you are familiar

3. Write a technical description of a farm or of a manufacturing plant with which you are familiar, or of your school shop.

After you have finished the technical description, write an artistic or imaginative description of the same place.

4. Read again the examples on pages 126 and 127; then try to write an artistic description of the place you work or of your school shop when everybody is busy. For example, you might describe your shop just before school starts—What is your instructor doing then? What are some of the students doing? Is some of the machinery just being started? Are some of the students just ringing in on the time clock while others are getting under way with their work? etc.

5. Try to write an imaginative description of some machine when it is in operation.

Picturing People

The explanation given at the beginning of this chapter applies also to describing people. You will find too that the outline previously given will help you in making a description of some person who has attracted your interest.

Examples of Descriptions of Persons

A Cowboy of the Skies

He was standing out on a steel girder, with a blue-print map in his hands. He wore brown canvas trousers tucked into his boots, a grimy jumper, a shirt wide open at the throat, buckskin gloves frayed by hard use, and an old slouch hat on the back of his head. His lean tanned face was set in a puzzled scowl as he glanced now at the map and now downward at the steel frame of the building. I came cautiously nearer, looked over, and drew quickly back, for there was a sheer drop of five hundred feet between him and the pavement. A gust of wind blew the map up into his face. With an ejaculation, he leaned slightly out to brace himself and impatiently struck the map open. Then he jammed his hat over his eyes and continued his looking and scowling.— Ernest Poole, *Cowboys of the Skies,* Charles H. Kerr & Co.

Mr. Bray

Mr. Bray—lantern in hand—climbs down and walks in the rain and swaying shadows, a slow deliberate figure like a farmer going about chores, to the tower, to return presently with instructions to wait for an east-bound train to get off the west-bound track. . . . —Edward Yeomans, "Pacific 4–6–2" (*Atlantic Monthly*).

Applying Your Knowledge

PROBLEMS:

1. As Ernest Poole has done, describe some worker that you have seen. In your description of his appearance, clothes, and actions try to show how his job affects these things.

2. Bring to class a copy of a good description of a person. You can easily secure such a description from some book, magazine, or newspaper.

3. Read over the following notes carefully. Make similar significant notes of your own characterizing some one well known to you. Expand your notes into a carefully written description of the person.

clear-eyed boy—tall—well built—short brown hair—blue work shirt under blue overalls—hammer in right hand—blueprint in left hand—face and hands dirty from work

4. Describe some person known to the class but without naming him. Have the class attempt to guess the person's name from your description.

Chapter 11

SPEAKING AND WRITING FROM AN OUTLINE

Most of us give an explanation with greater ease and accuracy when we answer definite questions asked by another person. Similarly, it is easier to give a talk or to write a good paper by answering a series of questions about the subject. In other words, it is possible to construct an outline for a speech or for a written paper by writing a list of questions that another person might ask about the subject. You can then give an interesting talk or write an effective paper merely by answering one at a time the questions that you have listed.

In Chapter 9 the descriptions of copper and of cast iron were developed by answering such questions as: How hard is copper? What are its characteristics? How well does it conduct electricity? etc. Again in Chapter 10 the descriptions of "A Scene in A Steel Mill," of "Pacific 4–6–2," and of "A Cowboy of the Skies," all answer questions. In other words, in order to write a description of anything, it is necessary to answer certain questions. This chapter explains how to develop these questions in order to make the writing clearer and the explanation more orderly.

Typical Outlines

Read over the following question outlines carefully so that you will understand better how they are constructed:

Coal

1. What different kinds of coal are there?
2. Where is each kind of coal found?
3. How was each kind formed?

4. What properties does each possess?
5. What are the chief uses of each kind of coal?

Varnish

1. What is varnish? (Describe it and give its ingredients.)
2. What are the different kinds of varnish?
3. How should the material be prepared for varnishing?
4. What are the commercial methods used in applying varnish?
5. What are the various treatments given work between coats?
6. What are the different methods of finishing a varnish job?

The Two-cycle Gas Engine

1. What is the principle of operation of internal-combustion engines?
2. What is a two-cycle gas engine?
3. How is a two-cycle gas engine constructed?
4. How does the two-cycle gas engine operate?
5. What are the uses of the engine?
6. What are its advantages over other types of engines? Its disadvantages?

FIGURE 4. You can become a better speaker by following a few simple but practical suggestions given in this chapter.

Points to Watch

When you develop question outlines of your own, you should be especially careful to observe the following points:

1. There should be enough questions to cover the subject thoroughly.

2. The questions should be arranged in the proper order, so that one answer will naturally follow the preceding one without any noticeable break in the thought of what you are saying or writing; for example, the question about the preparation of work for varnishing should come before the question concerning the ways of finishing varnish jobs.

3. In writing or speaking, the answer to each new question will begin a new paragraph.

4. When you are speaking from such an outline, you can write the questions on a small card which you can hold.

The methods outlined in this chapter were used to develop the following student theme and talk:

What Are the Problems of Jet Piloting?

Introduction
1. Why is heat a problem?
2. Why is the blackout a problem?
3. Why is speed a problem?
4. Why is fuel consumption a problem?
5. What is the major problem in jet piloting?
Conclusion

The Problems of Jet Piloting

Intro-duction   Here are a few of the problems that are encountered in jet piloting today. Some of these difficulties existed with the propeller-driven plane, some did not. The dangers of the airplane must be conquered for practical and safe transportation.

No. 1   *One of the first problems encountered in jet flying was the heat caused by the friction of the air against the plane.* When the Navy's experimental plane, the Skystreak, flew at 650 miles per hour, the temperature in the cockpit rose to 170

:egrees F. A refrigerating system had to be installed. That
-rought the temperature down to 105 degrees F., which is
much more bearable to a pilot. This heat problem is one of
the biggest limiting factors in the speed of present-day
aircraft.

No. 2   *A second problem encountered in all types of airplanes is
the blackout.* When a pilot pulls out of a fast dive, or is
suddenly catapulted forward, or makes a sudden sharp turn,
the force of gravity or inertia pulling on the body quickly
increases from normal to several times that much. That has
the effect of greatly increasing the pilot's weight.

A 160-pound man suddenly weighs a half a ton. His blood
becomes as heavy as molten lead. His heart isn't able to pump
enough of that heavy blood to his brain. Blood already in
his brain drains down into his abdomen. Deprived of blood,
his brain ceases to function normally. He becomes temporarily
blind, then deaf, then unconscious. This condition will continue until this tremendous force on his body is relieved.

No. 3   *Another problem occurs when the attempt is made to travel
faster than the speed of sound.* As he nears the speed of
sound, the pilot notices a strange buffeting effect. Why? When
one moves his hand through the air, or when a plane is flying
at less than sonic speed, it sets up pressure waves like the
waves when a stone is thrown into a pond. They warn the
air ahead that something is coming, and the molecules of air
start to move out of the way. But the maximum speed of
these pressure waves is approximately the same as the speed
of sound.

Thus, when a plane flies as fast as sound, the air ahead has
no warning. This results in an abrupt change in the air flow
around the plane. Shock waves are thus built up in front of
the plane, and produce the buffeting effect. Once an airplane
has passed the speed of sound, the turbulence of the air flow
disappears and the buffeting ceases. All one can hear is the
air stream and any noise that originates in the cockpit. The
same buffeting effect is created when one goes from above
to below the speed of sound.

No. 4   *Still another problem is that of fuel.* Jet engines burn fuel
so fast that, instead of an ordinary gauge, they carry a
liquidometer which constantly ticks off the number of gallons
remaining. Two Sabrejets on a mission will use as much fuel

as did a squadron of planes in World War II. On missions, pilots must often estimate so closely that they reach home base with only enough fuel for one go-around in case they misjudge a landing. Just for one go-around, the average jet fighter needs about 22 gallons of fuel.

When a Sabrejet is flying at a low speed and at a low altitude, it burns about a gallon of fuel every four seconds. Fuel sprays into the combustion chambers like water from a wide-open kitchen faucet. As far as fuel is concerned, no jet engine is efficient flying at a low speed and altitude. It burns about as much approaching a landing field at 200 miles per hour as it does traveling 600 miles per hour at 40,000 feet.

The average fuel consumption for the reciprocating airplane engine is about 60 gallons an hour. The average fuel consumption of the jet engine is about 1600 gallons an hour. With an afterburner on, the average consumption of the jet engine is about 7000 gallons an hour.

No. 5   *The major problem of jet piloting, however, is "bailing out."* If the jet pilot were to try to bail out in the usual way while traveling at a high speed, he would probably find himself pushed back into the cockpit by the tremendous force of the air stream. If he opened his mouth, the air pressure ramming down his throat could rupture his lungs and kill him. The air stream might even tear the flesh from his face, break his arms, or if he did not get clear, flatten him against the tail of his plane. Even if he did somehow escape, the shock of his parachute opening could disable him. If he were at a high altitude, he would probably die from cold and lack of oxygen before he got down to the lower altitudes where the air is dense enough and warm enough to support life.

In order to avoid these dangers, the U. S. Navy and Air Force have developed the "ejection seat." In the ejection seat, a small cartridge of explosive is placed under the pilot's seat. If the pilot must bail out, he trips a switch which explodes the cartridge. This literally blows the whole cockpit out of the plane. The cockpit is like a capsule, and is used to protect the pilot from the extreme conditions of speed and atmosphere.

Concluding statement   Undoubtedly, many more problems will be encountered in the future as man tries to fly faster and higher, and man will have to solve them as he has all the earlier ones.

The Introduction

The introduction is an important part of a speech or article. It has two purposes:

1. To explain anything that your listeners may need to know in order to understand what you have to say.
2. To secure favorable attention for your ideas.

In other words, the introduction leads up to what you have to say. Once you have the favorable attention of the group and they know your purpose, then you are ready to go ahead with the body of the speech. Some common methods for gaining attention in the introduction are:

1. To tell a story which can be connected with what you have to say.
2. To start with a situation:

A jet plane streaking across the sky at 750 miles an hour. . . .

Your audience will visualize the picture and they will want to know the outcome or where it leads.

3. To start with a statement of the problem:

a) The automobile and the airplane today carry so many people that passenger business is less and less profitable for the railroads . . .

b) The first atomic bomb ever used in warfare killed 78,000 people. That was on August 6, 1945, in World War II . . .

c) The curtain is now going up on our annual Sunshine Follies. Between now and Labor Day some fifteen million persons, trying to acquire a whole summer's tan in a single weekend, will burn lobster red, blister, swell, and peel. Some will be burned seriously.

By learning and heeding the facts . . .

Exercise. Can you suggest or can you find other good introductions?

The Conclusion

The conclusion should draw the threads or points together and round off the subject. The conclusion may end your speech or article in one of several ways depending upon the nature of your discussion. Here are some of them.

1. In some short, informal talks it may simply round off the subject, as "*I want to thank you for your courtesy in listening to me . . .*," or see the Conclusion on page 137.

2. You may summarize your points or arguments, as "*Gentlemen, may I review briefly the points which I have made . . . (a) . . . (b) . . . (c) . . .*," etc.

3. You may attempt to move the audience to take action as you want them to act. "*Now, will you permit this sort of thing to continue? . . .*"

Exercise. Can you suggest or find other good conclusions?

Applying Your Knowledge

HELPFUL QUESTIONS:

1. Usually, how many paragraphs will you need to write in order to answer one question in an outline?

2. Why is it easier to give a short speech or talk by following a question outline than by merely trying to follow a list of items about which you want to talk?

3. What rules or principles should you follow when developing question outlines?

PROBLEMS:

1. Select some subject in which you are interested and learn all you can about it in a reasonable length of time. On this subject, prepare a question outline such as you might use in giving a short talk.

2. Construct another question outline on another subject. Using this question outline as a guide, give a short talk to the class. During the talk, you may refer to the questions in your outline, but to no other notes.

3. Assume that you are to write an explanation of some job that you have done in your shop, how to operate some machine, or how to make some article. Construct a question outline and follow it in writing your explanation.

4. Construct a question outline on some subject pertaining to the work of your local, state, or national government. If your instructor so directs you, be prepared to give a talk before the class using this outline as a guide.

5. From a trade theory or a science book select an explanation of a manufacturing process or scientific principle. Make a clear outline of this explanation, following exactly the order given in the book. Using only your outline, try to give the same explanation yourself, either orally or in writing as your instructor directs. If the book uses a sketch or diagram have such illustrative material ready to use in your explanation.

6. Suggested topics for question outlines and discussions:

How to Forge and Temper Steel
How to Make a Simple Motor
Lubricating Oils
The Blast Furnace
How I Made . . .
How a Radio Tube Works
How an Electric Refrigerator Works
Electric Welding
Oxyacetylene Welding
Cutting Glass
Polishing Glass
Making Automobile Tires
Making Shoes
Battery Care in the Winter
Our Most Interesting Industry
How to Lay Roll Roofing
How to Fit and Repair a Door
Safe Working Practices in . . .
What Makes a Helicopter Fly

What Makes an Airplane Fly
How to Patch Fabric on an Airplane
Civil Air Regulations for . . .
Television
Radar
Reaction Engines
Atomic Energy
Photography
Transistor
How to Use a Chisel
How to Repair a Damaged Cord
Labor or Trade Unions
Our City Council
The United Nations
The Problems of a Teen-Ager
Where to Get Summer Jobs
Getting Along With Others
Why Stay in School
How to Write Better

Chapter 12

MAKING A DETAILED OUTLINE

Chapter 11 explained the construction of simple outlines in which each question was a rather large topic. This chapter discusses the development of detailed outlines which contain references to all subtopics as well as to the main topics.

All games must be played according to rules. These rules tell us how the game should begin, how the players shall conduct themselves during the game, how long the game shall last, and all other necessary details. Would an article about the football game last Saturday discuss the quarters in this order?

1. The fourth quarter
2. The second quarter
3. The first quarter
4. The third quarter

This arrangement would not be used because it does not follow the actual plan of the game. The four divisions would be arranged in the order in which they actually occur in the game; namely,

1. The first quarter
2. The second quarter
3. The third quarter
4. The fourth quarter

Looking at it from another viewpoint the game consists of two main divisions much larger than the quarters. They are

I. The first half
II. The second half

The rest period allowed between the halves is also longer than the rest period allowed between the quarters, isn't it? Wouldn't it be better to say then that the first and second quarters are merely parts of the first half? Likewise the third and fourth quarters would be considered divisions of the second half. If these statements are true, a diagram of a football game would look something like this:

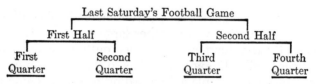

Now, instead of using the lines, the relationship of the different parts of the game may be shown by the use of numerals and letters.

LAST SATURDAY'S FOOTBALL GAME

I. The first half
   A. The first quarter
   B. The second quarter

II. The second half
   A. The third quarter
   B. The fourth quarter

The largest divisions of the game or of any subject are designated by Roman numerals. The next biggest divisions are marked by *capital* letters.

Interesting incidents in any quarter of the game may be shown by a diagram in the following way:

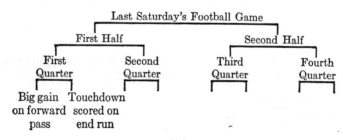

PROBLEM:

Now suppose that you make up your own diagram, completing it for the third and fourth quarters.

Complete the outline started below; that is, add details to the third and fourth quarters.

LAST SATURDAY'S FOOTBALL GAME

I. The first half
   A. The first quarter
      1. Our team made its first big gain by a forward pass
      2. The first touchdown was made by a long end run
   B. The second quarter

II. The second half
   A. The third quarter
   B. The fourth quarter

Notice that the roman numerals designate the main topics; the capital letters the large subdivisions of the main topics; the arabic numerals the smaller subtopics; etc.

The skeleton given below illustrates the details of such an outline.

TITLE OR SUBJECT

(Place at this point a brief statement of the purpose of this particular explanation or article, and the meaning of any unusual technical terms used in it.)

I. First main topic.
   A. First subdivision of main topic. This must be about, or in explanation of, the main topic.
      1. First secondary subdivision explaining or illustrating A.
      2. Second secondary subdivision also explaining or illustrating A.

   B. Second subdivision of main topic.
      1. First subdivision of B.
         a) Explanation of point 1 above.
         b) Second explanation or illustration of point 1.
         c) Third subdivision of 1.
      2. Second subdivision of B.

II. Second main topic.
    A. First subdivision of second mai. topic II.
        1. First subdivision of A.
        2. Second subdivision of A.
        3. Third subdivision of A.
          a)
          b)
          c)

    B. Second subdivision of II.
        1.
        2.

III. Third main topic.
    A.
        1.
        2.
    B.
        1.
    C.
        1.
        2.
          a)
          b)

Notice that the same system of letters and figures is used throughout the foregoing outline. The indention of topics and of the subdivisions indicates the relative importance of the various ideas they contain. Because of this grading of ideas, practically any one can look at an outline and grasp at once the main ideas and their relationship.

The form of the outline should be the same throughout. Each of the points may be written as a topic—groups of words which are not complete sentences but which give the idea. The subdivisions may be written as complete sentences or as short paragraphs. The important thing to remember, however, is that the same form of expression should be used throughout the entire outline.

The Written Standard Practice sheet, duplicated here in part, shows how one company outlines the procedure which its employees must follow.

WRITTEN STANDARD PRACTICE

Subject	DOCTOR AND NURSE	No. WI–19
By	D. J. Gilmore	Effective 9/12/—
Approved	C. L. W.	Revised

Reviewed	**I. PRINCIPLE** A. To maintain a close follow-up on the physical well-being of all employees. **II. PERSONNEL** A. Doctor, Nurse, Industrial Relations Manager. **III. PROCEDURE** A. The doctor's duties are: 1. Make all physical examinations prior to employment. 2. Give first-aid and treatment to employees injured while at work. 3. Examine all employees who have been absent because of illness or injury before they return to work. 4. Give medicines to employees for temporary relief only. a All sickness cases shall be referred to the employee's own doctor for treatment. b The doctor is subject to the call of employees who are absent from work due to conditions arising from their employment. B. The Nurse's duties are: 1. Assist the doctor with all medical examinations. 2. etc. 3. etc.
Copies to	

FIGURE 5. Written Standard Practice Sheet Used by a Large Manufacturing Concern. An actual use of the detailed outline giving the duties of a company physician and nurse.

You will find other practical applications of outlining in the chapter on "Report Writing."

Applying Your Knowledge

1. Select one of the following topics and develop a detailed outline on the subject. The outline should be developed so that it could be used later in writing up a report, preparing a speech, or for some other practical purpose. If you wish, you may select another subject more to your liking.

   a) The Various Methods of Heating a House. (Give the cost, advantages, and disadvantages of each.)
   b) Automobile Storage Batteries, Their Construction and Care.
   c) The Three Main Types of Business Organization. (Single Proprietorship, Partnership, Corporation. Develop the outline so that you could explain from it how each is organized, and the advantages and disadvantages of each.)
   d) The Most Widely Used Tool in Our Shop. (Take a tool, for example, a plane, and develop an outline to explain the different kinds of planes and the purposes for which each kind is designed.)
   e) The Problem of Conservation.

Use your outline as a guide in making a short speech to your class group or in writing a short paper on the subject that you have selected.

2. If you are working in a manufacturing plant or business office, develop a detailed outline to show the standard procedure to be used by the employees under a certain situation.

Chapter 13

HOW TO MAKE CLEAR EXPLANATIONS

A set of blueprints so complicated as to require long study to understand is almost useless. Exactly the same thing is true of any writing or speaking that you do—the easier it is to understand your writing or speaking the more useful it will be. Probably much of the writing and speaking that you may do will be giving explanations of many different things; for instance, you may need to explain the operation of a machine to another workman, you may need to explain what is wrong with your automobile to a mechanic, or you may need to explain how to perform small tasks about your home, such as how to replace electric fuses after they have burned out. Since an explanation is useful only to the extent that it is clear, let us study the following method suggested for making explanations clear.

When you prepare to explain something, you will have to answer two questions; namely,

1. What shall I include in the explanation?

Answer. Include as much material as is necessary to make the explanation perfectly clear.

2. How shall I arrange it?

Answer. You should arrange the facts of your explanation in the order in which they occur. Whatever is done first, you will probably mention first; whatever is done second, you will probably mention second, etc. Perhaps the skeleton outlines given here will help you in this respect.

Introduction	Step 1	Step 2	Step 3	Summary if any

Now, if you were to explain how to paint a house your outline might look like the one below.

Introduction	Step 1	Step 2	Step 3	Step 4	Concluding Remarks
General information as to types of woods, paints, etc.	Preparation	First coat of paint	Second coat of paint	Third coat of paint	Concluding remarks as to uses of each coat.

From an outline such as this, you will find it comparatively easy to explain clearly how new wood should be painted. This outline has been developed into just such an explanation by Arthur Wakeling in his book *Fix It Yourself.**

Painting New Wood

Introduction One of the principal things the painter learns from his years of experience is the proper preparation of painting materials with thinners, according to the condition of the particular surface he is painting. While no information can be given which will supplant the painter's experience, there are certain fundamental principles and general directions which will help greatly in assuring a good job.

The important thing with new wood surfaces is to have the painting material adapted to the absorption requirements of the wood. Generally speaking, woods may be divided into three different groups: extremely porous or absorbent, including red and white cedar and California redwood; medium absorbent, including white pine, poplar, basswood, and elm; close-grained, oily, and nonabsorbent, including southern or yellow pine, hemlock, spruce, northern pine, and fir.

The more porous and absorbent woods require a priming coat that is unusually rich in linseed oil, with a small amount of turpentine added. The less absorbent woods need less oil but more turpentine to help the oil penetrate well into the wood.

* Arthur Wakeling, *Fix It Yourself* (New York: Popular Science Publishing Co.).

Step 1   New unpainted wood requires only a small amount of preparation. Remove any loose dirt or mortar. Fill the nail holes and open joints with a plastic wood filler or putty. If the wood contains knots apply a coat of orange shellac to all pitchy places.

Assuming a three-coat job, which is generally required for the satisfactory painting of new wood surfaces, let us take up each coat as follows:

Step 2   First Coat: The first or priming coat should always carry enough linseed oil to satisfy fully the oil-hungry, bare wood and still leave enough oil in the paint film to bind and hold it together. Some turpentine should always be used in the first coat. The amount of oil and turpentine, however, will vary according to the kind of wood.

Step 3   Second Coat: The second coat should always contain a liberal amount of oil, although not so much as the priming coat, and a considerably larger amount of turpentine in proportion to the oil. The additional turpentine tends to make this a very hard coat with little gloss, permitting the following coat to adhere closely. There need be little difference in the thinning of the second coat, regardless of the kind of wood. This coat will be heavier-bodied and of greater hiding power than the priming coat.

Step 4   Third Coat: This coat should be a full-oil, glossy, finishing coat with very little, if any, turpentine added. The oil in this coat does not soak into the surface but remains in the paint filler to give it resistance against the weather and also to provide its attractive luster.

Concluding remarks   As will be seen, the absorption demands of the wood are only partly met with the priming coat, and part of the oil in the second coat is required to satisfy completely the demand of the wood for oil, while the third coat is needed for added protection.

Read carefully the following explanation, "How an Electric Bell Works"; then make an outline similar to the one on page 148 showing the different parts of the explanation.

How an Electric Bell Works

The electric bell is one of the simplest applications of the electromagnet.

When the button P in the switch S is pressed, the electric circuit of the battery is closed, and current flows in at D, over the closed contact at B, through the coils of the magnet, and out again at D, the other binding post or terminal. But as soon as this current is established, the electromagnet M pulls over the armature A, and in so doing breaks the contact at B. This stops the flow of the current and demagnetizes the magnet M. The armature A is then thrown back against the contact screw B by the elasticity of the spring V which supports it. No sooner is the contact made at B than the current again begins to flow and the former operation is repeated. Thus the circuit is automatically made and broken at B, and the hammer H in consequence is set into rapid vibration against the rim of the bell.

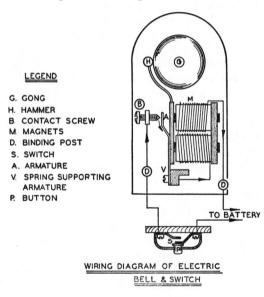

LEGEND

G. GONG
H. HAMMER
B. CONTACT SCREW
M. MAGNETS
D. BINDING POST
S. SWITCH
A. ARMATURE
V. SPRING SUPPORTING ARMATURE
P. BUTTON

TO BATTERY

WIRING DIAGRAM OF ELECTRIC BELL & SWITCH

Explaining Science

The following explanation about one phase of television is reprinted from William H. Crouse's *Understanding Science.**

How the Picture is Telecast

Before a picture can be broadcast, or telecast, it must be broken down into a series of tiny fragments. To get some idea of how a picture can

* William H. Crouse, *Understanding Science* (New York: McGraw-Hill Book Co., Inc., 1948), p. 143.

be broken down in this manner, look closely at a newspaper picture as you did when we were thinking about the way the rods and cones in the eye work to produce a picture. Note that this newspaper picture is made up of row after row of tiny dots. Some of the dots are large, some small. Many large dots together produce a dark area, small dots together produce a light area.

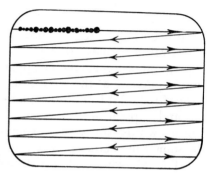

FIGURE 6. Dot Changer.
"The dot changer would move across the screen like this, but the lines would be much closer together, in order to cover every dot."

If every one of these dots were changed into an electrical impulse (strong impulses for large dots and weak impulses for small dots), the first step in telecasting the picture would have been made. Suppose that, for the moment, we call the instrument that changes dots into electrical impulses a "dot changer." To telecast the picture, the dot changer starts in the upper, left-hand corner of the picture and moves across the top line of dots. As it comes to each dot in turn, the dot changer changes the dot into an electrical impulse. If the dot is small the impulse is small. If the dot is large, the impulse is large.

After the dot changer has scanned the first line, it jumps to the left and starts across on the second line of dots. This is the same way that your eyes move when you read a book. You read from left to right, moving down from line to line toward the bottom of the page.

As the dot changer thus changes one dot after another into electrical impulses, the receiver changes these electrical impulses of varying strength into "dots" of varying sizes. If you viewed the receiver screen, you would then see a reproduction of the original picture, dot for dot.

When the television transmitter and receiver do these jobs, they do them very rapidly. In fact, the dot changer in the transmitter scans the entire picture or scene thirty times a second. This means that thirty pictures appear on the receiver screen every second. These pictures blend, much as on a motion-picture screen, to produce a moving scene of the action that is going on in the television studio.

When Several Things Occur at the Same Time

Thus far in the illustrations you have studied, all the steps of operation have occurred in regular order, one after the other. However, it often happens that you are called upon to explain the operation of a machine or apparatus in which several things are happening at the same instant.

When this is the situation it is best to explain one step, and then come back and explain any others that occur at the same time. In other words, you would explain all the steps that occur at the same time before proceeding to explain the remaining steps. The following outline will make this somewhat clearer to you.

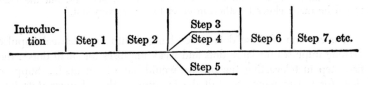

After Step 3 has been explained, it is necessary to show that Steps 4 and 5 are occurring at the same time. This can be done, and the reader assisted in understanding that several things are happening at once, by using such expressions as the following:

at the same time
while this was taking place
during this time

In a situation where Steps 3, 4, and 5 occur at the same time, 3, 4, and 5 must be explained before Step 6 is discussed.

The following explanation tells how a four-cycle engine operates. The italicized words indicate that something else is happening at the same time the piston is making a stroke.

The Four-Cycle Internal Combustion Engine

An internal combustion engine derives its power from rapid gas expansion resulting from the burning of a mixture of an inflammable vaporized liquid and air compressed in its cylinder. The fuels in common use are gas, gasoline, kerosene, and alcohol.

An engine is of the four-stroke cyle type when its cycle of operation is completed in four strokes of the piston or two revolutions of the flywheel. Each movement of the piston is known as one stroke; hence, the term four-cycle engine means an engine in which the piston makes four strokes for every explosion or expansion of the ignited gas.

The first stroke of the piston toward the bottom end of the cylinder draws in by suction a combustible mixture of the fuel. On the second stroke the piston returns to its original position at the head end. *When the piston starts this return stroke,* all the valves are closed so that the gas mixture is compressed by the piston as it moves to the head end of the cylinder. *Just before this stroke is completed,* the compressed gas mixture is ignited by an electrical spark from the spark plug. *As the gas mixture burns,* it expands very rapidly and drives the piston toward the bottom of the cylinder. This is the third stroke of the piston and it is the stroke which does the work. On the fourth stroke the piston returns again to the head end of the cylinder. *During this fourth stroke,* the exhaust valve is held open, and the piston forces the burned gases out of the cylinder as it nears the head end of the cylinder.

The Use of Drawings

In an earlier chapter the use of drawings as illustrations was discussed at length. At this time you will find it to your advantage to review those sections because in almost every case you can make your explanation clearer by using a sketch or drawing. If you are giving an oral explanation you can use an actual piece of apparatus or make a sketch on the blackboard to illustrate what you are saying.

Applying Your Knowledge

HELPFUL QUESTIONS:

1. What two questions must you answer before you start to explain anything?

2. Why is the ability to explain things clearly a valuable asset?

3. Why are skeleton outlines such as those given in this chapter easy to use when planning an explanation?

4. Suppose that you are explaining the operation of a machine which has a number of moving parts. Several of these parts perform their operations at the same time. If you were attempting to explain the various operations in the order in which they occurred, what would you do when you reached the situation mentioned above?

PROBLEMS:

1. Select a subject about which you know something and prepare an explanation of it. If you write your explanation, prepare a drawing to help make your explanation clear and easily understood. If your instructor asks you to make the explanation orally, place a sketch on the blackboard or bring in apparatus. Make an outline of your explanation before proceeding with it.

Suggested Subjects

How does a simple telephone work?

How does a telegraph instrument work?

What happens when you turn in a fire alarm through a box provided for that purpose?

What happens when you step on the starter pedal of an automobile?

Explain the operation of a two-cycle or a four-cycle gas engine.

Explain the operation of a radio set.

Explain the operation of some machine in your shop.

(NOTE: Begin with the source of power and trace the path over which the power travels until it is applied to the actual work.)

Explain the operation of an electric motor.

How are camera films developed?

How does a storage battery work?

Explain how to read the Essex board measure table on a steel square.

2. Explain how some article is made. The following articles are suggestions:

wire	pens	varnish	gasoline
rope	bricks	shellac	concrete road
coins	soap	paint	camera film
files	leather	paper	butter
saws	matches	glue	glass
pencils	cable	chain	wire rope

3. Explain how you performed a job in shop or an experiment in the laboratory.

4. Additional suggestions for explanations.

The Atom

The Atom Bomb

How the Steam Engine Works

How the Steam Turbine Works

How the Internal Combustion Engine Works

How the Electric Light Gives Off Light

How We Hear Sound

How We See Light

How the TV Set Works

How Radar Works

What Makes an Airplane Fly

How a Jet Engine Works

Chapter 14

HOW TO EXPLAIN SHORT CUTS AND SHOP-KINKS

A shop-kink is a short-cut method or an especially effective method for doing some job in the shop that saves time, labor, materials, or money. Most trade and technical magazines conduct departments in which short articles that explain these practical hints are published. The section of the magazine containing such articles often bears a title, such as *Hints from Practical Men, New Wrinkles for the Shop, Practical Ways to Cut Costs,* or *Practical Job Pointers.*

FIGURE 7. The Short Cut.

Several of these articles are given in this chapter. Read them so that you understand how each one illustrates the following directions and explains clearly the suggested method.

How to Write a Shop-Kink

Each article of this kind usually consists of definite steps which you should follow when attempting to write a similar article of your own:

1. A statement of the problem or purpose of the article.
2. An explanation of the useful or quick method.

3. A statement showing the advantages of the idea, or other remarks by the author.

4. A drawing, sketch, or photograph showing the idea as it is worked out.

Title

1. Shop Bins from Old Varnish Cans

Author

Frank C. Hudson

Simple statement of the problem

Old varnish cans make very good metal bins for bolts, nuts, washers, and the dozens of small parts that any small shop has to carry. A small-boat builder of my acquaintance uses dozens of these cans to good advantage. He simply cuts off the corner containing the spout, as in the illustration. The handle is located just right to act as a drawer-pull, and in all the larger sizes there is ample room for a label below the handle.

Description or explanation of idea

Statement of advantages of using this idea, or other remarks

Varnish cans are standardized sufficiently to make a very good-looking collection of drawers or bins, and they come in such different sizes that they are particularly convenient for small shop supplies.

Most of us consider varnish cans too sticky and messy to bother with when empty, but a little tur-

Sketch or illustration of idea

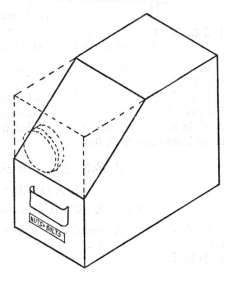

pentine cleans them easily and they will help keep the average shop looking better than is usually the case.

—American Machinist

2. Laying Asphalt Shingles

Joseph J. Zar

Instead of laying the first row of asphalt shingles along the edge of the roof, in the usual way, lay a strip of similar roll roofing first, as shown in the sketch. This gets the roofing started more quickly and with less nailing, as the roll requires a few nails only. The second layer of regular shingles is nailed sufficiently to hold the roll material in place. Since the usual first layer of shingles is entirely covered by the second layer, there is no apparent difference in the roof. The roll roofing is cut to the width of the shingles being used.

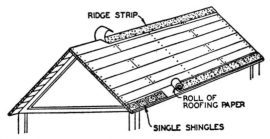

Roll Roofing Used at Eaves and Ridge with Asphalt Shingles Saves Time and Makes a Better Job. Sketch Shows Comparison.

In finishing the ridge use another piece of roll roofing as shown in the sketch. This not only quicker than laying single shingles, but it reduces the chance of a strong wind getting underneath and raising the roofing. With single shingles, sometimes some of the nails fail to catch in solid wood with the result that these shingles may raise and cause leaks.—*American Builder.*

3. False Jaws for the Vise

F. S. Doughty

Windhill, Shipley, Yorkshire, England

While dealing with some delicate electrical parts, we were using the usual loose vise jaws of copper or lead to preventing damaging the parts held.

It occurred to us to make a change to fiber for the false jaws and to attach them permanently to the vise, as shown in the illustration. The fiber jaws were softer than the ones made of metal and gave a better grip on the small brass parts with less likelihood of damage. One vise among a number, fitted up as described, is excellent for small parts that are likely to be damaged by holding them in metal jaws.

—American Machinist.

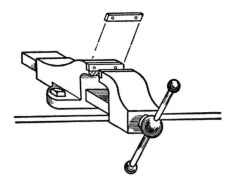

Applying Your Knowledge

PROBLEMS:

1. Study Examples 2 and 3 to determine how closely these articles follow the four steps given at the beginning of the chapter.

2. Find at least four different magazines that publish shop-kinks. Copy in your notebook the name of each magazine and the name of the department in which these articles are published.

3. Find and copy in your notebook two articles on practical ideas that you consider worth while. Give a bibliography of each article.

4. Write two such articles of your own. You can probably find in your school shop some practical ideas that have been used and about which you can write. If the idea is not yours tell where you secured it. Attach a sketch of the idea if it will make your explanation clearer.

5. Write up some idea that has been used in your school shop or some place where you have worked that has improved working conditions or safety in the shop.

Chapter 15

GIVING DEFINITE INSTRUCTIONS

Regardless of what we do for a living or what we become—carpenters, machinists, farmers, store clerks, printers, truck drivers, or engineers—we must at times give instructions to others. This is not so easy as it first appears. The main difficulty in giving instructions is, of course, to give them so clearly that they cannot be misunderstood.

How to give the directions depends, to a great extent, on how much the person to whom you give the instructions knows about the job to be done. A safe rule to follow when you are in doubt is always to give the instructions as if the other person knows very little or nothing about the item or job in question.

Unlike other forms of composition, it is usually better for practical purposes not to write instructions in the form of paragraphs. Instead, it is better to write each separate direction in a sentence and to place each new sentence on a separate line. You will find the following rules helpful in writing or giving oral instructions:

1. Be sure that you understand the job thoroughly.
2. Use only words or expressions the reader will understand.
3. Use short, clear sentences.
4. Place only one direction in each sentence.
5. Start another line with each new instruction.
6. Make drawings or sketches when they will be helpful, but letter or number the various parts of the drawing so that it can be understood readily.
7. Whenever it is necessary to a complete understanding, give reasons for your instructions.
8. Be courteous.

SAFETY INSTRUCTIONS

JOINTER

This machine is dangerous unless you observe the following:

1. Never talk while operating this machine.
2. Never run stock which is shorter than 10 in. long across this machine.
3. Set the machine for a light cut on all work.
4. Use the push block on all short work.
5. Never adjust the fence until the machine has stopped.
6. Keep the guard in place while machine is running.
7. Keep the fingers away from the knives at all times.

FIGURE 8. Safety Instructions for a Machine Operator.*

(Lyle M. Garnett, *Industrial Arts & Vocational Education Magazine,*
Bruce Publishing Co.)

* These safety instructions were posted at the machine.

Applying Your Knowledge

PROBLEMS:

1. How could the above safety instructions on the Jointer be improved?

2. Read carefully the safety instructions for the operation of some machine in your shop or for doing some job safely. Print your instructions on a sheet approximately 8½ by 11 inches so that it can be posted on a bulletin board.

A sketch or drawing is often helpful in illustrating specific points.

FIRE EXTINGUISHERS
Carbon Dioxide Type

Use on:

CLASS B FIRES—oil, gasoline, alcohol and other flammable solvents.

CLASS C FIRES—electrical equipment.

Carbon dioxide is not recommended for deep-seated fires in wood, rubbish and similar materials.

How to use:

1. Carry the extinguisher to the fire; release the hose and horn.
2. Release the gas ("snow") by removing the locking pin and turning the hand wheel, or by squeezing or pulling the operating lever.
3. Direct the "snow" toward the base of the fire or back toward its source.

After use, recharge and replace for re-use.

 SAFETY INSTRUCTION CARD **No. 652**

National Safety Council   PRINTED IN U. S. A.

(Courtesy National Safety Council)

FIGURE 9. How to Operate a Fire Extinguisher.†

† The National Safety Council issues on different subjects a large series of instruction cards similar to the one above.

<u>**Instruction Sheet**</u>

or

<u>**Job Analysis**</u>

HOW TO DRIVE A TEN-PENNY NAIL

Tools: 12-oz. or 16-oz. claw hammer.

Materials: 10d nail; soft wood stock.

Procedure: (Assuming that you are right-handed)

1. Grasp the hammer firmly in the right hand, well toward the rear end of the handle, so that the weight of the hammer may fall easily without force from the hand.

2. Grasp a 10d nail between the thumb and forefinger of the left hand, with the head of the nail up, and the point away from your body.

3. Place the point of the nail in the desired position on the wood and hold the nail at the proper angle.

4. Strike the head of the nail a light blow or two with the hammer to start the point into the wood.

5. Remove the left hand from the nail.

6. Strike a sufficient number of heavy blows upon the head of the nail to sink it into the wood to the desired depth.

FIGURE 10. Job Analysis Sheet.

The job analysis sheet here shows how a job can be analyzed in detail so that exact directions can be given for each operation.

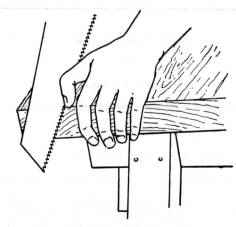

FIGURE 11. The Correct Method of Starting a Hand Saw.

With the aid of the above picture can you give definite directions on the correct method of starting a hand saw? Try it.

Applying Your Knowledge

PROBLEMS (*Continued*):

3. After studying carefully the job analysis or operation sheet on page 163, analyze some small job that you have done in the shop and develop your own operation sheet for a particular job.

The operations should be so clearly stated that another workman could do the same job by following your directions.

4. Write definite and clear instructions for doing some job in your school shop.

Use a drawing or a neat sketch if it will help you make the instructions clearer.

5. In many schools the different shops have students serve as Student Safety Engineers. Before they are permitted to serve,

however, they are sometimes required to pass an examination covering, among other things, the following points:

  a) How to operate the different machines safely.
  b) What to do in case a student cuts himself.
  c) What to do in case a student burns himself.
  d) What to do when foreign matter gets in a student's eye.
  e) How to use fire extinguishers.
  f) How to make accident reports properly.
  g) How to keep accident hazards at a minimum in the school shop; for example, keeping the aisles clear of obstacles, keeping grease spots on the floor at a minimum, etc.

Your instructor may think it profitable to have various members of the class give talks on some or all of these points, permitting you to secure what information you can beforehand.

A good project would be the preparation of a safety pamphlet in which is given, in condensed form, information on *How To Work Safely in the Shops.*

6. Be prepared to give orally in class the instructions for anything about which you have written in the four previous exercises. You may draw on the blackboard a sketch to help make your instructions clear.

7. A young man attending a trade school recently wrote to a friend:

Although I have made good progress in shop work, I am somewhat discouraged because I have so much difficulty getting my classwork. I believe that many of my friends are no brighter than I am, so that some of them must know better than I do how to study. Since you have been so successful with your class subjects, will you tell me about any methods of study that you have found especially helpful?

Many others have the same difficulty. Have you ever found ways of learning and understanding your work quickly? Write out such directions for studying classwork as you think might be helpful to any one having difficulty. Make your directions as definite as possible.

8. Many of you have served as a shop foreman at one time or another in your school shop. As shop foreman there were certain duties which it was your responsibility to perform. Using your

experience as a basis, develop an Instruction Sheet for Shop Foremen which students might use in the future when the shop instructor gives them such a job.

9. Write a short set of instructions on the proper handling of firearms during a hunting trip. Include in your composition a series of specific directions for the handling of a gun.

Chapter 16

WRITING NOTES OF INSTRUCTION

Frequently all of us have occasion to write short notes to others. At work we need to write short messages to some person in the same office or factory; at home we frequently write notes to the milkman, to the storekeeper, to a friend, or to some member of the family.

It is important that such messages be as brief and at the same time as clear as possible, so that the meaning will not be mistaken. The following suggestions for writing such messages will help you:

1. Use short sentences.
2. Place each idea in a different sentence.
3. Wherever possible write your note concerning only one thing.
4. If you mention more than one item in the note, place each item in a separate paragraph or on a separate line.
5. Make your message as short as convenient. Frequently the clearest notes are those which are the shortest.
6. Unless the note is personal or informal, it is better to give it a subject.

Read carefully the following notes which have been actually written by industrial executives while at work. Notice the short sentences and short paragraphs, each dealing with only one item. Notice also the heading that is used. Although you can begin a note by merely using the name in a salutation much as you do in a letter, a form similar to that given here is preferred in business or industry.

January 5, 19—

To. All Foremen & Dept. Heads
From: J. S. Martin
Subject: Securing Stationery Supplies

Effective immediately no storekeeper will be
maintained in the Stationery Department.

When you need stationery supplies, leave your
requisitions in the mail-basket and the supplies
will be delivered to you on the next mail trip.

October 5, 19—

To: All Foremen and Staff
From: A. V. Ostby
Subject: Conserving Electricity

It is more important than ever that we avoid
burning unnecessary electric lights during the
next few months because any unnecessary electric
load might increase our demand load. If this
happens, the result will be an increased cost for
the twelve months following.

In ordinary weather it is recommended that the
following schedule be adhered to as closely as
possible:

During October turn off lights at 8:00 A.M.
During November "   "   "   " 8:30 A.M.
During December   "   "   "   " 9:00 A.M.
During January   "   "   "   " 9:00 A.M.
During February   "   "   "   " 8:30 A.M.
During March   "   "   "   " 8:00 A.M

Figures 12a, b. Typical Memorandums from Industry.

May 16, 19—

To: Dept. Heads
From: C. L. Hartman
Subject: May 30th Holiday

The factory and office departments will not operate on May 30 or May 31.

As far as the office is concerned, it is assumed that each department head will so schedule the work that necessary reports and forms will be prepared on time.

FIGURE 12c. Typical Memorandum from Industry.

December 11, 19—

Service Department
Penna. Power & Light Co.

Please turn on the gas and electricity at 119 East Avenue, Wednesday, December 13.

Ralph S. Cost

119 East Avenue

Mr. Smith:

Please leave no milk on Saturday or Sunday mornings of this week.

Mrs. Gilmore

FIGURES 13a, b. Typical Notes from Everyday Life.

November 15, 19—

Jim:

The foreman asked me to tell you not to report for work tomorrow morning.

He will send you word just as soon as he can use you.

Fred

FIGURE 13c. Typical Note from Everyday Life.

Applying Your Knowledge

HELPFUL QUESTIONS:

1. Make a list of five things about which a man might have to write notes to another outside of his daily work.

2. Why are short sentences better than long sentences in writing of this kind?

3. Why is it better to place only one idea in a sentence?

4. When writing a memorandum, of what advantage is the use of the headings:

To:
From:
Subject:

5. What is the meaning of memorandum?
6. What is the plural of memorandum?

PROBLEMS:

1. Suppose that you go to the office of the local light and power company to ask that the electricity be turned off in your home on a certain date because you are leaving town, but find that the office is closed when you arrive. Write a note to the service de-

partment which you could push under the door to take care of the situation.

2. Write a note to the milkman asking that he leave no milk for several days, but that he begin leaving milk again on a certain date.

3. Assume that you are working in your shop or in a factory and that one of your machines breaks down. You cannot find the foreman at the moment, so you write a note telling him about the trouble and place the note on his desk. Write such a note. Be definite.

4. You have been asked be your foreman to tell a fellow worker to report for work Monday morning at seven o'clock. When you go to your friend's home, he is not there. Write a note giving him the foreman's message. Give any definite instructions that you believe necessary in regard to the job, the time, and place.

5. You are working in a grocery store. The store manager has gone out on business. While he is gone, the district superintendent comes in to see him about changes in the prices of various articles for the next week. Write a short note giving the manager all the necessary information.

6. In the absence of your superiors where you work, you answer the telephone. The person who calls leaves a message and requests that you deliver it to the foreman or manager. Write such a message as you might give to your superior.

7. Assume that your stock of some material is low. Write a memorandum to your superior giving the present inventory and requesting more material.

Chapter 17

WRITING NOTICES FOR THE BULLETIN BOARD

Those of us who participate in school activities find that frequently we must write notices for posting on the school bulletin boards. Men who hold offices in clubs or who have jobs with responsibility need constantly to write short notices for office and factory bulletin boards. It is, therefore, worth while that we be able to write clear and interesting notices suitable for posting.

Directions

In writing bulletin board notices it is important that the following principles and directions be observed:

1. Use a good, short title.
2. Mention only one item at a time.
3. If more than one item is mentioned in the same notice, place each item in a separate paragraph or on a separate line.
4. Use simple words and short sentences.
5. Use friendly language when giving orders.
6. Use positive, not negative forms. Avoid unpleasant suggestions. Notice the examples given in this chapter.

Like other writing, which tries to give information, it must be clear and complete. To bring this about the notice must answer the questions—what, when, where, who, why, how. It is true, however, that all the above questions do not appear in every notice, but they will be found in most notices.

Good Bulletin Board Practice

In order to post notices as effectively as possible so that they will attract the attention of employees or of students, you should keep in mind these principles:

1. Place the notice on the bulletin board at eye level.
2. Be original in posting; that is, if there is anything that you can use on the board to attract attention, use it. For example, you might use colored ink or chalk, you might make some kind of sketch or drawing, or you might arrange the notices in an unusual way.
3. Be sure to remove the notice when it is out of date. Notices are very seldom read after they have been posted two or three days. If necessary, it is better to remove the notice and post it again in a short time.
4. Don't overcrowd the bulletin board. You will find that a few notices at a time are much more effective than a large number.

The following notices are typical of those posted on factory and office bulletin boards. These have actually been used. The names of the persons mentioned, however, have been changed.

FIGURE 14a. An Effective Bulletin Board. Notices are well arranged and up to date.

FIGURE 14*b*. Few persons read a bulletin board so poorly arranged.

Important Notice to all Employees

An Employees' Dance will be held Saturday, January 17th, from 8:00 until 12:00 in the Elks' Ballroom, East Fourth Street.

Tickets will be on sale throughout the various departments by Friday, January 9th.

A concert will be given by the Lycoming Division Employees' Band and Glee Club from 8:00 to 9:00. Dancing, with music by "Ducky" Geese and his fourteen musicians, from 9:00 until 12:00. Door prizes for the ladies.

Price of admission—50¢ per person.

C. W. Shaffer
Chairman
Employees' Dance Committee

January 7th, 19—

FIGURE 15*a*. Poor Form of Bulletin Board Notice.

EMPLOYEES' DANCE

WHERE   — Elks' Auditorium
        36 East Fourth Street

WHEN   — Saturday evening
        January 17th, 19__

TIME   — Concert — 8:00 to 9:00 p.m.
        Dancing — 9:00 to 12:00 p.m.

DRESS   — Informal

TICKETS — On sale in departments throughout the plant

Door prizes for the ladies.

Several square dances will be held during the evening
at the request of the employees.

MUSIC   — "Ducky" Geese and his
        14 Musical Ganders.

CONCERT — Aviation Band and Male Chorus

                        C. W. Shaffer, Chairman
                        Employees' Dance Committee

FIGURE 15*b*. Better Form.

                                        May 16, 19—

HOLIDAY SHUTDOWN

    The factory and office will not operate on

Friday, May 30th, or on Saturday, May 31st.

                        C. L. Hartman
                        Factory Manager

FIGURE 15*c*. Bulletin Board Notice.

PAY NOTICE

Effective April 4th, and continuing until further notice, all operators will be paid in their respective departments each Thursday after 10:00 A.M.

Operators absent on Thursdays may obtain their back pay by calling at the Employment Office at the following times:

> Monday, Tuesday, Wednesday, and Friday between 11:00 A.M. and 12:00 M.
>
> Saturday between 9:00 A.M. and 11:00 A.M.

No back pay will be given out on Thursdays.

> C. L. Hartman
> Factory Manager

HAVE YOU A SUGGESTION ON SAFETY?

Beginning the week of March 4, 19— a series of Safety Posters will be shown on departmental bulletin boards each week for a period of several months.

Every employee is urged to turn in suggestions on the regular suggestion blanks on <u>how accident hazards can be reduced.</u>

— SAFETY HABITS PUT SAFETY FIRST —

FIGURES 15d, e. Bulletin Board Notices.

LOST

LOCKER KEY #531

If found, please return to

RAYMOND SMITH
Auto Shop

ATTENTION SENIORS

March 22, 19—

Measurements for caps and gowns will be taken

after school Thursday, Friday, Monday, and Tuesday

in room 207. The price is $12.25 and must

accompany order.

William Gehron, President

NOTICE

Sophomore boys, interested in trying for position
as football manager, are requested to give their
names to Mr. Landis in Room 407 at once.

FIGURES 16a, b, c. Typical Notices from School Bulletin Boards.

Applying Your Knowledge

HELPFUL QUESTIONS:

1. Of what practical value is the ability to write bulletin board notices that attract attention?

2. Give several definite directions for writing effective notices.

3. Name several ways to make a notice catch and hold the reader's attention.

PROBLEMS:

In doing the following exercises write out the notices exactly as you would want them to appear on the board.

1. Write a notice calling a meeting of some school club or other organization.

2. Assume that you are a foreman in a local factory. Write a notice requesting the employees in your department to turn out all lights when they are not needed. Draw a sketch showing how you might place such a notice on the bulletin board so that it will attract favorable attention.

3. You have lost some tool in your school shop. Write a notice about it.

4. Write out a safety notice for your shop. It should be one that could actually be used.

5. Copy three notices that have appeared on your shop bulletin boards. Write your opinion of each of these notices. Rewrite any that you can improve.

6. The following notices are poorly written and have omitted essential questions. Correct these notices, if possible, or rewrite them.

    a) Auto mechanics will wipe up the grease on the floor of the garage.

    b) *Attention Crib Boy for Today*
       See that all tools are in position before you hand out. Accept signed tool slips when necessary have student sign slip in front of you.

c) *Danger*

Never watch the light in the blueprint machine. See that your paper is laid flat. Roll the canvas over the paper even. Let the light shine only a short time. Take the blueprint out in a. hurry.

d) *Carpenters*

Place all wood not used on the rack. On June 10, 19— a boy was hurt because someone left wood on the floor. This is not at all necessary and besides the wood may be wasted. Remember that wood costs money, and just when you need that kind of wood you may not have any. Remember also that there is a place for each tool and that each tool when not in use should be in place. Heed this warning.

7. Suggested practice: Write one or more notices concerning:

a) A demonstration of a machine or process in your shop or plant.

b) The care of stock in your shop.

c) The change of foreman in your shop.

d) The change of the position of stock in your shop.

e) An article you lost.

f) A glee club or band rehearsal.

Chapter 18

MAKING SUGGESTIONS ABOUT YOUR JOB

At home, at school, in business, or in industry all of us are performing in a more or less satisfactory way jobs of various kinds. We learn in school that the person who is courteous, who does the best he knows how, and who thinks for himself is usually successful. These same qualities are essential to success in business or in any kind of industrial work.

The Reasons for Plant Suggestion Systems

Every company is interested in manufacturing its product in a better, quicker, cheaper way. Since the workers often see things about their jobs that can be improved, the management of progressive companies asks employees to suggest better ways of doing their jobs. The company places suggestion blanks at convenient points about the factory so that the worker can secure one easily at any time and write his suggestion on it.

When blanks are not available, suggestions are often written in the form of letters. If the suggestion is a good one and is practical, usually the worker who made it is rewarded in some way. A suggestion can be written about anything from saving paper clips to installing expensive machinery to improve the job.

The purpose of an Employee Suggestion Plan is twofold:

1. To encourage workers to think constructively about their work, thereby developing greater interest in the work, greater initiative, and better performance on the job.
2. To enable the management to get the benefit of any good ideas which employees may have for the improvement of any phase of the business.

The Importance of Making Suggestions

If you can suggest a better way of doing anything in the plant in which you work, it is very important that you do it and get credit for it, because this is one of the few ways you have of standing out from the rest of the employees and letting your superiors know what you can do.

Suggestions Should Be Written Carefully

The ability to use English correctly and clearly is very important in the making of suggestions. Too often employees write out good suggestions so poorly that the men in the office cannot understand exactly what it is that the worker is recommending. The way in which a suggestion is made often determines whether it will be clearly understood and received as a good suggestion or whether it will be considered another foolish idea.

How to Write a Suggestion

A suggestion may consist of just a single sentence or it may be composed of several different parts. If you will study the examples of good suggestions that follow, you will notice that each consists of several parts; namely, a statement of the suggestion, the reason for making the suggestion, the advantages and disadvantages of the suggestion. Sometimes it is necessary to attach a sketch or a drawing in order to make the suggestion clear. This is usually made on another sheet of paper and attached to the suggestion blank. Memorize the different parts of a well-written suggestion. They are:

1. The suggestion itself.
2. Reason for making the suggestion.
3. The advantages of the suggested method.
4. The disadvantages if any.
5. A sketch or drawing illustrating the suggestion.

SUGGESTION BLANK

Lycoming Rubber Company

We welcome suggestions on: No. _____

1. Improvement in the Quality of our Products
2. Development of New Products
3. Improvement of Factory or Office Methods
4. Savings in Labor, Time, or Materials
5. Labor-Saving Devices or Equipment
6. Reduction of Waste or Damaged Goods
7. Salvaging Material and Equipment
8. Reduction of Light, Heat, and Power Cost
9. Reduction of Other Overhead Expenses
10. Reduction of Fire and Accident Hazard
11. Better Service in the Salesroom or Cafeteria
12. Improvement of Working Conditions and Factory Cleanliness

I suggest the following:

Make the top of the outsole-rollers' work benches six inches narrower.

Reason for the Suggestion:

At present there is too little clearance between the shoe rack and the work bench. This not only makes it difficult to remove and replace the lasts on the bottom stick of the shoe rack, but it also causes considerable damage to shoes that are unavoidably bumped against the bench or the shoes on the stick above.
The tops of these benches are sufficiently wide to permit making this alteration without causing any inconvenience to the operators rolling soles.

Advantages:

1. Reduce the number of damaged shoes.
2. Eliminate small delays caused by bumping the shoe racks.

Disadvantages:

1. The operators may have a little difficulty becoming accustomed to the rather narrow work bench.

Date ___February 15, 19–___

Signed *Eldon McKean*

Dept. ___Waterproof___

Make only one complete suggestion on each blank.
The Planning Department or your foreman will be glad to help you make out your suggestion.
Send this suggestion to C. L. WANAMAKER, FACTORY MANAGER. Mark CONFIDENTIAL if so desired.

FIGURE 17. Suggestion Blank Used in a Manufacturing Company.

PUT YOUR IDEAS TO WORK SUGGESTION No. 7178

John L. Stearns & Co.

SUGGESTION BLANK

In making suggestions care should be taken to define and explain as clearly as possible, naming article, part number, and operation affected: When applicable to a machine or a part thereof, please give machine number and its location. If additional paper is required use plain sheets. Do not use more than one numbered sheet for each suggestion, nor submit more than one suggestion on a sheet. Receipt of this suggestion will be acknowledged through your Pay Envelope.

To the Suggestion Committee:

I would suggest _____

_____

_____

_____

_____

_____

_____

Coupon No. 1 is detached by Secretary and must not be sent or shown to committee or any individual.

Do not write name above this line as the suggestion number will be sufficient for the committee.

Coupon No. 1 Suggestion No. 7178

Date_____

Suggestor's
Name_____ Dept._____No._____

Write your name, dept., check number, and date on Coupon No. 1.

Coupon No. 2 Suggestion No. 7178

READ CAREFULLY

Before placing suggestion in the envelope tear off Coupon No. 2, sign your name and HOLD Coupon.

All suggestions will be carefully considered. Awards will be given when the merit and value of the suggestion have been proven.

When notified that your suggestion has been approved, you are asked to bring this coupon to the Suggestion Committee Secretary as a means of identification.

Name_____ Dept._____No._____

Sign your name here in ink to identify you in case this coupon is lost or stolen.

FIGURE 18. Another Form of Suggestion Blank.

No. __196__

SUGGESTION BLANK

COMMUNITY COLLEGE & TECHNICAL INSTITUTE
Allentown, Pennsylvania

The following suggestion is offered for consideration by the faculty:

Suggestion:

> I suggest that spring clips from which copy can be hung be suspended over the composing stone in the print shop.

Reasons for the Suggestion:

> The composing stone is barely large enough to accommodate four boys, and when they are working with large chases there is no room for copy.

Advantages:

> 1. The copy would not be blown or knocked on the floor as it is now when several boys are working at the stone.
> 2. If the copy can be hung on a level with the eyes it will not have to be handled so much; hence, it will be possible to make better progress on a job.

Disadvantages:

> 1. It is easier to refer to copy when it is lying beside the form on which you are working. The method suggested above would be somewhat inconvenient for this reason.

Date __March 18, 19—__   Signed _John Thomas_

                                      Class _____ Senior _____

                                      Trade _____ Printer _____

Make only one suggestion on each blank.

Send this suggestion to your English instructor. If it is well written and seems to be practical, he will submit it to the other instructors for consideration.

FIGURE 19. A Suggestion Blank Used in a Technical School.

October 1, 19—

Mr. J. G. Halsey, Supt.
Faxon Silk Company
Elmira, New York

Dear Mr. Halsey:

For some time we have been having difficulty with defective material getting past our inspectors. I believe that this is due, to some extent, to the inspection machines being operated at too high a speed.

May I suggest that the machines be geared for a somewhat lower speed.

I believe that such a change would permit the inspectors to see a greater percentage of the defects without reducing in any way the production of the department or the earnings of the inspectors.

Very truly yours,

Harold R. Robinson

Harold R. Robinson, Foreman
Inspection Department

Figure 20. A Suggestion Written in the Form of a Letter in a Plant Where There Was No Suggestion System.*

* The above suggestion could also have been written in the form of a memorandum using the headings

To:
From:
Subject:

as shown on page 168.

Applying Your Knowledge

HELPFUL QUESTIONS:

1. Why is it a good plan to write out the reason for the suggestion?

2. Why should the person making the suggestion write the disadvantages as well as the advantages on his suggestion blank?

3. If you were working for a company which had no suggestion system, in what form could you make your suggestions?

4. What is the difference between items 6 and 7 on the Lycoming Rubber Company suggestion blank?

5. What are the purposes of an employee suggestion system?

6. Why is it important that you make a suggestion in writing rather than simply telling a foreman or other supervisor about it?

7. What are the different parts of a well-written suggestion?

PROBLEMS:

1. Make a list of the different parts of a well-written suggestion.

2. Make a list of five items about which you might make suggestions in your school or the plant in which you work.

3. Make a suggestion on some way in which you think material could be saved in your school shop.

4. Assume that you have been working in one department of a local factory for several years, but you have never seen the other parts of the factory; you do not know how the work is done in other parts of the factory or how your work affects the man in the next department. You believe that it would be a good thing if the company would arrange short trips through the factory for employees when they are hired. Write a suggestion making such a recommendation.

5. Sometime during the next two weeks write two suggestions concerning something in your shop or school which you think can be improved. Attach a sketch to at least one of these suggestions in order to make the suggestion clearer.

6. Assume that you are working in a shop which has no suggestion system. Write a suggestion and send it to the superintendent in the form of a letter or memorandum.

Chapter 19

EXPRESSING YOUR OPINION

Most trade and technical magazines conduct departments devoted to discussion of various kinds. Some of these articles are written by the editor of the magazine and take the form of editorials similar to those found in our daily newspapers. Other short articles which dicuss various questions and which give us the opinions of foremen and workmen are written by men working at the trade throughout the country.

In some magazines such as the *American Machinist, The Inland Printer,* the *Automotive Digest,* and others, articles written by workmen are found in departments known as "The Executive Forum," "Round Table Discussion," "Letters to the Editor," etc. Some of the more common subjects of these articles are:

1. Items of general interest to the trade.
2. Technical improvements and their possible effects.
3. News items and their significance.
4. The education of apprentices, journeymen, and technical men.
5. Trade and business practices and ethics.
6. The worker and his relationship to his company and to the rest of the world.

How to Prepare Your Opinion

Although there is no set form in which these editorial-like articles should be written, you will find the following helpful:

1. Write or talk about a single topic.
2. Have a clear and definite point that you wish to make.

3. Be constructive; that is, if you make a negative criticism, you should suggest a remedy.

The following method of writing such an article expressing your opinion is recommended. Usually the editorial or article should consist of three paragraphs as follows:

Shortest   1. The first paragraph should state the issue or the subject.

Longest   2. The second paragraph should discuss the issue—tell what your opinion is.

Second shortest   3. The third or last paragraph should summarize what you have already said so as to draw a definite conclusion. In this paragraph you can try to persuade others to think as you do.

You will find many editorials and articles expressing opinions that are shorter than three paragraphs and many more that are longer. Experience shows, however, that the article of three paragraphs is the best length on which to practice.

Read the following editorials and editorial-like articles which have appeared in different trade magazines.

The short article below is typical of many others which appear in the *American Machinist*.

Carelessness

Statement of the subject   The man habitually causing or being in accidents is a doubtful asset to any company or shop.

Discussion and the writer's opinion   The probability is that when the services of such a man are most needed, he will "be on the shelf" due to one of his frequent and periodic accidents. It is possible, of course, that an accident might be due to an honest error of judgment. The main difference between carelessness and an error of judgement is that carelessness is either laziness or lack of desire and willingness to find out the facts or have any regard for consequences; on the other hand, an honest error of judgment may be caused by a decision made after considering all available information with some important fact missing.

Summary and conclusions   An honest error of judgment is excusable; but a careless error of judgment should never be tolerated, and chronic accident men should be discharged for their own good and the protection of other workers.—E. E. Gagnon, Mechanical Supt., U. S. Asbestos Division.

The following rather long editorial considers whether or not auto mechanics should be required to pass a test for a license to do business as does the registered plumber or the airplane pilot. Read the editorial carefully in order to get the writer's point of view.

Automotive Service of Tomorrow

Introduction

The public rides in airships, but only after the U. S. Department of Commerce has placed its seal of approval on the aircraft. Passing over the temptation to grow wordy and enter a long discussion of what the Government expects in a ship and uncorking a lot of eight and twelve cylinder scientific words descriptive of these qualifications, the whole proposition can be characterized in a few words: "The Government expects the aircraft to be right."

After the ships are placed in service only those men who enjoy the privilege and bear the responsibility of Department Licenses may work on the craft to perform either the routine maintenance service or repair operations.

In another field civil authorities see to it that the health and safety of society are protected against ill-trained and irresponsible workmen. That is the field of sanitation.

Statement of the subject

The question which is in the minds of thinking auto men the nation over is this: Would some system of testing, rating, and licensing be of value in protecting the interests of trained and efficient workers in the trade and insure a supply of *new material* (men) for trade work which would build rather than impair standards of service, and lessen the number of accidents due to faulty repair work?

The lot of the auto mechanic is not easy. Many owners want high quality work on their cars and being discerning men they are quite willing to pay. Price and quality, they deem synonymous. Other men expect high-grade work at low prices, trying to convince themselves that the two can be reconciled, which is impossible. Still others know that cheap repairs are really cheap and makeshift, but are willing to take a chance with their property and persons, and the persons and property of others.

Opinion   The size of the shop has nothing to do with the situation. Who ever heard the public condemn a one-man doctor's establishment or a one-man plumbing shop? It is simply a question of preparation, training, skill, and absolute honesty.

Our recent contest conducted to learn what readers thought an auto mechanic ought to be shows conclusively that he ought to have five or six years' experience. Incidentally, the Federal Government allows credit for years in accredited aviation schools for the aviation man and the same could be done for the auto man.

In view of the experiences in other fields the testing, rating, and licensing of automotive mechanics would be one step toward improving the situation.

Conclusion   The good effect of proper automobile repair and service standards wisely administered is a proposition worthy of consideration of all automotive men interested in the good name and well-being of our great industry.—Ray F. Kuns, *Automobile Digest.*

Expressing Your Opinion in a Meeting

Every one of us finds it easy enough to say what he thinks while standing on a street corner and talking with other persons, but we usually have difficulty expressing our opinion in an organized meeting or before a group of people. The average workman finds frequently the opportunity to tell what he thinks about current subjects in a lodge meeting, in a factory-council meeting, or in a trade union or labor union meeting. If he can express his ideas clearly and forcefully in meetings of organized groups, his remarks are heard with respect, and he also probably stands out from the rest of the group.

An opinion expressed in a meeting should be arranged in much the same manner as the three-paragraph editorial:

1. In the first few sentences tell what you plan to discuss.
2. Next discuss the subject, or give your opinion.
3. Finally, summarize what you have said and give your conclusions.

Applying Your Knowledge

HELPFUL QUESTIONS:

1. What principles should you follow when expressing your opinion in a short article?

2. In a three-paragraph editorial or article expressing an opinion which paragraph will usually be the shortest, which the longest?

3. How do editorials differ from news articles?

4. Trade and technical magazines frequently conduct special departments in which they place all short articles expressing the opinions of the men in the field. Find several such magazines. What names are given these departments?

PROBLEMS:

1. The following article was published not long ago in a trade magazine in the department known as "Discussion of Former Topics." Read it carefully and then rewrite it more clearly than it is now written. Use three paragraphs as suggested earlier in the chapter. The first paragraph should state the subject, the second should discuss the subject or give your opinion, and the third should summarize what you have written and give your conclusion.

Who Pays the Bills?

Looking at the matter from a businesslike viewpoint, it would seem justifiable to hold a man responsible and make him pay for tools he has drawn out on checks and for which he is unable to account. Let us not forget, however, that the circumstances under which he is working might be just as responsible for the loss of tools as his own negligence. Habitual losers should be penalized strictly, but one such offense may be excused.

A man is given a specified number of tool checks. A check is placed on every tool he draws out, and upon termination of connections with the company, he is required to render a signed release from tool liabilities before final payment is made. If he is further required to account for his checks at least once a week, reporting any discrepancy immediately, the plan should prove effective and tool losses should be reduced.

2. Make a list of five subjects about which editorials or other editorial-like articles have been written in trade or technical magazines.

3. Find in a trade or business magazine a good example of a short article expressing the opinion of a workman, foreman, or superintendent in some plant.

4. *Your opinion of your school.* Prepare an opinion of some good feature of your school or shop.

You might make a survey of what students think they want the school to be. The students should determine what areas they want the survey to cover, such as buildings, regulations, attitudes, club opportunities, etc. Probably a questionnaire could be prepared listing the questions, the student body surveyed, and the results tabulated. The results can be placed in report form and used in class discussion.

SUGGESTIONS:

a) A committee of students might develop and secure the results of the survey and tabulate them.

b) The questionnaire might first be tried out on the class.

5. *Your opinion of your trade.* Write an editorial on some question or subject of current interest in your trade. You can find a number of ideas in the current issues of trade or technical magazines.

6. *Your opinion of social and economic problems.* Under the direction of your instructor select several social or economic problems for class discussion. Before the next meeting of the class, secure some information on one of these subjects. Be ready to tell what you think about this problem when the class meets next time.

Your discussions may be more interesting if you ask your instructor to help you organize several panel discussions on these subjects.

7. *Your opinion of a motion picture or TV program.* All of us see the movies or TV, and all of us tell others what we think of the pictures that we have seen. For your next assignment, prepare to tell the rest of the class your opinion of a motion picture

or TV play that you have seen recently. You should discuss points such as these:

a) Was the acting good or poor?

b) Were the actors well chosen for their respective parts?

c) What do you think of the plot or story?

d) Did the picture deal with any important present-day problem? Do you think that it presented a fair picture of this problem?

e) Was the picture based on a book or a stage play? How closely did the motion picture follow the book or the play?

f) In your opinion, has this picture exerted a good or a bad influence on those who saw it?

8. *Your opinion of books.* Nearly every magazine and newspaper nowadays contains book reviews. These reviews tell who wrote the book, who published it, how much it costs, and what it is about. Usually they also tell whether the book is well written and whether it is worth reading.

Find and read several book reviews, then write a similar concise review of a book that you have read recently.

9. *Express your opinion in a "Town Meeting."* Students inevitably form opinions, yet have little opportunity to express their viewpoints. Students might be encouraged to conduct their own "Town Meeting of the Air" to discuss problems and issues in which they are interested—local, national, or world-wide.

If sufficient interest is aroused other classes might be invited to participate. As much as possible the students would have the total responsibility for running the forum—topics, speakers, presiding, conducting.

Chapter 20

CONDUCTING A MEETING

Training for Group Participation

A hundred years ago, American civilization was a frontier and horse-and-buggy civilization. One-man power and one-horse power were still important. American civilization today is a jet-engine, atomic-energy civilization powered by millions of horsepower.

One-man power is no longer enough to guide our society in one direction. Now the individual must work through groups of men to be effective. The individual as a group leader is often more effective than the rugged individualist.

Training for group leadership and participation in group activities is also training for citizenship. Citizenship is not a set of rules or facts. It is a way of conduct, and of living. The good citizen now must know how to work with a group or to lead a group; consequently, citizenship training includes training in how to do these things.

We have found that the best way to determine the majority opinion of a group on a particular question is through the making of a specific motion, followed by discussion and voting on the question. But this must all be done in an orderly and systematic way in group meetings.

In school and in outside activities most people have opportunities to participate in the meetings of different organizations. Since almost every one at some time has occasion to take part in the business of a meeting, it will be well to study briefly the proper method for conducting the business of an organized meeting.

What Is Parliamentary Procedure? *

If you are a member of a club, of a labor or trade organization, or of a lodge, you realize how important it is that order be maintained so that the business can be completed. Therefore, to get the most out of the meetings and to get the business transacted within a reasonable length of time, meetings are conducted according to established rules. These rules which govern the conduct of meetings are known as Parliamentary Procedure.

Organize Your Class as a Club

Since this chapter deals with the methods of conducting meetings, the group should organize itself into a club so that you have an organization for practicing the procedures outlined here.

To effect an organization some individual should serve as temporary chairman and call the first meeting. The business of the first meeting will probably be that of

1. Electing officers.
2. Deciding on the purpose of the club or organization.
3. Appointing a committee for the drawing up of a constitution and bylaws to govern the club and its members.

The Officers of a Club

A club usually has the following officers:

Officer	Duties
President	Presides at and conducts meetings. Usually the by-laws give the president such powers as:

* In this chapter the adverb meaning *yes* is spelled *I* instead of *aye* because *aye* has two pronunciations and meanings. *Aye*, pronounced *I*, means *yes*. *Aye*, pronounced *A*, means *forever*. These two different pronunciations lead to confusion, since some persons use one pronunciation and some the other. This confusion is avoided here by the use of the old spelling *I* for the adverb meaning *yes*.

1. To appoint committees.
2. Serve as ex-officio member of all committees.

Vice-President Performs the duties of the president when the president is absent.

Secretary Keeps a record of proceedings.
Prepares a roll of members and calls the roll when necessary.
Calls the meeting to order in the absence of a presiding officer.
Keeps safely all papers of the organization intrusted to him.
Gives each committee chairman a list of members of that committee with any instructions for it.
Gives the presiding officer at the beginning of each meeting the order of business for that meeting.
Reads to the assembly all communications or papers which should come before it.
Keeps on hand the constitution, bylaws, and regulations of the organization.
Keeps on hand a list of all committees and members.
Carries on the correspondence of the organization. (If the correspondence is especially heavy there may be a corresponding secretary.)

Treasurer Cares for financial business of club; custodian of funds.
Pays bills when directed.
(Sometimes the same person may serve as secretary and treasurer.)

A Suggested Order of Procedure for a Meeting

1. Call meeting to order.
2. Call roll if desirable.
3. Reading and approval of minutes.
4. Reports of officers and standing committees.
5. Reports of special committees.
6. Unfinished business.
7. New business (programs can be carried out here).
8. Adjournment.

Getting Permission to Speak in a Meeting

If you wish to speak in a meeting, you should rise and address the presiding officer as "MR. CHAIRMAN" or "MR. PRESIDENT," "MADAM CHAIRMAN" or "MADAM PRESIDENT," and wait until you are recognized by the chairman before you speak. You are free to speak as soon as the chairman recognizes you. This he does by repeating your name aloud. Usually no one may interrupt you while you are speaking unless the chairman or some one wishes information about the points you are discussing.

How to Nominate Officers

To nominate an individual for office, first gain recognition from the chairman, then present the name of the person by saying, "MR. CHAIRMAN, I nominate John Reynolds." *No second is necessary to a nomination.* After several nominations have been made and no one wishes to make another some one should say, "I move that the nominations be closed." This motion is then seconded and voted upon.

A person who has been nominated may withdraw his name with the permission of the person who nominated him.

CHAIRMAN: Nominations are in order for the office of. . . .

MEMBER: Mr. Chairman (*waits for recognition*).

CHAIRMAN: Mr. Smith.

MEMBER: I nominate Ernest Lehman.

CHAIRMAN: Ernest Lehman has been nominated. Are there any other nominations? (*Chairman waits for any other nominations, then speaks again to the members.*) If there are no further nominations, a motion to close the nominations for the office of . . . is in order.

Opening the Meeting and Conducting Routine Business

CHAIRMAN: (*Sounds gavel.*) The meeting will come to order. (*Chairman waits for members to become quiet.*)

CHAIRMAN: The Secretary will read the minutes of the last meeting.

SECRETARY: (*Reads the minutes.*)

CHAIRMAN: Are there any objections to or corrections of the minutes?

(*Pauses to hear any objections or corrections.*) If not, the minutes stand approved as read.

(*If there are any corrections, the corrections should be voted upon by the members.*)

CHAIRMAN: We will have the Treasurer's report.

TREASURER: (*Gives oral statement of financial condition of club.*)

NOTE: When the treasurer makes a report at each regular meeting to inform the members of the financial condition of the organization, the report should be made orally from a memorandum and no action should be taken by the chairman or assembly.

When the treasurer makes his regular written report quarterly, semi-annually, or annually the report should be audited before it is read; then as soon as the auditor's report is read the chairman says, "The question is on the adoption of the auditor's report." The adoption of the auditor's report certifies that the treasurer's report is correct.

If the report has not been audited, it should be referred to the auditing committee before being approved.

CHAIRMAN: The . . . Committee will present its report at this time. (*The Committee Chairman gives the report of the Committee's activities.*)

CHAIRMAN: We will now have the report of the . . . Committee.

NOTE: If a committee report merely outlines an account of what the committee has done, no action is taken by the assembly and the chairman merely calls for the report of the next committee as is done above.

Only when a committee report makes recommendations does the assembly take action. In such a case, the member making the report moves the adoption of the recommendations, and the assembly takes action on the motion.

Making a Motion

Although a nomination need not be seconded, in most cases a motion must be seconded and voted upon. Only one motion can be considered by the assembly at a time. In other words, there cannot be two motions before the meeting at the same time. The following outline presents the essential steps in the making and the handling of motions:

MEMBER: Mr. Chairman (*Pauses for recognition*).

CHAIRMAN: Mr. Jones.

MEMBER: I move that we. . . .

CHAIRMAN: Is there a second to the motion?

ANOTHER MEMBER: Mr. Chairman, I second the motion.

CHAIRMAN: It is moved and seconded that we . . . (*states motion*). Is there any discussion? (*If there is no discussion, or after the discussion by the members, the chairman proceeds with the question.*) Are you ready for the question?

MEMBERS respond by saying: Question.

CHAIRMAN: The motion is that we. . . . Those in favor of the motion say "I."

MEMBERS IN FAVOR: I.

CHAIRMAN: Those opposed to the motion say "No."

MEMBERS OPPOSED: No.

CHAIRMAN: (*If the vote is in favor of the motion*) The motion is carried. Is there any further business?

CHAIRMAN: (*If the vote is against the motion*) The motion is lost. Is there any further business?

To Change or Amend a Motion

We have stated that only one motion at a time can be placed before the assembly. However, it is sometimes desirable to change a motion so that it is clearer or so that it is more acceptable to the members. A motion may be changed or amended by:

1. Adding words.
2. Striking out words.

3. Inserting words.
4. Substituting words.
5. Dividing the motion.

MEMBER: Mr. Chairman.

CHAIRMAN: Mr. Lehman.

MR. LEHMAN: I move that we amend the motion by (*substituting, striking out, inserting*) the words . . .

CHAIRMAN: Is there a second to the motion?

MEMBER: Mr. Chairman. I second the motion.

CHAIRMAN: It has been moved and seconded that we amend the motion by (*states the proposed change*). If the motion is amended, it will read that . . . Is there any discussion on the amendment? (*Discussion.*)

CHAIRMAN: Are you ready for the question?

MEMBERS: Question.

CHAIRMAN: The vote is on the amendment that. . . . Those in favor of the amendment give their consent by saying "I." (*Pause for the vote.*) Those opposed to the amendment say, "No."

(*If the I's win, the chairman proceeds.*) The I's have it and the amendment is carried. The next business is the amended motion which now reads that. . . . Is there any discussion on the motion as amended? (*The amended motion is then put to a vote.*)

If the No's win the vote, the amendment is dropped, and a vote is taken on the original motion.

To Withdraw a Motion

A motion may be withdrawn by its mover at any time before it is voted upon, providing that no one objects to its withdrawal. If some one objects, then another member must move that the motion may be withdrawn. This motion to withdraw must then be voted upon.

MEMBER WHO MADE MOTION: Mr. Chairman (*Waits for recognition*). I wish to withdraw my motion that. . . .

CHAIRMAN: Mr. Bower asks permission to withdraw his motion. Is there any objection? (*Pause.*) If there is no objection the motion is withdrawn.

To Adjourn a Meeting

If the meeting is scheduled to adjourn at a set time the chairman says, "It is two o'clock and you stand adjourned."

If there is no set time for adjournment or if it is advisable to adjourn before that time, then a motion to adjourn should be made.

MEMBER: Mr. Chairman (*Pause for recognition*). I move that the meeting be adjourned.

CHAIRMAN: (*Has the assembly vote on this motion the same as on any other.*)

Applying Your Knowledge

HELPFUL QUESTIONS:

1. Jim introduced a motion which he wished he could withdraw, but did not know how. What could he have done?

2. Howard introduced a motion; the chairman asked for a second, but there was none. What happened to the motion?

3. The chairman appoints a committee, but he does not definitely name the committee chairman. Who is assumed to be the chairman of the committee in this case?

4. Should a chairman take part in a discussion before the assembly?

5. William has made a motion. The rest of the assembly is in favor of the motion providing a part of it can be changed. How can the motion be changed after it has been moved and seconded?

6. The treasurer has been asked to make a monthly report to the club. How should he make the report? Should he have it audited before making it? What should the chairman do with this monthly financial report?

7. A group of men or boys wishes to start a social club or an athletic club, but they do not know how to proceed. What should they do?

8. A meeting of the club has been called and the members are assembled. As yet the president and vice-president have not appeared. The secretary and treasurer are present. Who should call the meeting to order?

9. The club meets from 1:30 to 2:00 in the afternoon during a special period at the school. A speaker has taken up all the time and it is two o'clock. Can the chairman adjourn the meeting without asking for a motion from the floor?

PROBLEMS:

1. Trace a motion through its various possible steps from the time it is introduced until it is passed.

2. Write out several carefully worded motions. Write out in full the parts that the chairman and the assembly would take in either passing or rejecting them.

3. Write out the order of business or the order of procedure followed by a club or organization to which you belong. Can you suggest any changes?

4. Organize your English class into an English club. Go through the steps necessary to organize any club.

5. For several days, if your instructor thinks it wise, conduct your class according to regular parliamentary procedure. For practice, a different boy should act as chairman each day.

6. Bring to class several carefully worded motions. For drill, have your English club put through several of them from beginning to end. Do not rush this practice; on the other hand, do not let it drag.

7. Write out each of the following in preparation for the meeting to be held in class, at which time each will be used.

    a) Report of a nominating committee to nominate officers for the club you are forming.
    b) Report of a committee appointed to hold a dance.
    c) A nomination for each of the officers of a club.
    d) A motion to appoint a committee.
    e) A motion to discharge a committee from further duties.
    f) A motion to adjourn the meeting.

8. After your English club has learned well the procedure used in passing motions, state some motions and then offer amendments

to them. Write on paper at least one of these amendments and the procedure for handling it before you come to class.

Writing the Minutes of Meetings

The minutes of a meeting are an exact official record of that meeting. Since they are often needed later as records of what actually occurred, they must be written accurately, clearly, and concisely. Although different organizations use different forms, most sets of minutes contain the following items:

1. Name of the organization.
2. Date of the meeting.
3. Time and location of the meeting.
4. Names of those present and those absent.
5. Reading of minutes of previous meeting.
6. Reports of officers and committee.
7. Unfinished business.
8. New business.
9. Informal discussion or comments.
10. Adjournment and time of adjournment.
11. Signature of secretary.

Suggestions for Writing Minutes

1. Minutes should be brief. Only important facts or discussions should be included.
2. Write all motions exactly as stated. Record the name of the person making the motion and of the person making the second.
3. Record the number of positive and negative votes cast on the question whenever it is possible to do so.
4. Include in the records copies of all documents such as notices, legal papers, charters, special reports, etc.
5. Record the names of the officers present and those absent.
6. If the meeting is small, you can also record the names of those present.

7. Record the time of adjournment.

8. Sign the minutes.

Correction of Minutes

If just a few words must be corrected, it is best to draw lines through the incorrect words and write the correct words just above the line.

If entire sentences or paragraphs must be corrected, then it is best to cross out those sentences or paragraphs and place the corrected material at the end of the minutes or on another page. Where the incorrect passages are crossed out, write a note in the margin telling where the corrected statements appear.

Never destroy or tear out any part of the minutes. They should be kept in the record for possible future reference.

Items in these
Minutes

Name of
Organization   Minutes of Student Safety Committee

Date, Time,   A regular meeting of the Student Safety Com-
and Place   mittee was held in room 329 in the main
                  building, November 1, 19__, at 1:30 p.m.

                  Wilfred McCaslin presided over the
                  meeting. LaRue Bieber was the recording
                  secretary.

Names of   Officers present were:
Members   Wilfred McCaslin, Chairman
Present   LaRue Bieber, Secretary
                       Mr. J. Corbin, Faculty Adviser

                  Members present were:
                       Paul Bussler
                       Lloyd Haag
                       Charles Kent
                       Charles Blatchley
                       Herbert Godfrey
                       Harold Guthrie

Reading of   The minutes of the previous meeting held
Minutes   on October 15, 19—, were unanimously approved
                  as read.

Reports of
Officers
or Committees   Herbert Godfrey, chairman of the Bulletin Board Committee, announced that he had received a new lot of safety posters from the National Safety Council.

Unfinished
Business   Paul Bussler, automotive representative, was asked to have another student from his shop elected to the safety committee. This representative is to take the place of William Riley, who quit school recently.

New Business   Two accidents had not been reported by either the students involved or any one else in the shops. These accidents were discussed at some length. Charles Smith, print shop, ran a screwdriver into the palm of his hand. Walter Johnson, electric shop, cut the first finger of his left hand with a knife.

Lloyd Haag moved that "these shops be penalized for these unreported accidents as provided in the safety contest rules." The motion was seconded by Charles Kent. Upon being put to a vote the motion was unanimously carried.

Comments   Wilfred McCaslin announced that the next regular meeting would be held on November 15, 19—.

Adjournment   Herbert Godfrey moved that the meeting be adjourned. Lloyd Haag seconded the motion. The motion was unanimously approved and the meeting adjourned at 2:00 p.m., November 1, 19—.

                    (Signed) LaRue Bieber
                             Secretary

FIGURE 21. Minutes of a Student Committee Meeting.

_____ MANUFACTURING CORPORATION

MINUTES OF SUPERVISORS' MEETING

Date: December 6, 19—

Time: 3:30 p.m.

Place: Conference Room

Present: W. M. Knerr   E. H. Sears   W. A. Jackson
         C. W. Laurenson   R. D. Shore   I. H. Hamilton
         E. R. Gilbody   H. P. Rider   C. W. Williamson

Absent: K. E. Carl   E. U. Kast

1. ORDERS AND SHIPMENTS

    a. V-Type Engines

        Mr. Sears reported a total of 125 engines shipped
        last month. No report available for December as
        yet.

        Mr. Gilbody is to check on delivery dates of new
        equipment scheduled for this month.

2. OPERATIONS

    a. Castings

        Number of castings received weekly will not
        increase materially before January 30, 19—.

    b. Safety

        Mr. Knerr explained that the plant is still having
        a great many medical cases, especially cuts,
        bruises, and puncture wounds, but that the number
        of eye accidents has decreased.

        Mr. Rider reported that a uniform system of cleaning
        tanks and cleaning materials will soon be in
        operation.

        Mr. Williamson informed the group that effective
        immediately no more gasoline is to be used in the
        plant for cleaning or for any purpose whatever.

3. GENERAL

    a. Suggestion Plan System

Mr. Knerr discussed the new Employee Suggestion System, explaining its method of operation and stating that the new suggestion boxes would be placed throughout the plant during the coming week.

J. M. Wolfe

FIGURE 22. Minutes of a Supervisors' Meeting.*

* The above minutes are those of a supervisors' meeting held to discuss plant problems in a manufacturing plant.

June 25, 19—

MINUTES OF MEETING BETWEEN MANAGEMENT

AND REPRESENTATIVES OF THE EMPLOYEES' UNION

At the request of the Secretary of_____, a meeting was held in the Conference Room on Monday, June 23, 19—, at 2:00 p.m.

Shop Representatives
Present:

James Bender	Harold Yoder
Harold Staib	Charles Simcox
James Felix	Arthur Downs
Harold Smith	

Management Represent-
atives Present:

Charles Zimmerman	W. B. Mitchell
	Kelley Frank

OLD BUSINESS

VACATIONS FOR HOURLY EMPLOYEES

Vacation notices have been delivered to all employees who are entitled to vacations, and checks will be distributed with the regular pay on July 7.

SENIORITY

Mr. Zimmerman is to check with several members of the Employees' Committee with reference to questionable cases which have come to the attention of the Employment Office.

UNION PICNIC

The Union has decided to hold its picnic at the Community Park, Saturday, August 30. Mr. Zimmerman informed the group that the plant picnic would probably be held about the middle of September.

DEPARTMENT 15

    It was reported at the meeting that Charles Jones, one of the older employees in the department, had a grievance with reference to the division of work which has reduced his earnings. A meeting was arranged with Mr. Zimmerman, Mr. Downs, and Mr. Ireland, and the matter was corrected to the satisfaction of Mr. Jones.

NEW BUSINESS

HOSPITALIZATION INSURANCE

    Mr. Zimmerman reported that forty-one (41) claims totaling $2863.85 have been paid to date and that eight (8) claims are pending.

    The average claim amounts to $69.85.

CREDIT UNION

    Mr. Zimmerman reported that we now have 257 employee members in the Credit Union as of the end of June.

PRODUCTION POOLS

    One of the representatives asked why the foremen were checking individual production in some of the pools. Mr. Mitchell and Mr. Frank both advised the representatives that the foremen were not checking these jobs with the idea of changing rates, but did wish to know what production each machine was good for in order to rearrange machine lines. If possible, machine lines must be rearranged to secure a more even flow of production.

                          J. E. Osborne
                          Secretary

FIGURE 23. Minutes of a Management-Union Meeting.

MINUTES OF PLANT OPERATIONS COMMITTEE MEETING

MEETING DATE: Thursday, March 5, 19—, 4:00 P.M.

PRESENT: W. P. Hauck — Chairman, E. F. Corkery,
                P. H. Gensemer, P. M. Lubin, C. W. Morse,
                E. A. Wagner, and E. W. Warwick.

DISCUSSION:

1. COST REDUCTION—
   E. F. Corkery reported that some sixty-two (62)
   Cost Reduction ideas are in the process of investigation. There is a definite need for all of us to
   stimulate necessary concluding action.

   It was agreed that the present _____ Plant
   Operations Committee will comprise the Cost Reduction Committee, and will devote ten (10) or fifteen
   (15) minutes at the end of each weekly Operations
   Meeting to the review of Cost Reduction matters.
   To accomplish this, all necessary spade work must
   be done in advance so that the Operations Committee
   will be able to make necessary final decisions.

2. SUGGESTION SYSTEM—
   P. M. Lubin reported that the number of suggestions
   received per hundred employees has been getting
   progressively less each year. The year 19—
   represented the lowest point in this trend. For
   an effective Suggestion System to function, it is
   essential that prompt conclusive review is made of
   each suggestion and the employee is informed as
   soon as possible.

3. SAFETY COMMITTEE—
   Interest in employee safety must be stimulated from
   the top down. In the future, the Safety Committee
   will consist of Messrs. C. L. Spalding (Chairman),
   B. F. Bohner (Secretary), P. M. Lubin, E. W. Warwick
   (or someone he may designate), L. L. Simmons, and
   Fred Crush.

4. TELEPHONE SERVICE—
   C. L. Spalding will inaugurate a record keeping
   system next week to help determine whether present
   facilities are adequate. A progress report will be
   made at a future date.

   Some employees are now making outside personal calls
   lasting for over one-half hour, usually between the

hours of 2:00 to 4:00 P.M. Each of us must remind our employees to discontinue such practice.

5. PARKING ARRANGEMENTS—
E. W. Warwick will submit a progress report next week.

6. UNIT BINDER ASSEMBLY—
E. A. Wagner reported that from his point of view, it was not possible to accomplish what was suggested for product service purposes. It was concluded that the idea be abandoned.

7. GENERAL ITEMS
   (a) E. A. Wagner will arrange a meeting of Messrs. Miklas, Richards, Morse, and any others for the purpose of spelling out gauging methods, type of pack, inspection procedures, basis for rejection, etc. with reference to future coffee maker parts deliveries by Landers, Frary and Clark.
   (b) E. F. Corkery will investigate a possibility of our buying our own truck for transportation purposes.
   (c) E. W. Warwick will report at the next meeting on a better way of waste paper disposal in our present office building.
   (d) P. M. Lubin urged that —
      1. No office personnel be hired without initial clearance through Personnel.
      2. No exempt employees be hired without consideration being given to the matter of Position Guides and salary evaluation.

8. IT WAS AGREED that next week's meeting will start at 3:30 P.M.

P. M. Lubin, Secretary

FIGURE 24. Minutes of a Plant Operations Committee.

The men on this committee constituted the top management of a manufacturing concern employing about 500.

Applying Your Knowledge

HELPFUL QUESTIONS:

1. What differences do you notice between the minutes of the Student Safety Committee meeting and the minutes of the two industrial plant meetings?

2. What would you think of writing minutes for all meetings in a form similar to that common to industrial plant organizations?

3. Why do all organization meetings use the same order of business?

PROBLEMS:

1. Write the minutes of one session of a class meeting so that they can be presented for approval at the next session of the class.

2. Write the minutes for a meeting of some shop committee to which you belong. If this is not possible select any meeting which you have attended recently; or if necessary, write the minutes of an imaginary meeting. Use an outline form in writing this set of minutes.

3. Write the minutes of a recent assembly program or other meeting that you have attended.

PART III

Conducting Business by Correspondence

Chapter 21

THE LETTERS WE WRITE

One principal test of our ability to use English correctly is our skill in writing letters. Perhaps this is true chiefly because most of us do little writing aside from the composing of letters.

In spite of this, however, many of us fail to realize that letter writing should be studied and cultivated. At one time or another the ability to write good letters becomes especially important to us. Sometimes we need to resort to letters in applying for jobs, in making adjustments in business transactions, or in securing the attention of an executive who either does not have the time to see us or does not care to see us.

The following general directions will prove helpful in writing letters:

1. After writing a letter read it aloud so that you hear how it sounds. Imagine that you are talking over the telephone or directly to some one.
2. Place only one main idea in a sentence.
3. Place each new subject in a new paragraph.
4. Avoid the use of such words and stock expressions as *beg to acknowledge, beg to inquire.* Don't beg at all.
5. Never end your letter with a sentence that is introduced by a word ending in *ing*, such as *trusting, hoping, thanking,* etc.
6. Keep the letter neat and attractive in appearance.
7. Type your letter if possible.
8. Always use courteous language.
9. Frequently, it is a good plan to keep an important letter over night and reread it in the morning before mailing it.

Make a Set of Blueprints for Your Letter

A contractor will not figure the cost of a job until he has studied the blueprints and specifications for that job. He knows that he must use accurate plans and specifications in order to compute accurately the cost of labor, the time, and the materials required. It is the same with a letter. Unless you plan your letter, you cannot do as good a job as you might.

The following points are worth your consideration when planning a letter:

1. Get before you all previous correspondence that is pertinent.
2. Bring together all the facts that bear on the situation.
3. Make a list of the things you wish to say or discuss.
4. Arrange the thoughts in the order in which you wish them to appear in the letter.
5. Write as concise a paragraph as possible covering each idea.

The Layout of the Letter

The Six Essential Parts of a Letter. The six essential parts of a letter are (1) heading, (2) inside address, (3) salutation, (4) body, (5) complimentary close, (6) signature. These parts are illustrated in the short letter on the following page.

Punctuation of the Heading and the Address. The tendency today is to use as little punctuation as possible. For example, periods are used only after abbreviations, and commas only inside the lines to separate items. Proper punctuation is illustrated in the examples which are shown on page 219.

Heading. The heading tells where and when the letter was written. Usually it is placed in the upper right-hand corner of the first page, an inch or more from the top. When a

Heading

15 South Broad Street
Salem, Massachusetts
August 5, 19—

*Inside
address*

Mr. Dixon O. Marshall
60 East 42nd Street
New York 17, New York

Salutation

Dear Mr. Marshall:

*Body or
contents*

Thank you for your letter of August 3, containing the information about which we wrote you. I shall see you when I get to Boston next week.

*Complimentary
close*

Very truly yours,

Signature

Alfred A. Marks

Alfred A. Marks

FIGURE 25. The Layout of a Letter.

printed letterhead is not used, the complete heading should contain the street and the number of the writer's address, the city, the state in which the letter was written, and the date on which it was written. Although the block form is preferred, the heading and the inside address may be arranged in either the block or the indented form.

Inside Address. The inside address contains the name and the address of the person or company to whom the letter is written. It is usually placed two spaces below the date line of the heading. If the heading is written in block form, the inside address should also be written in the block form; if the heading is in the indented form, the address should likewise be in the indented form.

Salutation. The salutation or greeting is written two spaces below the inside address.

The business salutations most frequently used today are:

Gentlemen: This form is used for addressing a
               company or group of men or of both men
               and women.

```
Dear Mr. Jones:   This form is the most popular. It is
Dear Dr. Lyon:    friendly, but it is also courteous.
Dear Miss Fry:    When we meet some one for the first time,
Dear Mrs. Moore:  this is what we usually say.

Dear Paul:        This form is informal and friendly.  Use
Dear Helen:       it only to address some one you know very
                  well.

Dear Dick:        Use this form in a business letter only if
Dear Peg:         you would use the same form in writing a
                  personal letter.
```

Body of the Letter. The body of the letter begins two spaces below the salutation. It is best to indent the paragraphs regularly and uniformly, although the blocked paragraph is widely used. Liberal margins of not less than one inch should be used on both sides of the paper and at the top and the bottom. The pages should be numbered in sequence as are the pages of a book or pamphlet, but the first page is never numbered.

Complimentary Close and Signature. The complimentary close is placed two lines or spaces below the last line of the body. It is usually followed by a comma. Only the first word should be capitalized. The complimentary close of a business letter is generally one of the following forms:

```
Very truly yours,
Yours very truly,
Yours truly,
```

In friendly business letters one of the following may be used:

```
Sincerely yours,
Cordially yours,
```

The signature should be written about a half inch below the complimentary ending. In most modern business correspondence, the name of the writer is typewritten below the space provided for the signature.

Forms for Business Letters

```
                                    916 Market Street
                                    Wilmington 9, Delaware
                                    December 5, 19—


Firestone Plastics Company
Chemical Sales Division
Pottstown, Pennsylvania

Gentlemen:

Please send me.......................................

....................................................

....................................................

Yours truly,


Charles A. Barclay
```

FIGURE 26. Block Form. All the Letter Parts Begin at the Left Margin.

```
                                    916 Market Street
                                    Wilmington 9, Delaware
                                    December 5, 19—


Firestone Plastics Company
Chemical Sales Division
Pottstown, Pennsylvania

Gentlemen:

      Please send me................................

....................................................

....................................................

                         Yours truly,


                         Charles A. Barclay
```

FIGURE 27. Indented Form. In This Form the Paragraphs Are Indented.

The Envelope

The envelope should be properly addressed. The *address* of the sender should be placed in the upper left corner. This is known as the *return address*. The address of the person to whom you are sending the letter is placed on the front much as that indicated in Figure 28.

Return address

```
Alfred A. Marks
15 South Broad Street
Salem, Massachusetts
```

The address

```
                              Mr. Dixon O. Marshall
                              60 East 42 Street
                              New York 17, New York
```

FIGURE 28. The Form for the Envelope.

Chapter 22

LETTERS OF INQUIRY, REPLY, AND THANKS

The mechanic or technical man frequently finds it necessary to ask for information by means of letters. In some cases the information required has to do with his trade or business and is technical; in other cases it may be personal. Whatever the kind of information required, it must be accurate to be of any value. Inexact, vague, or incomplete information is of little value to any workman, no matter for what purpose he wants it. On the other hand, specific information is of considerable assistance.

To secure exact information by means of letters is not a difficult task if the writer knows exactly what he wants and how to ask for it. However, if the writer does not know exactly what he wants, how can he expect the reader to know?

Any one desiring information should ask these questions before writing the letter:

1. Exactly what information do I want?
2. Do I need the information?
3. Is the person to whom I am writing the best source of information?

Clearness Is Essential

Word your letter so clearly that any one can understand it readily. The following plan contains the points to which you should give attention in the development of a letter of inquiry:

1. State the subject of your inquiry. If you are requesting information on several items, list them in order.
2. Add any necessary explanation.

3. Give the reasons for your inquiry.
4. Be courteous always. A *please* and a *thank you* will help induce the reader to consider your letter favorably. Express appreciation, but never end the letter with the expression *Thanking you in advance, I am . . .*
5. Enclose a stamped, self-addressed envelope when you are asking a favor which you will be unable to return.

The kinds of letters of inquiry most commonly written are:

1. Letters asking for catalogs or other printed material.
2. Letters asking for trade or technical information regarding methods of doing jobs and operating equipment of various kinds.
3. Letters asking for prices.

Requests for Printed Materials

A letter requesting a catalog or a printed booklet requires only a brief, courteous, and definite sentence:

January 15, 19—

```
Pittsburgh Plate Glass Company
Paint Division
Pittsburgh 22, Pennsylvania

Gentlemen:

        Please send me a copy of your new revised booklet
"Color Dynamics in Industry" as advertised in the January
issue of Mill and Factory.

                        Very truly yours,
```

FIGURE 29. Request for Printed Material.

Requests for Technical Information

Letters in which a number of questions are asked must be especially clear and easy to read. These letters are made easy to understand by listing each question separately and numbering it. The following letter illustrates this method:

January 5, 19—

American Type Founders Sales Corporation
13th and Cherry Streets
Philadelphia 7, Pennsylvania

Gentlemen:

     As you know we have been considering the installation
of offset printing equipment. We appreciate the information which you sent us recently. However, we wish to
secure some additional information.

     Will you please write us your answers to the follow-
ing questions as soon as convenient:

     1. Does anyone make plates commercially in our area?

     2. What are the usual or approximate prices currently
       charged for the various types of plates?

     We shall appreciate any specific information that you
can send us on these points.

              Very truly yours,

FIGURE 30. Letter Requesting Information.

Letters of Reply to Inquiries

Whether the requested information is supplied or withheld,
answer the inquiry as courteously and as promptly as possible.
Whenever possible, give the exact information in the briefest
possible form. If several different questions have been asked,
answer them in the same order in which they were asked.

Letters of Thanks

Too frequently a favor or kindness is forgotten after it has
been done. If you receive a helpful reply to an inquiry and
are not in a position to return the courtesy in some way, mail
a letter of thanks expressing your gratitude or appreciation.

A Complete Letter Series

Watrous, Penna.
July 15, 19—

Mr. Charles S. Smith
Diesel Instructor
Williamsport Technical Institute
Williamsport, Pennsylvania

Dear Mr. Smith:

You will recall that last winter I attended your class in Diesel Engine Maintenance.

Unfortunately I have lost the diploma which was given me upon my successful completion of the course. Is it possible for you to secure for me a duplicate diploma?

At present I am driving a truck, but in the near future I have a good chance of securing work on diesel maintenance in the North Penn Power Company's plant. One of the diplomas would help me considerably in securing this job.

I shall appreciate very much anything that you might be able to do for me in this matter.

Very truly yours,

Charles Campbell

FIGURE 31. Letter of Inquiry.

Applying Your Knowledge

HELPFUL QUESTIONS:

1. What quality is essential in a letter of inquiry?

2. List several specific directions for writing a letter of inquiry.

3. How long should a letter requesting a booklet or a catalog be?

4. How should you arrange a letter in which you inquire about several different items?

WILLIAMSPORT TECHNICAL INSTITUTE

Phone 2-4691

A DIVISION OF THE SCHOOL DISTRICT

1005 WEST THIRD STREET
WILLIAMSPORT, PENNSYLVANIA

July 20, 19—

Mr. Charles Campbell
Watrous
Pennsylvania

Dear Mr. Campbell:

We are sending you with this letter a duplicate copy of the diploma you were granted last year.

We are glad to hear of your chances for future employment. If there is anything that we can do for you in the future, please feel free to request it of us.

Very truly yours,

Charles S. Smith

Charles S. Smith
Diesel Instructor

FIGURE 32. Letter of Reply.

Watrous, Penna.
July 25, 19—

Mr. Charles S. Smith
Diesel Instructor
Williamsport Technical Institute
Williamsport, Pennsylvania

Dear Mr. Smith:

The duplicate copy of the diploma and your letter arrived today. Please accept my thanks for your kindness in sending me the duplicate and for your offer of further assistance.

I am sure that the diploma will help me considerably in securing the job which I mentioned to you in my first letter.

Very truly yours,

Charles Campbell

FIGURE 33. Letter of Thanks.

5. Should you refuse to answer a letter of inquiry under any conditions?

6. When do you consider it advisable or necessary to write a letter of thanks?

PROBLEMS:

1. Select from a popular magazine or from some trade magazine the name of a company which advertises a catalog or other printed literature for distribution. Write a letter to the company requesting a catalog or other printed material concerning their product. Mail the letter.

2. Write a letter inquiring about the subscription rates for a magazine having to do with your trade or with some related trade.

3. Write a letter to one of your fellow students requesting some information concerning his shop. Exchange the letters in your class. Answer the letter that has been written to you; then write a letter of thanks upon receiving the reply that has been handed to you.

4. Write to a manufacturer of equipment or tools used in your shop asking for a catalog. Ask two or three definite questions about certain equipment.

5. In a trade or technical magazine select and read an article on some subject in which you are interested. Write to the editor of the magazine for more information on the subject. Write the editor a letter of thanks for sending you the information.

6. The school's basketball or football team has several open dates on its next schedule and wishes to play some schools within a radius of a hundred miles on these open dates. In your letter give the open dates, and such other information as will enable the other school's faculty manager of athletics to make a definite and intelligent reply.

Chapter 23

LETTERS OF REFERENCE, RECOMMENDATION, AND INTRODUCTION

Letters to References

When a person is being considered for a job, the prospective employer often writes to the individual or companies whose names are given as references. These letters are written to secure definite and reliable information about the ability and the character of the applicant. Some concerns use a printed form which they ask the reference to fill out. This saves time and standardizes the records of employees.

When printed blanks are used, the reference letter is written the same as one asking a favor. It may follow this outline:

First paragraph: Statement that the reader's name was used as a reference.

Second paragraph: The request or favor asked.

Third paragraph: Expression of appreciation.

Because they may employ people only occasionally, many small business men have little use for printed reference blanks. Whatever questions are asked are placed in the reference letter itself. The reference letter is similar to the letter of inquiry discussed in the preceding chapter, and it is written in much the same way. However, some of the following specific directions may prove helpful:

1. Ask definite questions in order to secure definite answers.
2. Ask no more questions than necessary.
3. Number and list the questions when more than two or three are asked. The next example illustrates this point.
4. Use an outline similar to that given above. The questions are merely a part of the request.

Dear Mr. Markley:

Lester R. Ensminger, who has applied to us for work as a toolmaker or safety inspector, has given your name as reference. He informs us that he was employed in your toolmaking department approximately six years, and as safety inspector about the same length of time.

Since we are considering him for the position as safety inspector, we have enclosed a reference blank which we shall appreciate your filling out and returning to us in the enclosed envelope.

We shall appreciate any information that you can give us and shall be glad to return the courtesy at any time.

Very truly yours,

FIGURE 34. Letter to Accompany a Reference Blank.

Applying Your Knowledge

HELPFUL QUESTIONS:

1. Why do some companies use printed questionnaires to secure information from references?

2. Of what three parts may the outline of a reference letter consist?

3. When several questions are asked in a letter, why is it a good plan to list them rather than place them in a paragraph?

4. What two different types of reference letters are discussed here?

5. What specific directions should be followed when writing a reference letter which is not to be accompanied by a printed questionnaire?

PROBLEMS:

1. Assume that you are operating a garage. Herman Sweet has moved to your town from a city about a hundred miles distant.

When he applied to you for work as a mechanic, he gave Charles S. Snyder, proprietor of the Black & White garage, as reference. Write Mr. Snyder for complete information regarding Herman Sweet. Ask a number of specific questions. If you wish, you may assume that you are operating a business other than an automobile garage.

Dear Mr. Markley:

We are investigating the record of Lester R. Ensminger, who informs us that your company employed him from December, 19— to September 1, 19—. Mr. Ensminger has applied to us for work as either a toolmaker or safety inspector.

Since we desire to secure reliable information concerning his record, we shall appreciate your answering the following questions as definitely as possible:

1. When did you employ Mr. Ensminger?

2. Was he thoroughly reliable and trustworthy while in your employ?

3. What is his record with your company so far as his ability and accomplishments on the job are concerned?

4. Why did he leave your employ?

Will you please write us about Mr. Ensminger as soon as you find it convenient. If we can be of any help to you on similar matters, we shall be glad to reciprocate.

Very truly yours,

FIGURE 35. Example of a Letter to a Reference, Asking Several Questions.

Letters of Recommendation

Many men have been aided in securing their present positions through using effective letters of application, and letters of recommendation, and by supplying a list of carefully chosen references to whom the prospective employer could turn for additional information. Certain facts concerning letters of recommendation are important and should be kept in mind when a recommendation is requested. In this chapter the important principles which should be applied in writing letters of recommendation will be considered.

General hints for writing letters of recommendation:

1. Make your letter sound sincere.
2. Make specific statements. Definite statements mean much more to an employer than a letter full of general statements containing high-sounding compliments.
3. Be truthful about the ability and character of the individual. If his ability and habits are commendable, say so; if he has weaknesses, say that also.

There are two types of letters of recommendation:

1. Specific—written to a particular individual.
2. General—written for any interested individual. These letters usually begin with "To Whom It May Concern":

A specific letter of recommendation is more effective when it is sealed and mailed to the particular individual to whom it is written. Since it gives definite information, it is much more valuable than the general letter of recommendation.

A general letter of recommendation is not much more than a certificate of good standing or a letter of introduction. As a general rule, employers pay little attention to letters beginning with "To Whom It May Concern."

Applying Your Knowledge

Helpful Questions:

1. What two types of letters of recommendation are presented in this chapter?
2. When is each used?

AJAX MANUFACTURING COMPANY
Cincinnati 9, Ohio

September 15, 19—

Electric Furnace Company
65 River Street
Buffalo 2, New York

Gentlemen:

Mr. Lester R. Ensminger, about whom you inquired in your letter of September 12, originally entered our employ December 2, 19—, as a machinist in our Machine Repair Department. He served in this capacity until he was promoted to the position of Safety Inspector, February 1, 19—.

We have found Mr. Ensminger to be a conscientious and willing worker. He has been prompt and regular in his attendance, and his duties as Safety Inspector have required that he frequently work overtime.

In regard to his ability, we wish to say that since 19—, our lost-time accidents have decreased approximately fifty per cent. Our lost-time accident rate in 19— was approximately 20 accidents per 100 men. For 19—, we had only 2.4 lost-time accidents for every one hundred men.

Mr. Ensminger is a machinist and an experienced toolmaker by trade. His work for us along these lines was also very satisfactory.

If you are in need of either a toolmaker or a Safety Engineer, we can recommend Mr. Ensminger and know that he is capable of doing a good job for you.

Very truly yours,

AJAX MANUFACTURING CO.

Earle Markley

Employment Manager

FIGURE 36. A Specific Letter of Recommendation.

AJAX MANUFACTURING COMPANY
Cincinnati 9, Ohio

September 15, 19—

TO WHOM IT MAY CONCERN:

This will introduce Lester R. Ensminger, who has been employed as a Safety Inspector at our Emory Street Plant since February 1, 19—.

It is necessary for us to lay off Mr. Ensminger because of business conditions.

While in our employ Mr. Ensminger has proved to be a conscientious and willing worker. He has been prompt and regular in his attendance. He is an excellent man on Safety Work of any kind.

Very truly yours,

AJAX MANUFACTURING CO.

Earle Markley

Employment Manager

FIGURE 37. A General Letter of Recommendation.

3. Which type, generally speaking, is the more valuable to a man seeking employment? Why?

4. Is it better policy to give the man himself the letter of recommendation or to mail it direct to the person to whom it is addressed? Why?

PROBLEMS:

1. As a foreman in a local factory or other business concern, you have been asked to write to another foreman in the same city a specific letter of recommendation for a man who formerly worked under you. Write a letter which you could mail directly to the other foreman.

2. Fred Jones, who has worked for you for five years, plans to move to another city to live with his aged parents. He is planning to secure work in the same type of business as you are operating.

He asks you for a general letter of recommendation. Comply with his request.

Letters of Introduction

A letter of introduction is used to establish business or social contacts.

For example, suppose that you are seeking work. A friend of yours knows a foreman or works under one in a local plant. He gives you a letter of introduction to the foreman. When you go to the plant, you present the letter to the foreman. As a result of the introduction through a person known to him, he may consider you more favorably than he would otherwise.

When writing a letter of introduction, tell who your friend is, and why you are introducing him. The following plan is suggested for a letter of this kind:

1. Introduce the person.
2. Give briefly your reason for introducing him.
3. Give briefly some definite information about him.
4. Express your appreciation of any courtesy that might be shown your friend.

When the situation does not require a letter, you can use a business card bearing the words "Introducing Mr. . . ."

Applying Your Knowledge

HELPFUL QUESTIONS:

1. For what purposes is a letter of introduction used?
2. Of what four parts does a letter of introduction usually consist?
3. How should an envelope containing a letter of introduction be addressed?

November 15, 19—

Mr. Albert V. Whiteman, Foreman
John N. Stearns & Company
Hopewell 4, Virginia

Dear Mr. Whiteman:

Introduction   This will introduce William Zeiders, who has had several years' experience as a loom-fixer.

Reason for   Because of his past experience you may
introduction be interested in him as a prospective employee.

Information   Mr. Zeiders has worked for the Susque-
about friend hanna Silk Company where he made a good record. He is not working at present because the plant in which he was employed is closed. I have known Mr. Zeiders personally for several years and can assure you that he is energetic, honest, and loyal to his friends and superiors.

Expression of   Any aid that you may be able to give him
appreciation in locating work at his trade will be appreciated personally.

Very truly yours,

Robert A. Wood

FIGURE 38. Typical Letter of Introduction.

Robert A. Wood
957 W. Third St.
Elmira, New York

Mr. Albert V. Whiteman, Foreman
John N. Stearns & Company
1500 Memorial Avenue
Hopewell 4, Virginia

Introducing
Mr. William Zeiders

FIGURE 39. How the Envelope Should Be Addressed.

PROBLEMS:

1. A friend of yours is planning to move to another town. You have an old friend living in this town. Write a letter introducing the former to the latter individual.

2. You are working in a local factory or for a local company. There is a job open for which a friend of yours wishes to apply. Write a letter of introduction to the man who will do the hiring for this job.

3. You are a member of a social or athletic club. A friend wishes to secure a membership in the club. Write a letter of introduction to the secretary or the chairman of the membership committee.

Chapter 24

ORDERING GOODS BY MAIL

The Order Letter

Since a large amount of the business of both small and large concerns is done by mail, the letter ordering materials or equipment is especially important. When an order is accepted by a company, it usually becomes a contract enforceable by law, and for this reason every sentence in the order letter should be carefully written and closely read by the writer.

An order letter is easy to write if you state exactly and carefully what you want. Always give all necessary details so that anybody can fill your order. Note carefully the details of information that a company requests when you order something from it.

When you write an order letter be sure to follow these directions:

I. Arrange the order carefully.
   A. List the articles wanted and separate them from the rest of the letter. Place each item on a separate line. Give the quantity of each article wanted.
   B. When possible, put the prices in a column at the right side of the page. The unit price should come first and the total price in the price column.
   C. Capitalize the trade name of each article; for example, *Tydol motor oil.*
   D. Use figures, not words, to express quantities.
   E. If possible, give the size, color, and catalog number of each article.

II. Give shipping instructions.
   A. Specify whether the articles are to be shipped by mail, ex-

press, freight, or truck; whether they are to be shipped collect
or prepaid (C.O.D. or f.o.b.*).

B. Give the exact address to which the goods are to be sent.

C. Tell when you want the articles shipped.

III. Make provisions for payment.

A. If you enclose any remittance, state definitely in what form
and amount. If you want the bill to be charged, say so or refer
to your credit account if you have one. Don't just neglect
saying anything about payment because such a procedure
frequently causes long delays.

IV. Special considerations.

A. Here make any special requests as to quality, discounts,
promptness of shipment, or give the seller any information
that will help him meet your wishes.

An order letter should give definite directions by answering these questions:

1. Where
2. When
3. How   To send
4. What   the goods
5. How much
6. On what terms

Memorize this brief outline. Whenever you write an order
letter, be sure that your letter answers each of these six questions.

* C.O.D. and f.o.b. are abbreviations commonly used and almost as frequently misunderstood. C.O.D. means *collect on delivery.* The purchaser
pays all charges, the cost of the articles plus the shipping charges. F.o.b.
means *free on board.* The seller places the goods on the railroad cars free
of charge and the buyer pays the express or freight charges from that
point.

Typical Order Letters

RADER'S MACHINE SHOP
Atlanta, Georgia

September 5, 19—

Norton Company
Worcester, Mass.

Gentlemen:

Please send by express the following repair parts for a Number 1, Belt–Driven, Norton Universal Tool and Cutter Grinder, bearing serial number M–1974:

Quantity	Catalog No.	Article	Price
2	U–2670	Back Bearing @ $3.50	$7.00
1	U–2671	Spindle Sleeve	6.50
1	U–2672	Spindle	4.25
1	U–2673	Spindle Check Nut	1.25
		Total	$19.00

Please charge this order to our account subject to your terms of thirty days net.

Since we need these repair parts very much, we shall appreciate your shipping them immediately

Very truly yours,

John A. Rader

John A. Rader
Proprietor

FIGURE 40a. An Order Letter.

When ordering only one or two items, it is probably best to omit column headings, such as *Quantity, Catalog No., Article,* and *Price*; but when more than two items are ordered, the use of such headings helps to make the letter clear and to prevent mistakes.

1223 Vine Avenue
Rochester, New York
January 15, 19—

Modern Plastics
575 Madison Avenue
New York 22, New York

Gentlemen:

Please send the Modern Plastics magazine for one year, beginning with the February issue, to

Mr. Alfred B. Snyder
1223 Vine Avenue
Rochester, New York

I am inclosing a personal check for six dollars in payment for the subscription.

Very truly yours,

Alfred B. Snyder

FIGURE 40*b*. A Brief Letter Placing an Order for a Magazine.

157 West Third Street
Nashville, Tennessee
October 1, 19—

The Ronald Press Company
15 East 26th Street
New York 10, New York

Gentlemen:

Will you please send me one copy of Effective Business Writing by Williams and Ball, listed at $4.25. Please send the book C. O. D.

Yours truly,

Joseph L. Payne

FIGURE 40*c*. A Typical Letter Ordering a Book.

Applying Your Knowledge

HELPFUL QUESTIONS:

1. What six definite directions should an order letter contain?

2. For what do the abbreviations C.O.D. and f.o.b. stand?

3. On which side of the letter (right or left) do you put the prices of the articles you are ordering? Should these prices be totaled and the total written under them in the order letter?

4. If you are ordering several articles of the same kind, how can you indicate both the unit price and the total price for the several articles? (Unit price refers to the price of a single article.)

5. In how many different ways could you write the price of the book mentioned in Figure 40c?

PROBLEMS:

1. List the names and complete addresses of at least five manufacturing companies that produce articles which can be used in your trade or occupation.

2. Order some machine for your school shop.

3. Write a letter subscribing for a technical or trade magazine over a specified period of time.

4. Write a letter ordering repair parts for some machine.

5. Assume that you are going to take a camping trip in the Adirondack Mountains of New York State, but you don't want to get any provisions before you reach the mountains. Write a letter to the Saranac Lake Supply Company, Saranac Lake, New York, ordering a week's supply of provisions for your friend and you. Give the Supply Company all the necessary information and tell them when you expect to call for the provisions.

6. Have a magazine sent to a friend for one year as a gift.

7. Place an order with some supply company for various tools or equipment which you might need in your trade. Order at least five different items, and several articles of each item. The bill is to be charged to your company's account.

The Order Blank

A mechanic or other employee is frequently required to order parts used in making repairs. He may only select the parts and then have a clerk write the order, or he may have to write it himself. At any rate every one finds it necessary at times to order articles, and in doing so is often required to fill out an order blank.

Purchase Order Blank. Most shops or firms that place orders frequently have found that a carefully planned order blank is an excellent aid in avoiding errors on their part as well as on the part of the shipper. They are written at least in duplicate, so that one can be filed and there can be no future doubt as to the original order. The term *order blank* is used to designate the blank that is supplied by the seller to customers. The term *purchase order blank* is used to designate the blank that the customer has printed and that he uses regularly in ordering from any seller. Order blanks may be arranged differently, but practically all of them ask for the same information.

How to Use an Order Blank. It is necessary to fill in correctly the information asked for on the blank, but regardless of other things you should give accurately the quantity, the catalog number, and the description of the article.

It is best to get the description of the article from a catalog, but when that cannot be done, give a complete description of the machine for which you want the part. For example:

1 emery wheel for a Stanley stone saw, serial number G-342, type CCS-9.

1 clutch shaft bearing for a Ford V-8, 1954 model, number F126068.

When ordering parts for automobiles or for other machinery, be sure that the following items are explained in some way:

Shipping directions (parcel post, express, or freight)
Quantity
Name and complete description of the part
Style, type, or model of machine or automobile
Machine number or vehicle number which appears on
    manufacturer's patent plate

Engine or motor number of machine
Color, if part is painted
Method of payment
Date wanted

Purchase Order

Send Invoice To   DU-RITE ELECTRIC COMPANY
Electrical Contractors
2004 R Santa Fe Avenue
Los Angeles 54, California

Date <u>September 25, 19—</u>

Order No. 631

To <u>Allen Electric Company</u>
<u>2460 East Slauson Avenue</u>
<u>Huntington Park, California</u>

Please ship to us by   Motor Express

Quantity	Material	Unit Price	Amount
2	Weller Soldering Guns, WB, 250 Watt, 60 Cycle, 125 Volt	10.00	20.00
10	Porcelain Bases, Concealed for Receptacles, Hubble, #158	.38	3.80
20	Boxes, Switch & Receptacle, Wiremold #5747	.45	9.00
	Total		$32.80

Observe strictly the following conditions to which this order is subject:
Purchase is for monthly account unless otherwise specified.
Send invoice in duplicate. Send freight bills with invoice.
Please put our number on all invoices, packages, and bills of lading.

THE DU-RITE ELECTRIC COMPANY

By   *H. Goodman*

Treasurer

FIGURE 41. A Form of Purchase Order Blank Used by an Electrical Firm.

Applying Your Knowledge

HELPFUL QUESTIONS:

1. What is the difference between the ordinary order blank usually found in a mail order catalog and a purchase order blank?

2. When would you consider a business large enough to require purchase order blanks for that particular business?

3. How should an article be ordered when you cannot find a description of it in a catalog?

4. To what seven items should you pay particular attention when ordering parts for a machine?

5. Why do all order blanks provide a space for the signature or O. K. of some company official?

6. What is the meaning of "Ship Via"?

PROBLEMS:

1. Study the illustration of a typical order blank shown in Figure 41 and make a list of the items of information for which a purchase order blank makes provision.

2. Assume that you are operating a small shop of some kind. Make up a purchase order blank that you might use in ordering supplies and materials.

3. Using a purchase order blank, order repair parts for some machine or machines in your school shop.

4. Using a purchase order blank, order materials or small supplies that you use in your school shop.

5. Secure, if you can, a regular order blank used by one of the mail order houses. If you cannot secure a blank, borrow one from another student and draw one of your own. Order with one of these some camping equipment, fishing equipment, or any other items that you might want at some time for your personal use.

Chapter 25

CLAIM AND ADJUSTMENT LETTERS

In spite of all precautions, the best firm will sometimes make mistakes or send wrong or defective material. On the other hand, orders will be cancelled, and shipments may be lost. At times the customer will be at fault, and at other times the railroad company or the trucking company will be the cause of errors and claims.

Claims are seldom pleasant; but if they are handled promptly, courteously, and fairly, their adjustment will ultimately result in increased good will.

A well-written claim letter should

1. State exactly what is wrong.
2. Give definite dates, order numbers, etc., to make identification and tracing easy.
3. Suggest an adjustment or remedy.
4. Close courteously.
5. Be addressed to the company or individual responsible for the mistake or damage.

Additional Suggestions

Before signing a freight receipt or other shipping receipt, the person receiving the goods should always make sure that there is no visible damage or shortage. When a shipping receipt is signed, it is an acknowledgment that the goods were received in good condition. When goods have been damaged in transit, the agent of the transportation company should be asked to put a notation of the damage on the shipping receipt. The buyer can then accept the goods and make a claim against the transportation company rather than against the shipper.

A claim may be made properly against the seller or shipper for:

1. A delay in the receipt of the goods ordered.
2. A shortage in the order.
3. Errors in filling the order.
4. Goods not up to specifications.

The letter should be courteous and should present the entire case fairly. A show of anger may result only in angering the other firm; further, it is humiliating to show anger in a letter only to find out later that the fault was your own.

Adjustment Letters

The principal objective of any adjustment letter is to satisfy the customer and, if possible, to keep the customer. To lose

October 27, 19—

Callahan Printing Company
2345 North Main Street
Dayton 14, Ohio

Gentlemen:

On October 20 we placed with you an order for 1000 letterheads to be printed on 24-lb. Fiscal bond. We received these letterheads from you today, but we are returning them to you immediately because of two errors in the filling of our order.

There is an error in the spelling of "Hirsch," which you have spelled "Hirsh." The original order also called for Fiscal bond, a better paper than you have used.

Will you please duplicate our original order as soon as possible.

Very truly yours,

Samuel J. Hirsch

Samuel J. Hirsch

FIGURE 42. A Letter Making a Claim and Asking for an Adjustment.

Callahan PRINTING COMPANY

SPECIALIZING IN COMMERCIAL STATIONERY • 2345 NORTH MAIN STREET • DAYTON, OHIO

Telephone BUTLER 3-3588

October 28, 19—

Mr. Samuel J. Hirsch
1024 North Third Street
Dayton, Ohio

Dear Mr. Hirsch:

   We thank you for the privilege of again filling your order so that the work will be entirely satisfactory to you. The incorrect spelling of "Hirsch" is our mistake.

   We are printing immediately another 1000 letterheads which, we feel sure, you will find satisfactory in every way.

   The paper which we used for the letterheads that you returned to us is slightly lighter in weight than your original sample, but it is a better grade of paper. However, we are glad to duplicate exactly the paper used in your copy.

   It is a pleasure to adjust this matter because we make it a point to please our customers. We shall appreciate very much the opportunity to supply your printing needs in the future.

                    Very truly yours,
                    Callahan Printing Company

                    George H. Marsh

FIGURE 43. A Letter Making an Adjustment.

a customer is one of the easiest things a business man can do; to secure a new customer, one of the most difficult. It is, therefore, necessary to adjust the claim to the satisfaction of the customer if it is at all possible and to work for future orders.

An adjustment should always be courteous and as generous as possible. No matter how offensive the letter of claim, the adjustment letter must have a courteous, friendly tone. Promptness also adds much to the effectiveness of an adjustment since it helps the customer feel that he is worthy of attention.

Planning the Adjustment Letter

Letters of adjustment are usually most effective when they follow a plan somewhat similar to the one outlined here:

1. Adjust your share of the difficulty immediately and tell why you make the adjustment.
2. Mention the customer's part tactfully and state your decision if you refuse the claim.
3. Give any further explanation necessary.
4. Close the letter with a cordial request for future business.

Applying Your Knowledge

PROBLEMS:

1. A month ago you sent a want ad to a trade magazine, such as *The Inland Printer, American Machinist, Automotive Digest,* etc., for insertion in this month's issue. When you received your copy of the magazine, you found that your address was omitted. Inasmuch as the ad is of no value to you without your address and you have been out of work for several months, you are not inclined to pay for the ad. Write a letter to the editor asking for an adjustment.

2. Answer the letter that you have written in Problem 1. Offer to refund the money or to give the individual another insertion free of charge.

3. Assume that you have purchased a used automobile in a nearby town, but that no tools came with the car as promised. Write a letter asking for an adjustment of the matter.

4. Answer the letter that you have written in Problem 3.

5. You have ordered some tools for use in your trade. When the order arrived, some of the tools were missing, but the company charged you for them on the invoice. Write a letter explaining the situation to the company.

6. Harold Peters, who works for you as a mechanic, has made a claim for overtime pay. Here are the facts: You needed a gasoline engine repaired to operate a small concrete mixer on a contracting job. You hired him July 5, and he promised to be at work the first thing the next morning. He arrived at ten o'clock; and because the job required eight hours' work, he stayed until seven o'clock to finish the job. He presents a bill for four dollars for overtime in addition to his bill for eight hours at regular rates. You feel that this is unjust. Write a letter offering to make a reasonable adjustment. (Mr. Peters had originally estimated that the job would require about six hours.)

7. One month ago you purchased a ½-hp. electric motor from a local electric shop in your city. The motor was guaranteed for 90 days. Two weeks ago it started to give you trouble. It has steadily become worse, and now it will not run at all. Write a letter to the company explaining the situation and asking for an adjustment.

Chapter 26

COLLECTING THE BILLS

The Importance of Making Collections When Due

A business man who makes a net profit of 10 per cent on the business he transacts loses all his profit on $1,000 of business every time he fails to collect an account of $100. It is better to lose a few sales than to run the risk of creating accounts that can not be collected. It is also better to insist that customers pay their accounts when due. Insisting that customers keep their accounts paid up often tends to increase business rather than decrease it, because a customer who is allowed to get behind in his accounts will often buy where he owes no money.

The first section of this chapter contains information on the use of printed forms to collect bills, the second section presents helpful information on the use of collection letters and other devices to collect delinquent accounts.

The Invoice, the Bill, and the Statement

An invoice, a bill, and a statement are all written statements of articles or services sold to some one. Although these business forms are similar in wording and arrangement, there are important differences in the purposes for which each is used. These differences will be discussed after several ways in which they are similar have been considered. Each of these forms usually contains the following information:

1. The name of the seller and the name of the buyer.
2. The kind, quantity, and price of the goods or services sold.
3. The discount allowed.

4. The terms upon which the sale was made.

5. The time and place where the transaction occurred.

In place of the goods sold there might be a statement of the work done or of the professional services rendered. For example, a person who has done some work for another might write "*For work on lawn, 10 hours @ $.75.........$7.50.*" A physician might write "*For professional services...$5.00.*"

INVOICE

JOHNSTON PAPER COMPANY

South Market Square

Boston 6, Mass.

		Terms:		
		2% 30 Days		
SOLD TO	The Williams Press	Net 31 Days		
		Shipped Via Frt.		
	Portland, Maine	Your Order No. 1531-A		
		F. O. B.		

3 M	Shts. Homestead Bond White 17x22 sub. 20		25.50	
3 M	Shts. Homestead Bond Pink 17x22 sub. 20		25.50	
				51.00
	ALL CLAIMS MUST BE REPORTED WITHIN FIVE DAYS FROM RECEIPT OF GOODS. NO CLAIMS ALLOWED ON PAPER AFTER IT IS CUT, RULED OR PRINTED. DO NOT DEDUCT UNADJUSTED CLAIMS.			

FIGURE 44. An Invoice Used by a Paper Company and Mailed When the Shipment Went Forward.

The Invoice. An invoice is mailed at the time a shipment of goods goes forward so that the customer may check the goods as they are listed to determine whether the order is complete; and if the prices are listed, to see that no mistake has been made in the charges. The word *invoice* usually appears prominently on the invoice blank.

The Bill. A billhead on which the bill is written is some-times mistakenly called an invoice, and contains similar infor-mation regarding the services or charges for merchandise that have been forwarded to the purchaser or consignee. The bill is mailed soon after the shipment goes forward or the job is completed; it is a notice that payment is due the seller (consignor) on a certain date. A bill is also made out for services rendered. Merchandise is usually sold to firms of good credit rating on thirty and occasionally on sixty days' time, or even longer. Frequently a cash discount is allowed from the net amount of the bill if the account is paid within a specified time such as ten days. The bill is mailed in time for the purchaser to avail himself of any discount privilege.

The Statement. A statement is a record of a customer's account which is sent to the customer about the first of each month as long as any part of his bill remains unpaid. State-ments, especially monthly statements, are used to inform the purchaser (debtor) of the amount of his account and to secure prompt payment of bills as they fall due.

As you study the examples on the following pages, you will see that these three forms are really very much alike but that they are used for different purposes. You will learn also that among tradesmen who operate small businesses, the billhead is the most commonly used of the three forms. In most cases in the trades, the billhead is the only form used; and if it is necessary to send a delinquent customer a state-ment at the end of the month, a billhead is merely used as a statement. It is well to remember, however, that as the size of the business increases the need for all three forms increases.

Trenton, N. J., __March 3. 19—__

Mr. James A. Dunn, Dr.

615 Seventh Avenue

To Mr. James A. McNamara

210 Elmira Street

March 2	Hauling 2 loads brick @ $8.	16	00			
March 3	Delivering 1 load of freight	5	10			
				21	10	

Trenton, N. J., __March 3. 19—__

James A. McNamara

210 Elmira Street

In account with

Mr. James A. Dunn

615 Seventh Avenue

March 2	Hauling 2 loads brick @ $8.	$16.00
March 3	Delivering 1 load of freight	5.10
		$21.10

FIGURE 45. These Examples Illustrate Two Different Types of Plain Billing Forms That Any Individual Might Use. They also illustrate two different methods of writing a bill.

Rochester 6, N. Y., July 15, 19__

Mr. V. B. Hann

708 Seventh Avenue

To CULVER'S GARAGE, Dr.

Service Station, General Auto Repairing
Oil, Gas and Accessories
Day and Night Wrecking Service

729 SIXTH AVENUE   BELL PHONE

July 5	5 qts. oil @ $.40	2.00	
	7 gal. gasoline @ $.30	2.10	
	Greasing car	1.50	
	2 lbs. grease @ $.30	.60	
July 15	Spindle bolts and bushings	3.20	
	Inspection	1.50	
	4 hrs. labor installing		
	spindle bolts @ $2.	8.00	
			$18.90

FIGURE 46. A Bill Given a Customer on Completion of Some Work Done on His Automobile.

NEYHARD HARDWARE COMPANY, INC.
Established 1871

WHOLESALE AND RETAIL HARDWARE
141-151 W. 3rd Street
Hampton, Va.

STATEMENT of your account for month of May, 19—

        Milton Auto Parts Company

        16 East Main Street

        Milton, Va.

TERMS:

Mo.	Day	Description of Articles	Charges	Credits	Balance
May	1	To previous statement rendered			15.75
May	5	Mdse.	74.25		
May	16	Mdse.	21.95		
May	25	Paid by check		80.00	
May	28	Mdse. returned		11.50	
					20.45

Month_____19___Date Paid_____Check No._____Amt. $_____

FIGURE 47. This Form Has Been Used by a Wholesale and Retail Hardware Company for Making Monthly Statements of Accounts. Notice that the merchandise purchased on May 5 and 16 is not itemized as must be done on an invoice.

Applying Your Knowledge

HELPFUL QUESTIONS:

1. What is an invoice, a bill, a statement? When is each of these forms used?

2. What information should appear on the printed part of each of these forms?

3. What is the meaning of the abbreviation @? When is it used?

4. What is the meaning of "*2–10, net 30 days*"?

5. Explain how the writing of a statement differs from that of of an invoice.

6. What is the fundamental distinction between an invoice and a bill?

PROBLEMS:

1. Copy in your notebook three different billhead designs, preferably the kind used by the man operating a small business.

2. Assume that you are operating a supply company selling to some particular trade. Design a form that you might use as an invoice, billhead, or statement.

- *a*) Write a bill for some services that your company has rendered.
- *b*) Write an invoice for supplies sold to the same customer in (*a*).
- *c*) Write a statement on a similar form indicating the amount of the account remaining unpaid from the previous month, several purchases made this month, and some credit allowed for returned supplies.

3. Assume that you have done some odd jobs for some one. Such jobs as trimming a hedge, painting a porch, or doing some odd repairing will serve the purpose very well. Using a plain sheet of paper, write a bill for your services.

4. Suppose that you are renting a garage, a small storeroom, or other type of building to some one operating a small business. Send him a bill for last month's rent. Do not use a printed billhead.

5. Assume that you are running a garage, an electrical business, a plumbing business, or any other moderate-sized shop.

- *a*) Design a billhead of your own.
- *b*) Using this billhead, bill a customer for some work you have done for him.

Collection Systems

Business firms have found that it pays to be systematic in collecting money. Some such plan as the one suggested below will be of great value to you.

Use the Telephone When Possible. If a local customer has not responded to your bills or monthly statements, you can often secure payment as the result of a telephone conversation. You can put a smile into your telephone conversation which you cannot readily put into a letter. Open your telephone conversation, if you wish, with a reference to work that you have done for the customer or to work that you have on hand at the time. For example:

Say, Mr. Miller, how soon do you need this job that you just sent us? . . . By the way, can you send us a check sometime this week for last month's bill? If you can, we'll certainly appreciate it.

Letters That Collect. A collection letter is successful when it secures the payment of the past-due account and holds the good will of the customer. Your job is twofold: to get the money, and to keep the customer. Most customers pay soon after they receive the bill or within a reasonable time. If this were not true, business could not be conducted on credit. When more than one letter is required, the collection procedure may fall into four divisions:

1. A reminder that the bill is past due.
2. A stronger reminder.
3. A discussion of the situation.
4. An urgent request for some action on the part of the customer.

Reminders: The kind of letters suggested by the following paragraphs will often bring a check:

We shall appreciate very much your sending us your check for $__   so that we can close our April accounts.

We get much more fun from selling goods and services than from writing letters asking for money. But,
as you realize, collections must be made in any business.

_____

The balance shown on the enclosed statement has
been due for_____, and we really need your check at
this time.

_____

Will you please give this your attention right
away.

_____

Dear Mr._____:

Will you please let us hear from you?

We are sorry to bother you. We assure you that we
dislike to send you letters about overdue bills as much as
you do to receive them. But we have now called your
attention several times to the unpaid items on your account
without result, and we are beginning to wonder whether
there is some mistake on our part.

Enclosed is another statement showing the items for
which you have not paid, according to the records we have.
If there is anything wrong with this record, will you please
sit down right now and tell us about it, so that we can
correct the mistake.

If, however, the account is correct, WILL YOU PLEASE
SEND A CHECK OR MONEY ORDER AT ONCE.

You can answer right on this letter, and enclosed
is a return envelope, which does not even need a stamp.
PLEASE ANSWER THIS MOMENT, so that it will not slip your
mind.

If your payment has been mailed to us, please
disregard this letter and accept our thanks.

Very truly yours,

FIGURE 48. Letter Discussing the Situation.

An Urgent Request for Action. Letters requesting immediate action and delivering an ultimatum to customers who

have thus far ignored previous letters are still more forceful. As a general rule, however, people do not like to be dunned or threatened, and there are very few exceptions to this. Hence, collection letters should be kept friendly and tactful as long as possible. Courtesy is possible and necessary even though the language of the letter must be firm and the action drastic.

Dear Mr._____:

   We have now written to you several times and have personally talked to you once about your account which has been past due for six months.

   We regret very much to inform you that unless you keep your former promise and make a regular weekly payment to reduce the amount of this obligation, we shall have to go to your present employer with our story or turn the account over to a collection agency. Either method will, of course, lower your credit rating and standing in the community. We feel certain that you do not care to have us do this. To forestall this unpleasant action it will be necessary that you make a payment as you originally promised on your account by September 5.

                              Very truly yours,

FIGURE 49. Letter Requesting Immediate Action.

Applying Your Knowledge

HELPFUL QUESTIONS:

   1. How can the telephone be used to advantage in the collection of past-due accounts?

   2. What four distinct types of collection letters are commonly used?

   3. Why do you think that a series of appeals for money is more effective than a single appeal?

PROBLEMS:

   1. Assume that you are operating a radio or TV service shop, a garage, a print shop, an electrical shop, or any other business with

which you are familiar. Prepare a plan for the collection of an overdue account of approximately $75. Your plan is to include one itemized bill, one monthly statement, one letter reminding the customer of the account, one letter discussing the situation, and one letter stating that some definite action will be taken. Write these different forms as you would prepare them for mailing.

2. A slow-pay customer who has always paid his bills has ignored several reminders. He finally answers a letter discussing the situation and asks for an extension of time, promising payment in a month. Write a letter granting the time extension but emphasizing that payment is expected four weeks hence. Write a courteous but firm letter.

3. Another customer who has always paid his bills answers a letter but asks permission to pay his bill in installments. Write a letter granting the request and fixing the dates on which installments shall be paid.

Chapter 27

GETTING AND HOLDING A JOB

Selecting Your Vocation

You attend school or study in order to develop your ability to render the greatest possible service in the most efficient manner—to develop your power *to think* and *to do.* In order to do this, you must secure training for definite lines of work; but before you can take training in a certain field you must decide what line of activity you wish to enter when you leave school.

Many different things should be considered when you are seeking a job. Although the amount of money a job pays is very important, there are other things that are equally important. The regularity of employment, the danger, the chance for advancement, and the working conditions all determine the desirability of a job.

Selecting the occupation for which you are best fitted and then, if possible, getting and keeping a job in that type of work is a very important problem. This chapter is designed to help you with it. If you need additional help go to your instructor.

What You Need to Know About Occupations

Before selecting an occupation, you should learn everything possible about it. Some of the more important things that you should consider when you investigate a prospective job or occupation are:

1. Nature and conditions of the work.
2. Advantages and disadvantages.

3. Demand for workers in that occupation; local, state, national.

4. Qualifications necessary.

5. Opportunities.

PROBLEMS:

1. Select a job or position you wish to secure. Make a thorough study of it, then prepare as complete a description of it as you can. Follow the outline given above in developing your description of the job you have selected.

2. Discuss the following statements pro and con with your classmates.

a) A boy should decide on his life work not later than his first year in high school.

b) Every worker should be flexible enough to do more than one thing.

c) It is just as well for a boy to take the first job he can get as to try to get work in a certain field.

d) Knowing all there is to be known about one job is better than knowing the fundamentals of the trade as a whole.

Filling Out an Application Blank

Before you apply for a job ask yourself these questions: *Would you hire yourself?* If not, why not? If so, why? Remember that you are not hunting a job so much as you are seeking an employer, and if you answer honestly the above questions you will see yourself much as an employer might see you. With this thought in mind, write down your answers to these questions on a piece of paper, then later, if you wish, destroy the paper and try to improve any shortcoming that you have found.

Can you answer quickly and accurately every question on the application blank shown in Figure 50? Many men when they apply for jobs cannot give exact names, dates, or reasons for changing or losing jobs. If there is any question on the application blank which you cannot answer quickly and accurately, you should find out the answer at once and

LYCOMING – SPENCER

Division – *AVCO* Manufacturing Corp.

APPLICATION FOR EMPLOYMENT

Position Applied for.. Date.......................19.......

Name in Full.. Social Security No..............................

           Last   First   Middle

Local Address.. Phone.....................

          Street   City   State   Since Date

Permanent Address.. Phone.....................

          Street   City   State   Since Date

In Emergency Notify.. Phone.....................

          Name   Address

Draft Status.............. Date Classified.............. Draft No.............. Board No.............. Location..............

PERSONAL	HOME LIFE	DEPENDENTS	PHYSICAL
Male................	Own Home............	Wife or Husband............	Height................
Female..............	Rent..................	Parents....................	Weight................
Married.............	Live with Parents.....	Children.................	
Single..............	Live with Relatives....	Ages:.................	Right Handed ☐ ǀ Left Handed ☐
Widowed ☐	Room.................		Physical Defects............
Separated ☐ Divorced ☐		Others..............	

BIRTH RECORD

NATURALIZATION

Date of Birth..

     Month   Day   Year   Age

City or County..

State or Country..

Date Entered United States..

Name Used When Entering U. S......................................

Port of Entry..

Country now a citizen of ....

Name of Ship ....

Birthplace of Father ....

Date of First Papers ....

Birthplace of Mother ....

Naturalization Certificate No. .... Date ....

Birthplace of Wife or Husband ....

Court Granting Final Papers ....

Birth Certificate—Yes ☐ No ☐

EDUCATIONAL RECORD

School	No. of Years	Year Graduated	Year Left School	Name of School	Location	Subjects or Training
Grammar						
High						
College						
Other						

PREVIOUS EMPLOYMENT

Names of Concerns worked for beginning with last employer	Dates of Employment	Kind of Work	Rates of Pay	Reasons for Leaving
Name.................... Address....................	From.................... To....................			
Name.................... Address....................	From.................... To....................			
Name.................... Address....................	From.................... To....................			
Name.................... Address....................	From.................... To....................			

(OVER)

FIGURE 50a, Application Blank.

Names and addresses of two references other than relatives.

Trade or Special Training................ What Experience................ Serve Apprenticeship.

Own Tools.......... Read Prints.......... Use Precision Instruments.......... Set up own work.

Were you ever employed by this Company.......... If so, when.

In what capacity.......... Why did you leave.

Are you now employed?.......... If so, by whom.......... Willing to work any shift.

Names of relatives employed by this Company.

Names and addresses of all members of immediate family. (If in a foreign country, give complete information as to name, address, country, age and what occupation engaged in.).

Have you ever had any injury or accident for which you received compensation or insurance.......... If so, give details.

Name and address of any relative in Government Service here or abroad.

Names and addresses of { Husband's } { Wife's } immediate relatives.

Wife's maiden name or husband's name.......... Husband's employer.

If over 45 years of age, state what you were doing between 1914 and 1918.

Have you a police record — Yes ...... No ...... If yes, state offense: when, where and disposition.

List all organizations of which you are a member other than labor unions.

Are you a member of or sympathetic to any foreign group such as Nazism, Fascism or Communism?.................................

Military or Naval experience (domestic or foreign) ....

Reason for termination of service.................................

Place and date of enlistment................................. Place and date of discharge.................................

Serial number of enlistment................................. Branch of Service.................................

APPLICANT'S REMARKS

....

....

I hereby declare that the foregoing answers made by me are true and correct and I hereby authorize my former employers to give any information regarding my employment and I also release them from all liability for any damage whatsoever for furnishing such information.

It is understood and agreed that any misrepresentation by me in this application will be sufficient cause for cancellation of the application and/or for separation from the Company's service if I have been employed.

....
Signature of Applicant   Date

DO NOT WRITE IN THIS SPACE

ATTACH PHOTOGRAPH HERE	REMARKS.................................

FIGURE 50b. Reverse of Application Blank.

memorize it. Make a copy of the application blank, fill it out, and place it in your notebook.

Suggestions for filling out an application blank:

1. If possible type your answers. If this is not possible, use a pen rather than a pencil.
2. Unless your handwriting is very good, *print your answers.*
3. Give exact names, dates, statements, etc.
4. Be frank and truthful.
5. If you have trouble remembering dates, the names of machines, etc., write them on a small card or piece of paper which you can carry with you and to which you can refer when filling out a blank.
6. Attach a small but good photograph of yourself.
7. Be sure to list all education and training.

PRACTICAL PROBLEMS FOR CLASS DISCUSSION

1. Assume that you are applying for a job in a local factory. You have no telephone in your home. Should you give the telephone number of a neighbor to the employment manager? What would you do in this case?

2. You wish to apply for a job and the employment manager has the door to his office closed. There is no one in the office with him, but he is busy working at his desk. If you just stand around and wait, an hour may pass before you get a chance to talk to him. On the other hand, he probably has the door closed because he does not care to be disturbed. What would you do?

3. Some men when looking for work go around to several employment offices the first thing every morning and ask whether any jobs are available. Are there any other methods by which you might profitably go about getting a job?

4. When you apply for a job, is it necessary that you know the names of the machines you have operated, the tools you have used, and the jobs you have done? Give reasons for your answer.

5. Imagine that it is noon, and that you have just been laid off at the plant where you have been working. As you leave the factory you learn that another company in another section of the city is hiring men. As it happens you are very dirty from your morning's work. Would it be better to go immediately to the

other plant and then go home; or would it be better to go home, clean up, and then go directly to the other plant?

6. You have applied for work several times at one place without success. Each time a clerk has simply told you that there are no vacancies. You believe that you would stand a better chance of securing work if you could see the employment manager himself. How can you accomplish this?

7. Assume that you were accepted for a job but you did not pass the physical examination, and the company physician or personnel director will not tell you the reason. What steps can you take to prevent a second such occurrence?

8. Assume that you have been graduated from school in some particular trade, but you have been unable to find work in that trade and you still want to follow it. How can you improve your chances of securing an opening in the trade you want to follow?

9. Assume that you have been graduated from school in a particular trade or field of work. Very few opportunities exist in that field in your home community. Either you must secure work in another section of the country or secure training in another field of work. How can you best proceed to solve this problem? Develop a definite plan of action to attain your objective.

10. You live in a depressed area, such as the coal regions where not enough jobs exist in mining, or once prosperous industries have left your community. How can you best proceed to secure work in other sections of the United States?

Applying for the Job

Employment is generally obtained through one or more of the six agencies listed below.

1. Friends who may know or learn of employment opportunities.
2. Advertisements in newspapers or trade journals.
3. Business news and items in newspapers and trade journals.
4. Public employment agencies, such as the State Employment Service.

5. Private employment agencies.
6. Organizations such as chambers of commerce, boards of trade, and trade or labor organizations.

Friends and Acquaintances. Many more jobs are obtained through friends than is commonly recognized. Too many men dislike telling their friends of having lost a position. If, however, the person seeking work faces a blank wall, he should tell all his friends about his predicament. Very often a friend can assist another in finding a job, or as frequently happens, a friend of a friend may help find the job.

Business News and Items in the Newspapers. Usually every newspaper and trade journal contains information about work that is being done or is to be done and about the operating conditions of various companies. Such items frequently give leads as to the more likely places to apply for work.

Employment Agencies. There are many fine employment agencies just as there are many poor ones. The public employment agency charges nothing for its services. The private employment agency generally charges a fee for registration or a percentage of your wages for a certain length of time when you are placed on a job. Even though you register with an employment agency, you should continue to look for your own job. Registration in any agency does not guarantee you a job, and it is far easier for you to secure your own job than it is for an agency to secure one for you.

Advertisements in Newspapers and Trade Magazines. As aids to securing work, you can use advertisements in two ways. You can answer advertisements that appeal to you in Help Wanted columns or you can insert an advertisement of your own in the Positions Wanted columns of a newspaper or trade magazine.

If you are seeking a specialized job, your advertisement should be placed in a trade or technical magazine as well as a newspaper. For example, an airplane mechanic or pilot looking for a job might advertise in one of the aviation magazines; a printer, in one of the printing magazines.

Study the following advertisements. Notice that the first advertisement is too brief and general to get good results. The second and third are better because they are more specific and detailed; they give a prospective employer more exact information.

I

KELLY PRESSMAN wants steady position; familiar with cylinder and can work in bindery. B-529.

II

RELIABLE YOUNG MAN, with 12 years' experience in composition, imposition, and presswork on Miehle automatics and cylinders, desires steady position in plant where advancement and future are assured; recommendations available. B-530.

III

THOROUGHLY TRAINED young man with 11 years' practical experience; knows composition, imposition, and presswork; also has had technical school training; good knowledge of costs, experienced in estimating and buying materials; desires position as estimator or assistant superintendent; now employed. B-438.

Figure 51. The Advertisement Is Important.

The Application Letter as a Business Letter

The application letter is a very special kind of business letter, but a very important business letter it is. Certainly much employment takes place without the use of application letters, but it is also true that application letters are used in securing at least half of the better positions in the industrial and business world.

From the employer's point of view, the application letter saves him time because a quick examination of, say, twenty letters will tell him which five of the applicants he wants to interview.

From your point of view as a job seeker, the application letter is a valuable means of presenting your qualifications to employers who would not otherwise talk with you. It helps you contact many more employers than you could possibly meet personally, and it helps not only with the first job, but also in securing new opportunities.

The Application Letter as a Sales Letter

The application letter is also a very special kind of sales letter. It is intended to sell your services in return for wages or a salary. The psychology of the application letter is much the same as that of other sales letters. The "you" attitude is important. You may need employment, but you will be hired not because of your need but rather because you have some ability or skills which the employer or company can use.

When you write a letter of application you are entering a contest—a competition with other persons in the appearance, form, and content of your letter. Your letter is only one of many entries in a game, and only the better letters will survive in the struggle for attention.

How to Write an Application Letter

A complete and well-written letter of application usually consists of the following parts:

1. A sentence or very short paragraph stating the purpose of the letter.
2. Personal characteristics such as age, height, weight, health.
3. Education or training.
4. Experience. (It is at this point after the paragraph giving your experience that you can give your reasons for wishing to change from your present job.)
5. References as to ability and character.
6. A request for an interview.

651 West Third Street
Baltimore, Maryland
September 5, 19--

Mr. Claire W. Bishop
Personnel Director
Aviation Manufacturing Corporation
Baltimore, Maryland

Dear Mr. Bishop:

Mr. John Heim of your toolmaking department has informed me that you need a machine operator capable of operating several different machines. He feels that I am qualified for the job. Will you please consider my application for this work.

Personal Qualifications: I am a young man of twenty-two, five-feet seven inches tall, 165 pounds in weight, healthy, and strong.

Education: In June, 19--, I was graduated from the Baltimore High School where I completed the course in Machine Shop Practice. In this course I learned to read blueprints and to operate all of the machines commonly used in a machine shop. At evening school during 19-- I successfully completed a course in Advanced Shop Mathematics.

Experience: During my senior year in high school I worked after school and in the evenings at Rader's Machine Shop, foot of Walnut Street. Since October 19--, I have been working as a lathe and milling machine operator for the Anderson Manufacturing Company, 615 Locust Street.

Reason for Change: I wish to secure the work in your plant because the job that you have open offers better opportunity for regular work.

References: With permission I refer you to the following men:

Mr. W. A. Koehler, Machine Shop Instructor, Baltimore High School, Baltimore, Maryland.

Mr. Clyde Smith, Superintendent, Anderson Manufacturing Company, 615 Locust Street, Baltimore, Maryland.

Mr. Charles Rader, Proprietor of Rader's Machine Shop, foot of Walnut Street, Baltimore, Maryland.

I shall be glad to come to your office for a personal interview at your convenience. My phone number is HE 4-7908.

Very truly yours,

Albert S. Snyder

Albert S. Snyder

FIGURE 52. A Sample Letter of Application.

State the wages that you expect only when you must, or when you are specifically asked to do so.

Study carefully the sample letter of application shown in Figure 52. Notice the headings for the paragraphs. Although they are not necessary, it is a good plan to use such headings. If you do not use them, be very careful that each paragraph is concerned with only one subject and that your letter is arranged much the same as is the specimen letter.

The Two-Part Application

In some respects the two-part application is better not only in appearance, but also in effectiveness of presentation, and easier to write than is the regular application letter. Note the differences between the letter shown in Figure 52 and that in Figure 53. The two-part application consists of:

1. A short letter emphasizing the important points in your application.
2. A personal data sheet containing all the important facts neatly and carefully tabulated.

When this two-part form is used, the short letter permits you to stress those few points that you might want to emphasize.

The Data Sheet. A data sheet should be neat, accurate, and complete. It should be arranged logically to show that you can plan and organize what you write. Your picture can be placed in the upper left corner or at another appropriate place. List on the data sheet those items which an employer would want to know about you. All dates, work experience, etc., should be arranged in order. You can readily see what details are usually placed on a personal data sheet by referring to the one in Figure 54.

1730 Highland Street
Allentown 5, Pennsylvania
June 1, 19

Mr. Samuel W. Christine
Superintendent of Training & Employment
Bethlehem Steel Company
Bethlehem, Pennsylvania

Dear Mr. Christine:

I wish to apply for work as an electrician at
Bethlehem Steel Company.

In June 19— I was graduated from the Course in
Technical Electricity, Allentown High School. During the
last two years, I have taken additional work in electricity
in the evening classes conducted by the Community College
and Technical Institute, Allentown, Pennsylvania.

I would be glad to secure an apprenticeship should
such an opportunity become available.

If you have an opening for a young man with a good
training in electricity, including electronics, I would
appreciate the opportunity of a personal interview.

Very truly yours,

Richard F. Dreisbach

Richard F. Dreisbach

FIGURE 53. A letter of application to accompany a personal data sheet
in Figure 54.

PERSONAL DATA SHEET

Photo

may be

attached here

Name: Richard F. Dreisbach
Address: 1730 Highland Street
Allentown 5, Pennsylvania

Phone: Hemlock 4-3454

Age: 24
Height: 5' 7" **Weight:** 150
Health: Excellent

Education:

1. Graduated from Allentown High School, in Technical Electricity, 19__.

2. Completed the following courses in evening classes of the Community College and Technical Institute: Public Speaking, Industrial Electricity, and Technical Mathematics.

3. I have passed successfully and with good grades all the courses ever taken.

Experience:

1. June 1, 19__ to July 10, 19__, United States Navy. Rank on discharge, Electrician's Mate.

2. August 1, 19__ to the present time, Northampton Electric Company as an electrician on construction jobs.

References:

1. Mr. Ralph Shimer, Head
Electrical Department
Allentown High School
Allentown, Pennsylvania

2. Mr. Thomas M. B. Schrader, Coordinator
Community College & Technical Institute
School District
Allentown, Pennsylvania

3. Mr. Dale J. Gilmore, Foreman
Northampton Electric Company
623 Main Street
Northampton, Pennsylvania

FIGURE 54. The Data Sheet To Accompany an Application.

The Interview

Do not expect too much from a letter of application; it seldom secures the job. The most that you can expect from an application letter is to secure an interview with the employer. It is also a mistake to assume that the job is yours because you have been called in for an interview. It is true, however, that you are usually granted an interview because your letter was better than the others in appearance, form, or content.

The way in which you conduct yourself during an interview often determines whether or not you get the job. The following list of statements will give you a few hints on how to conduct yourself during an interview.

Entering the Office and Meeting the Employer. Be punctual, dress neatly, and be clean.

Shake hands with the employer if he offers his hand first; not otherwise.

Carry your coat or hat in your left arm, thus keeping your right hand and arm free.

Sit down only when you are asked to do so.

If the door was closed before you entered the office close it after you, or find out whether the employer wishes it open or closed.

Sit erect.

What To Do During the Interview. Do not interrupt another person's conversation.

Tell the truth—do not claim that you can do something you cannot.

Do not talk too much. Let the employer do the talking, but answer respectfully and accurately any questions he asks. Be ready with your replies. Give exact dates.

Do not speak ill of any one. Every employer has heard too many hard-luck stories.

Should the employer have to use the telephone during the interview, try to divert your attention to something other than his telephone conversation. You might walk to the window and look out, or do any other small act that will tend to take your attention from his conversation.

Do not prolong the interview any longer than necessary, and do not apologize for taking up his time. On the other hand you should ask for any information you want about the job or the company. Do not hesitate to ask specific questions in order to get a good description of the job.

Applying Your Knowledge

PROBLEMS:

1. Write an advertisement that you could use in seeking a job. After you have completed the advertisement, estimate how much it would cost you to run it for three days in your local newspaper and for two issues of the trade magazine or journal representing your field. Place this information on the same sheet on which you have written the advertisement. Be sure to write the advertisement as you want it to appear in print.

2. Secure a trade magazine and find an advertisement of a job for which you might be able to qualify in the future. An advertisement from a newspaper will do if the job advertised is in your trade. Write a letter of application in answer to the advertisement. Make a copy of the advertisement and attach it to the letter you have written.

3. Write a letter of application for a job that has nothing to do with your trade. This letter can be either unsolicited or in answer to an advertisement.

4. You secured an interview with the manager of the company with which you wish to secure work. At the close of the interview he asked you to write him in one or two days, answering certain questions and explaining more fully your ambitions—what you think you are best fitted to do, what you are willing to do to get

ahead, what you have accomplished in your educational career that leads you to believe that you can accomplish in life what you hope to achieve.

5. Write a letter of application applying for work at some local concern during the summer season. Assume that you plan to return to school the next fall.

Chapter 28

SUBMITTING BIDS

Mr. Brown wished to build a garage on the rear of his lot. In order to have it built as cheaply as possible, he sent blueprints of the plans to four different carpenters or small contractors. Each man wrote to Mr. Brown telling how much he would charge to do the job as specified. The prices the contractors quoted Mr. Brown were $535, $568, $610, and $650. Naturally enough Mr. Brown gave the job to the contractor agreeing to do the job for $535.

The written form or statement by means of which such quotations are made might be known as a bid, a proposal, or a quotation. Although these terms have slightly different meanings, it is sometimes difficult to distinguish between them.

Proposals or bids play an important part in the daily work of the craftsman, the tradesman, and the business man. When a concern wishes to buy certain equipment or have some work done, executives usually ask others to give them a price or an estimate for doing such work. The seller then makes up a detailed written offer to furnish or install certain equipment, or to perform certain work at a specified price. When such a proposal or bid is properly signed or agreed to by both parties, it becomes a legally binding contract.

It is impossible to mention here all the types of service and equipment that are sold through bids and proposals. They are generally used by contractors in all types of building construction, by manufacturing plants, by printers, by men who operate small machine shops; in fact, by almost any one who sells goods or services to a number of customers.

Proposals or bids may originate in a hundred different ways. A customer may telephone to ask for a bid or a quota-

THE STANDARD AUTO REPAIR COMPANY
123 East Hennepin Avenue
Minneapolis 14, Minnesota

February 12, 19__

Bowman's Department Store
12 North Market Street
Minneapolis 3, Minnesota

Gentlemen:

Your letter of February 10, asking for quotations on various maintenance jobs on your 6-cylinder Chevrolet delivery trucks, is very much appreciated. Our quotations covering these jobs follow:

Carbon and valve job..........................$25.00
    Includes: All operations performed in
                tuning motor,
                cleaning carbon, re-facing
                valves,
                re-seating cylinder block,
                adjusting tappets.

Motor Reconditioning.........................$150.00
    Includes: All operations performed in
                tuning motor; grinding
                valves; ring, pin, and
                bearing job; reconditioning
                cylinder walls and fitting
                new pistons.

All prices are for labor only.
It is a pleasure to submit this bid. We shall be glad to give you quotations at any time on other maintenance or repair jobs such as greasing, relining brakes, etc. If awarded your work, we assure you our very best and prompt attention to every detail of it.

We shall appreciate your giving us the opportunity to do this work for you. A thirty-day guarantee goes with every job.

Very truly yours,

Martin Q. Ebersole

THE STANDARD AUTO REPAIR COMPANY

FIGURE 55. Letter Giving Quotation for Work on Automobile.

tion on a certain job. A city usually advertises in the local newspaper for bids on the construction of a bridge, a street, or a sewer. A business concern may send letters to several different shops requesting bids on certain work or services.

How To Submit Bids

As was mentioned before, these various terms designate different forms of statements. A bid is a competitive offer to accept a price for a contract. Although a proposal is written to accept a definite price for materials, work, or service, it is not always made in competition with other concerns. Bids and proposals, however, are usually written in about the same form.

Whenever a company has a contract to let, it usually tries to get as many bids as possible. The person who offers to do the work at the lowest price generally gets the job if he is thought to be reliable. Most municipalities furnish bid blanks on which all bids must be made, and they likewise furnish contract blanks when the contract is awarded. In much construction work, a bid is usually accompanied by 5 to 10 per cent of the total contract price submitted as an evidence of good faith by the bidder. A careful study of the examples given in this chapter will give you a better understanding of how this type of business correspondence is written.

Figure 55 illustrates one type of letter used to give quotations on work. The quotations given in this letter have been made in competition with other garages, and as a result, the letter is actually a bid for a job even though the term bid is not mentioned.

Notice the opening paragraph which refers to the letter of February 10 from the department store, and to the type of automobile for which these quotations are given. Notice also that following the name of each job appears a list of the specific operations to be performed. *In making any estimate or quotation always be especially careful that all specifications and details are given so that there can be no misunderstanding later, once an agreement has been made.* The quotation for each job is placed in the column to the right, but these figures are not totaled because each job is separate in itself.

A good ending is important. Here the proprietor of the garage invites the store to ask for quotations at any time, and then at the very end promises a thirty-day guarantee with every job.

In writing similar letters, remember the following principles:

1. List each job, operation, material, or supply separately.
2. Give the price for each individual job mentioned in the bid.
3. Indent beyond the line naming the job any specification as to just what the job includes.
4. Put in the last one or two paragraphs any item that you wish especially to emphasize such as the quality of work, the time required, or the guarantee that goes with the job.
5. Wherever possible, place all figures in a column rather than within sentences or paragraphs.

Figure 56 illustrates the kind of letter that many contractors, carpenters, printers, etc., who operate small shops or businesses of their own frequently find it necessary to write.

Notice that in the third paragraph the bid price is written in both words and figures. This is a standard procedure and should be done in any proposal or bid where a price is given. In case of a discrepancy, the written words should be considered as being the price bid.

The letter shown in Figure 57 makes a centered display of the quoted figures, which makes them particularly clear and understandable. This too is a standard type of letter.

PHONE WO 2-9771   ESTIMATES CHEERFULLY FURNISHED

HOMER L. BARTON
PLUMBING AND HEATING CONTRACTOR
608 East Fort Street
Detroit 26, Michigan

June 16, 19—

Mr. Earl A. Wagner
549 West Congress Street
Detroit 26, Michigan

Dear Mr. Wagner:

I am pleased to give you a quotation on the installation of a Thrush hot water heating system in your proposed residence as follows:

My proposal includes one #106-W Spencer hot water boiler, eleven (11) Richvar radiators containing 684.4 sq. ft. of cast-iron radiation, all the necessary pipe, fittings, floor and ceiling plates, hangers, radiator valves, union ells, air vents, bronze, pipe covering, and smoke pipe.

I shall furnish, deliver, and install the above described heating material for the net sum of NINE HUNDRED SEVENTY-FIVE DOLLARS ($975).

If the radiators on the second floor are omitted and material is furnished for the roughing-in only, deduct from the base price ONE HUNDRED FORTY DOLLARS ($140).

I shall appreciate the opportunity of doing this work, and I assure you that you shall receive a first-class job.

Very truly yours,

Homer L. Barton

Homer L. Barton

FIGURE 56. Letter Used by Small Contractor for Price Quotation.

THE CAMP CURTIN PRESS

1815 Tilghman Street,   Allentown, Pennsylvania

⬤Commercial Printing

October 26, 19__

Keystone Milk Products Company
2134 North Third Street
Detroit, Michigan

Gentlemen:

On the basis of the samples submitted to us, we propose
to furnish you the printing listed here at the following prices:

6-1/4" x 10" circulars on 50-lb. colored
book stock, four (4) forms, each M $11.75;
an additional M of any form at $5.50.

6" x 9" four-page folder, on book paper,
60-lb., flat finish, 1 M $35.75.

We thank you for the opportunity of quoting you prices on
this work, and we shall be glad to learn that they meet with
your approval.

Very truly yours,

THE CAMP CURTIN PRESS

By J. G. Wright

FIGURE 57. Proposal Letter by Printing Concern.

Return Original   **Main 2654**
All guarantees given by this Company are based on prompt settlement of
bills when due.

Location of Job _____	**PROPOSAL OF**
Type of Building_____	**THE ELKHART CO.**
Class Material _____	*"Always Dependable"*
Trim Material_____	Lemoyne, Pa.
Owner_____	
Architect_____,	——To——
Date_____19_____	

We purpose to _____
.

on the Property located at _____ in accordance with
ʀlans and specifications of _____Architect
as submitted to us_____19____for the sum of _____
_____Dollars ($_____).

This proposal does not include any other than above stipulated work,
and we expect at least_____days notification to start, so as to
get our materials and tools on the ground and afford us opportunity for
continuous operation from that time.
REMARKS:

Terms:_____
We will not be responsible for damage done nor delays caused by other
men than our own.
We will accept no changes of any kind on this contract unless authorized
by this Company in writing.
ACCEPTANCE OF THIS PROPOSAL WILL CONSTITUTE A CON-
TRACT BETWEEN US.

_____19_____   Yours truly,

                               THE ELKHART CO.

_____accept the above proposal.
(I or We)

_____   _____

_____   _____

It is agreed that the essential facts are covered in this proposal and no
verbal agreements with our representatives shall be recognized.
This Proposal Subject to Strikes, and other Conditions Beyond Our Control.

FIGURE 58. Proposal Blank To Be Filled in by Contractor.

Figure 58 is an illustration of a proposal blank that needs only to be filled in by the contractor. This proposal blank might be used to make a proposal as such, an estimate, quotation, or a bid.

Under "Remarks" would be written any stipulations or specifications not found in the architect's blueprints or in any other part of the proposal.

Quotation blanks similar to the one in Figure 59 are common among contractors and supply companies of various kinds. These forms are usually typed in duplicate so that the original or white copy can be sent to the customer and the duplicate or colored copy filed. Such a form does away with much unnecessary writing or typing because the various items and prices need only to be typed in their proper order. However, a letter from the company usually accompanies such a quotation.

In filling out a quotation blank of this kind several principles should be kept in mind, namely:

1. The date on which the quotation is made should appear on the sheet.

2. The name and address of the customer for whom the quotation is made should be given somewhere at the top.

3. A statement giving the exact job or work in question should appear either before or after the quotation itself.

4. Each item should be placed on a separate line.

5. When it is necessary to use more than one line to give the specifications of one material, the second, third, fourth, or more lines should be indented as is done in Figure 59 under *Cement*.

6. Statements giving regular terms of payment, conditions of delivery, and date when quotation expires should be placed where convenient. They are most frequently found at the bottom of the blank.

QUOTATION

from

SUSQUEHANNA SUPPLY COMPANY

Wholesale Building Materials

ERIE AVE. and CAMPBELL STS.

Mr. J. B. Fanshaw   New York 51, N. Y.
   General Contractor
      Newark 23, N. J.   January 12, 19—

Material	Price
Common brick—truck lots—delivered on job— per M	45.00
Hydrated lime—ton lots—delivered on job— per ton	30.00

Cement—carload—in paper—f.o.b. Newark—per
  bbl. Discount of 10¢ per bbl. for payment
  10 days from date of shipment. No allowance
  for return of paper bags.
	4.20

Plaster—USG brand—truck lots—delivered on job—per ton	28.00
Sand—cleaned and washed—for plastering and brick work—per ton	3.95
Sand—concrete grit—for mass concrete work— per ton del.	3.00
Sand—white—glass—for ornamental plaster— per ton del.	8.00

Above prices are based upon present freight rates and any increase thereof must be assumed by purchaser. Prices subject to change without notice.

Terms   Cement special disc. All other items 2% 10 days—
             30 days net.
Delivery   c.l. 4 days from date of order—l.c.l. when
             ordered from warehouse.
Expiration Date   15 days from date of this quotation.

SUSQUEHANNA SUPPLY COMPANY

By *J. Willis*

FIGURE 59. Filled-in Quotation Blank Used by Building Supply Company.

Applying Your Knowledge

PROBLEMS:

1. Write a letter offering to do a job for a definite amount. Select as a job something that you might get to do in your community if you were operating a small business.

2. Write a letter giving quotations on some job in your trade or on the making of a number of some article with which you have become familiar in your school shop.

3. Assume that you are in the supply business in your particular trade. Make out a quotation or a bid sheet similar to that presented by the Susquehanna Supply Company, listing a number of supplies used in your trade. Secure a price list to use in this problem. You may be able to find lists of prices in various catalogs.

4. Assume that you are contracting to do some work on a property in your community. Duplicate the proposal of the Elkhart Company and fill it in as you would if you were a contractor.

Chapter 29

SENDING TELEGRAMS

Telegrams are used when greater speed is required than the mail service offers. In our present industrial system, with its widely separated units of manufacture and distribution, swift communication is of vital importance. Here we find the telegram supplying the demand for a quick and relatively economical method of communication. In our personal and social life also, we frequently find need for using this method of sending fast messages to friends and relatives.

Because different degrees of haste are necessary, Western Union offers different types of messages, varying in degree of speed in transmission and delivery. These messages also differ in the number of words possible at a minimum rate of cost. Classes of service are: telegrams, day letters, night letters.

Writing the Message

Since the cost of a telegram depends upon the number of words transmitted and because of the way they are printed, certain principles should be followed when writing such a message. The main thing to keep in mind is that telegrams must be both clear and brief.

Brevity and Conciseness. In order to convey your message in as few words as possible, it is necessary to eliminate all words that do not directly affect the meaning of the message. If you are inexperienced in writing telegrams *it is wise to write out the message as you would an ordinary letter and then to strike out all unnecessary words*. This will help you learn to state the message clearly and briefly.

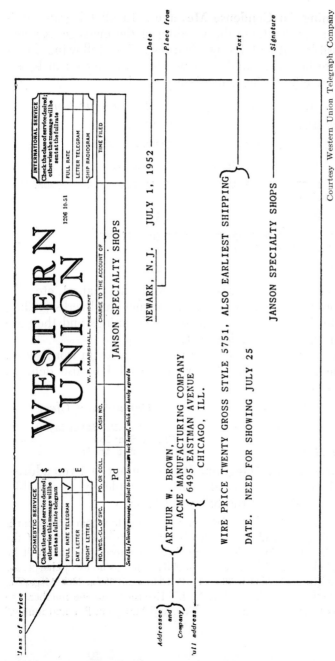

WESTERN UNION

DOMESTIC SERVICE

Check the class of service desired; otherwise this message will be sent as a full rate telegram

FULL RATE TELEGRAM	✓
DAY LETTER	
NIGHT LETTER	

$
$

1206 10-51

W. P. MARSHALL, PRESIDENT

INTERNATIONAL SERVICE

Check the class of service desired; otherwise the message will be sent at the full rate

FULL RATE
LETTER TELEGRAM
SHIP RADIOGRAM

NO. WDS.-CL. OF SVC.	PD. OR COLL.	CASH NO.	CHARGE TO THE ACCOUNT OF	TIME FILED
	Pd		JANSON SPECIALTY SHOPS	

Send the following message, subject to the terms on back hereof, which are hereby agreed to

NEWARK, N.J.   JULY 1, 1952 — *Date*

— *Place from*

ARTHUR W. BROWN,
ACME MANUFACTURING COMPANY
6495 EASTMAN AVENUE
CHICAGO, ILL.

WIRE PRICE TWENTY GROSS STYLE 5751, ALSO EARLIEST SHIPPING — *Text*

DATE. NEED FOR SHOWING JULY 25

JANSON SPECIALTY SHOPS — *Signature*

Class of service

Addressee and Company

Full address

Courtesy Western Union Telegraph Company

FIGURE 60. Example of Correctly Prepared Telegram. Every telegram you prepare should include each of the elements pointed out in the telegram on the sending blank above.

Learning To Condense Messages. In all telegrams it is necessary to condense the wording of the message as much as possible without losing clearnes . The following forms illustrate how the number of words 'n messages can be reduced by eliminating unnecessary words:

Long Form	Telegraphic Form
SHIP ON MONDAY	SHIP MONDAY
WE WILL SHIP TOMORROW	SHIPPING TOMORROW
WE WILL ARRIVE HOME TUESDAY	HOME TUESDAY
I WILL INSPECT THE PLANT TOMORROW	WILL INSPECT PLANT TOMORROW
THE ORDER	ORDER
WE WILL SEND MORE COMPLETE EXPLANATION BY LETTER	LETTER FOLLOWS
AT ONCE	IMMEDIATELY

Notice that such words as on, we, I, the, that, at, etc., are the words omitted above. Nouns (names) and verbs (telling what to do) best convey ideas and meanings and they are used more freely in telegrams.

However, it is always better to use a few extra words when they make a message clearer. Be careful to use definite, clear statements.

Not Clear	Definite and Clear
Arrive on 2 P.M. train	Arrive 2 P.M. Saturday Union Station
Please meet me	Please meet train

Addressing the Telegram. It is important that you address the telegram as accurately and as completely as possible. Western Union has the following to say:

The name of the person, firm, or corporation to whom a telegram is to be delivered should be written below the upper-left corner of the blank. In addressing telegrams, include all information that will be helpful in locating the addressee quickly. There is no extra charge, for instance, for the address: "George P. Oslin, care John Doe Mfg. Co., 7 Meade Terrace, Glen Ridge, N. J." Even a telephone number, the business title of the addressee or "Mr. and Mrs. John Roe and family," may be used without extra charge. Code addresses are not permissible in domestic telegrams.

Sometimes people address a telegram to "John Jones, Empire State Building, New York City," forgetting that there are thousands of people employed in that building. Use firm names and room numbers. The address "11 Forty-Second Street, New York City," may necessitate attempts at delivery on both East and West Forty-Second Street. If, however, the telegram is addressed to a well-known, nationally known business or bank, it is unnecessary to give the room number, building, and street address.

In addressing a telegram to a passenger on a train, airplane, or bus, give full details. For example: "John Jones, En Route Chicago, care Conductor (or Pullman Reservation if known, such as 'Lower 6, Car 92') N. Y. C. Train Three, First Section, due 10:35 P. M. Cleveland, Ohio."

Only one signature will be carried without extra charge, but titles, names of departments, or names of firms, may be added to let the addressee know just who the sender is. For example, "George J. Wilson, Standard Can Co." is all carried without extra charge. In family signatures, such as "Mary and Jack" or "Mr. and Mrs. J. A. Jones and family," no extra words are charged for.

Word Selection and Cost. The selection of the best word to use is perhaps the most important phase of writing telegrams. A wise choice of words may reduce considerably the cost of the message. The following comparison will show you the importance of the careful use of words and figures in the preparation of telegrams:

	Number of Words Charged
2,000	1
two thousand	2
15 dozens	2
fifteen dozens	2
$25.35	1
twenty five dollars and thirty five cents	7
16th	2
sixteenth	1
½	1
one half	2
percent	1

The date, the address, and the signature are not considered part of the message and are sent free of charge. Only the words actually used in the message are counted.

The following practices are observed in determining the number of chargeable words in domestic telegrams to all places in North America:

1. One address and one signature are free.

2. Dictionary words from the English, German, French, Italian, Dutch, Portuguese, Spanish, and Latin languages are counted as one word each, irrespective of length. Any word or group of letters not forming a dictionary word in any of these eight languages is counted at the rate of one word for every five letters or fraction of five letters.

3. Proper names in any language are counted according to the way they are normally written. Examples:

> United States   −2 words
> North Dakota   −2   "
> New York City−3   "

4. Abbreviations are counted at the rate of one word for each five letters. Examples:

> lb. −1 word
> AM−1   "
> PM−1   "
> NY−1   "

5. Personal names are counted in the way they are normally written. Examples:

> Du Bois   −2 words
> Van Dyke   −2   "
> Van der Gross− 3   "
> Vanderwater   −1   "

Initials, when separated by spaces, are counted as separate words but when written together as are J.O.R. in the case of J.O.R. Smith, they are counted at the rate of one word for five letters.

6. Punctuation marks are neither counted nor charged for, regardless of where they appear in the text of the message.

Sending a Message by Telephone

The telegraph company will accept over the telephone any one of the three types of message for transmission. The cost of the telegram is merely added to your telephone bill by the telephone company, and then you pay the charge for the message to the telephone company as a part of your telephone bill. This service is very convenient.

To send a telegraphic message by telephone follow these steps:

1. Write out carefully the message you wish to send.
2. Telephone the local office of the telegraph company.
3. Tell the person who answers the phone what kind of message you wish to send, and the person to whom you wish to send it.
4. Dictate your message clearly.
5. After dictating the message, give the clerk your address and telephone number, as well as the name of the person in whose name the phone is listed in the telephone directory.
6. If any difficulty arises in understanding a word, it is customary to spell it out as follows: *protest—P* as in *Paul*, *R* as in *Robert*, *O* as in *Oscar*, *T* as in *Thomas*, etc.
7. Listen carefully for errors while the clerk repeats what you have dictated.
8. Pay the charge to the telephone company as an additional part of your monthly telephone bill.

If you are away from home and not close to a telegraph station, you can send a telegram by using a regular pay phone. With but two exceptions the steps are exactly the same as those listed above. When using a pay phone, call the telephone operator and ask for the telegraph company. When you have finished giving the message to the telegraph clerk, ask for the cost of the message, and then drop the correct amount into the regular coin slots of the telephone just as you would pay for a long distance telephone call.

Applying Your Knowledge

HELPFUL QUESTIONS:

1. For what parts of a telegraphic message do the telegraph companies not charge?

2. Does it cost less to send the numerals *600* than words *six hundred*? Why?

3. Does it cost more to send *third* or *3d*? Why?

4. When writing a telegraphic message why is it a good idea to write out the message just as you would an ordinary letter and then cross out the unnecessary words?

5. Which of the following forms will it cost the most to send: *33*, or *thirty-three*?

6. On what part of a telegraph blank are the different kinds of messages described in detail?

PRACTICE IN WRITING TELEGRAMS:

1. Write the following statements in better form for telegraphic messages:

   a) I shall get to Chicago on the 15th of March.
   b) Please send 1000 sq. ft. of your No. 2, black, unglazed building paper.
   c) We are now able to ship the best grade of walnut veneer to you.

2. Write the following into a telegram of about ten words:

We wish to cancel our order for three 200 series electric hand drills, but we wish you to ship at once two 300 series electric hand drills. Please charge to our account.

3. You have planned a trip with a friend who lives in a nearby town. At the last minute you are unable to go. Since your friend has no telephone, the quickest means of reaching him is by telegraph. Write a telegram which you might phone to the nearest telegraph office.

4. You have been traveling away from home all day and have just reached your destination. Wire your parents telling them about your pleasant journey, safe arrival, or a pleasant meeting with your friends.

5. Write two telegrams such as might be necessary at some time in managing some school activity.

6. Write a friend or relative a personal telegram concerning a death or serious illness in the family, or congratulating him upon a birthday, marriage, or other event.

The Classes of Service

The Telegram. The telegram, which is the standard message, is sent and delivered before any other telegraphic message. It is accepted at any hour of the day or night, is transmitted as soon as it is accepted, and is delivered immediately when it is received at its destination. The minimum charge is for fifteen words, with an additional charge for each word over fifteen.

The Day Letter. The day letter is next to the telegram in the order of transmission and delivery. As soon as all the telegrams are sent, the day letters are sent out. If it is possible, they are transmitted and delivered the same day they are given the telegraph company. This class of service is usually used when the message is longer than fifteen words, and it is not necessary that it be delivered in a few hours. The minimum cost is based on fifty words.

The Night Letter. The night letter is a low-rate over-night service. Night letters may be filed up to 2 A.M. for delivery the ensuing morning. The minimum charge is based on fifty words.

Applying Your Knowledge

HELPFUL QUESTIONS:

1. What is the difference between a telegram and a day letter; between a telegram and a night letter?

2. What is the difference between a day letter and a night letter?

3. By which type of message can you send the greatest number of words at the least cost?

4. Which type of message is the fastest?

5. Find out the minimum cost for each of the three types of service from your community to several large cities. A committee can be appointed to do this. When the committee reports, record the information in your notebook.

PRACTICE IN WRITING MESSAGES:

1. Assume that you are an automobile dealer, a garage owner, a printer, a plumber, a grocer, etc. Ten days ago you ordered some material from a manufacturing concern which supplies your trade. Write three telegraph messages, the first one inquiring about your order; the second, from the manufacturers, stating that your order had not been received; the third, to the manufacturers, repeating your order and urging them to make shipment as soon as possible. Check in the upper left-hand corner of your blank the kind of message that you wish each to be.

2. Your company must reach A. L. Downs, one of its executives, and instruct him to order five more automobiles for delivery next month. He is now in Detroit, Michigan, at the Edgewater Hotel. You are asked to do this as you are leaving the salesroom about six o'clock in the evening, and Mr. Downs is supposed to leave Detroit the following afternoon. What kind of message would you send? Write such a message.

3. An order for Timken Roller Bearings due September 1 for installation in some machinery that must be delivered before September 15 has not been received. Write a telegram to the Timken Roller Bearing Company, Canton, Ohio. Assume that you are working for some local company in your home town. (If you wish, you may assume the same situation existing for another trade and another company.)

4. Write a message from the company to whom you sent a telegram in Number 3, explaining that the materials were shipped August 15. The company will have a tracer started after the

shipped goods; and if nothing definite is learned within a day or so, they will duplicate the order immediately.

5. Telegraph some company to send you via Parcel Post, Special Delivery, some part for one of the machines in your school shop. Ask the company to wire you in reference to shipping immediately. (Order some supplies instead of a machine part, if you wish.)

6. Write the following message in approximately fifty words so that it can be sent as a night letter at about the minimum rate.

Mr. Rock informs me that there is an opening in the Baltimore Y. M. C. A. boys' camp for a counselor. He wants a high school graduate or a college student who can pass the Red Cross senior life-saving test and drive a small truck. The job will pay thirty dollars a week, expenses to and from the camp, and all living expenses. Camp starts July 6 and closes August 10. I thought that you might be interested in it. Telegraph Mr. J. C. Rock, Baltimore Y. M. C. A.

PART IV

English in Advertising and Selling

Chapter 30

HOW GOOD ARE YOU AS A SALESMAN?

A great many alert, efficient automotive mechanics, plumbers, electricians, etc., who are experts in the mechanical phases of their trades, are unable to sell their services or products effectively. At the same time many good salesmen know about selling just what the shop men should know, but the salesmen cannot repair motor cars or other machinery. Of course, many salesmen are good mechanics, and many mechanics are also good salesmen.

Good salesmanship does not consist of high-pressure methods which induce a customer to buy unnecessary work or articles, nor does it consist of much easy-flowing language which attempts to make a customer feel that he just can't do without the article or service. Good salesmanship consists of another kind of selling. It is that method which a person employs when he shows or explains something worth while to a customer so well that the customer really sells the thing to himself.

English Between the Salesman and the Customer

Business transactions show constant need for a perfectly clear understanding between the salesman and the customer. The customer must often explain his wants; the salesman, on the other hand, must be able to ask useful questions, to discuss the different possibilities of the problem, and to explain the merits of the different materials or methods. In order to meet these situations the salesman must know his field or trade thoroughly, and he must be able to use accurately the vocabulary associated with it. The salesman who can speak correctly and convincingly can make a good impression on the customer and help him make a wise choice.

Both the manner and the speech of the salesman must show that he is willing and ready to serve the customer. Notice the poor and the good introductory expressions that are given below. The expressions listed on the right are much more likely to result in a sale.

Poor	*Better*
Do you want anything?	May I serve you, Sir?
Do you want some gasoline?	Do you wish ethyl or regular?
Is the oil O.K.?	May I check the oil and water?
The pistons are in bad shape.	Do you wish to see the pistons? They are badly worn.

The Principles of Good Salesmanship

Although it is not possible for you to become a forceful salesman as the result of studying a few paragraphs in a textbook, it is possible for you to become familiar with the important principles of selling, so that your knowledge of them will prove valuable to you.

The principles of personal salesmanship are the same as the fundamental principles used in writing a successful sales letter. The four main steps in a sales talk, like the four main steps in a sales letter, are:

1. To attract the customer's favorable attention.
2. To secure his interest.
3. To persuade or convince him.
4. To secure action through friendly suggestions.

Just as the writer of a sales letter selects carefully his opening sentence, so the salesman must choose carefully his line of approach. If possible, the salesman should approach the customer and attract his attention by mentioning something in which the customer is especially interested. For example, one man may be interested in the safety features of an automobile, another in the economy of operation, and still another in its acceleration or how easily it can be handled in traffic.

A sale is usually made only if the first three steps have been thoroughly covered and if the salesman has succeeded in making the prospect want the article. When the experienced salesman finds that the prospect is not yet convinced or ready to buy, he guides his discussion in line with what the prospect says and presents the strongest points possible as he nears the end of the discussion.

Meeting Objections

People usually want full value for their money. It is only natural, then, that the customer will raise questions and objections. How to meet the vast number of objections the salesman learns only through experience, but an observance of the following principles may help in many situations:

1. Find out what objections are raised most frequently and learn how to answer them.
2. Learn all that you can about your occupation or the article that you are selling. Only by becoming an expert in your field can you answer most of the objections and questions that are raised by customers.
3. Be ready with facts and information. When a customer asks a question, you must be ready to answer it immediately.

Applying Your Knowledge

HELPFUL QUESTIONS:

1. What experiences have you had which have convinced you of the value of effective English in the business world?

2. Of what importance is correct English in sales situations?

3. In what respects is personal salesmanship similar to the salesmanship displayed in the writing of a sales letter?

4. If other things are equal, why should an expert auto mechanic be a better automobile salesman than another individual who is not so skilled mechanically? Apply this question to the occupation in which you are interested.

Problems:

1. List three good sources of information that you can utilize to keep informed on new developments in your trade or occupation.

2. Imagine yourself to be a salesman of one of the following articles. Find out what you can about it, and tell the class what a salesman should know about it in order to discuss it intelligently.

weatherstripping	radios or TV sets
brass pipe plumbing for houses	electric refrigerators for homes
copper tube plumbing for houses	gasoline
cement	oil (lubricating)
maple furniture	electric lights for homes
upholstered furniture	some tool used in your occupation
personal stationery	oil burners

3. Write five remarks that you might use in opening a conversation with a customer. In each case name the thing you are selling.

4. Enact a sales situation with a classmate. Assume that you are attempting to sell some article or service to your classmate. Your classmate as the customer will raise questions about the product. You answer the questions and objections as best you can.

Planning a Sales Talk

A mechanic may urge a customer to have a repair job done on his automobile to prevent serious damage to the motor, to make the motor run more smoothly, or to prevent possible future breakdowns. In other words, the automobile mechanic sells Mr. Motorist the repair job by giving him one or several good reasons why the job should be done.

When a mechanic or shop man is trying to persuade a customer to have a certain job done, he should keep in mind certain principles during the conversation; namely,

1. Assume a *you* attitude; that is, tell the customer what benefits he will derive from having the work done.

2. Have several talking points around which to develop the sales argument.

a) Try to discover a principle on which to base your talking points, such as money saved, safety, convenience, etc. For example, if you are a plumber and are endeavoring to induce a customer to install copper tubing in a soft water area, you can approach him on the basis of convenience or freedom from the annoyance of rusty water as well as the economy of installing plumbing that will last.

1) Copper tubing lasts many times longer than iron.

2) Copper tubing requires no replacing, thus justifying the additional expense at the beginning.

3) Copper tubing eliminates the possibility of rusty water from rusty iron pipes.

4) Copper tubing assures good water pressure because the pipes do not tend to become clogged with rust.

b) Each of the sales points should be clearly explained and proved if possible and advisable. It would be an excellent plan to show the customer pieces of different kinds of pipe that have been in use.

3. Do not memorize any kind of sales talk. Instead, become thoroughly familiar with your job and your merchandise. You will then experience no trouble in answering intelligently any questions that you might be asked, or in advancing strong sales arguments.

4. The plan of a sales talk is much the same as that of a sales letter.

a) Attract attention—Secure attention through a contact sentence in which you mention something of interest to the prospect.

b) Stimulate interest—Secure the person's interest by giving your reasons for mentioning the subject.

c) Create desire—Make the person want the article or service by describing its benefits to him.

d) Convince prospect—Persuade him to believe your points by statements of fact or demonstration.

e) Secure action—Induce him to do something about it.

"There's a good buy. Best money's worth we have
on the lot."

"Look at that motor. Clean as new, tuned right
up to the minute."

"See that upholstery. Not worn at all and you
don't see any spots."

"Thank you very much. You are getting a first-
class automobile."

FIGURE 61. Good Salesmanship

Notice how these five steps are carried out in the following typical sales conversation between a mechanic and a
motorist. Of course, the different steps merge together so
that there is no distinct point at which the first step stops
and the second begins.

A Typical Sales Situation

Mr. Motorist has stopped at the garage to see how the carbon and valve job on his car is progressing. The mechanic

"We've cut the price three times on this one."
(No coat, smoking.)

"Sure, help yourself, look 'er over." (Prospect does the work.)

"Don't worry about that. You can clean those spots off all right."

"You won't find another buy like this. Hey, wait a minute . . ."

(Courtesy Motor Magazine and Town Auto Company, Allentown, Pennsylvania)

ersus Poor Salesmanship.

happens to be working on the car when Mr. Motorist comes in. Mr. Motorist is about to leave when the mechanic attracts his attention by starting the following conversation:

MECHANIC: By the way, do you know that the pistons are beginning to show signs of wear, and are becoming rather loose?
MOTORIST: No, I didn't. How badly worn are they?
MECHANIC: Oh, as yet they aren't very bad, but still they are loose enough to let the oil get by and burn.

MOTORIST: The motor uses about a quart now to every hundred and fifty miles. Is that the trouble?

MECHANIC: It probably is. Look at the clearance here between the piston and the cylinder wall. That's enough clearance to permit the oil to get by and to burn when combustion takes place.

MOTORIST: What do you think I ought to do about it?

MECHANIC: Well, you could put in oil rings or oversized pistons.

MOTORIST: Oil rings are cheaper than pistons, aren't they?

MECHANIC: Oh yes, a set of oil rings will cost you about $25 installed, but a good piston job will be about $65. However, the oil rings will not last so long as the new pistons. If you expect to drive the car for some time, I believe that the extra money spent on a piston job would be a good investment.

MOTORIST: If I did have you do a piston job on the motor, how soon would the motor again need attention? This car is beginning to get a little old and I dislike putting much money into it.

MECHANIC: When we do a job like that, we usually find it advisable to tighten up the bearings and to make other adjustments. If you permit us to do that, your motor will be as good as a new one after we have finished the job.

If you want us to do it for you, we can finish in good time since the head of the motor and the radiator are off already.

Give Your Reasons

In the foregoing conversation between the mechanic and the motorist, the mechanic was careful to give good reasons for his recommendations about additional work. Often it is only by explaining carefully and fully the reasons for your suggestions that you can sell your services. The customer will order work done only when he is convinced that he will get the results he wants. Hence, good selling involves much good explaining. For example, the following explanation demonstrates how a St. Louis painter sold a two-coat inside paint job to a woman who thought her dining room needed only one coat.

"You want this work done as economically as possible, Mrs. Crawford. That's why I recommend two coats. The first coat always soaks into the wall. In six months you wouldn't know the room has been done over at all. It's the second coat which makes permanent the real color effect we've been talking about.

"And there's another point. When the warm weather comes, you'll have these windows open. Dust will blow in from the street. By fall the walls will look a little dingy, and you'll want to wash them off.

"But if we put on only one coat, so much of the oil in it—oil is really what gives paint its life—will have soaked into the plaster that the color that's left will be all dried out. So that if you wash it, it will come off.

"Now, if I put on two coats, the first will give a real base for the second, so that the oil will not soak into the wall, but will stay in the paint. And when you wash the walls off at the end of summer, they'll look just as nice and attractive as if they'd just been done over fresh. And that's the way you'd like them to be, isn't it, Mrs. Crawford?"

—*National Painters Magazine*

Applying Your Knowledge

HELPFUL QUESTIONS:

1. Why is it not a good procedure to memorize a sales talk?
2. What is meant by the statement "assume a *you* attitude"?
3. In what respects is a sales talk similar to a sales letter?
4. If it is true that merely studying the proper methods of selling will not turn you into a first-rate salesman, what is the value of studying salesmanship?

PROBLEMS:

1. List the qualifications of a good salesman.
2. List the characteristics of a good sales talk.
3. Imagine yourself an automobile salesman. Draw up a sales plan (series of talking points) suitable for the sale of an automobile. (If you wish, you may use some article other than an automobile.)
4. From a carefully prepared plan talk to your classmates on one of the following suggestions:

Selling the school paper to everyone in the school.
Selling a season ticket to all basketball games.
Selling a set of tools to . . .
Selling automotive service to . . .

Selling good plumbing to home builders.
Selling electrical service or fixtures to . . .
Selling good rather than cheap printing to a customer.
Etc.

5. Listen to a sales conversation between two other persons or engage in one yourself with some one outside the school. Write on paper the conversation as it progressed. In the left-hand margin, write any criticisms that you might have of the conversation.

6. Bring to class a sample of some article. Keep it in your hands or on the table in front of you while you engage in a sales discussion with some one. While you are talking or as a part of your sales procedure, point out the principal features in connection with your statements. Any article such as the following will do: book, magazine, fountain pen, chair, tool of some kind, electrical fixture, cut-away section of an automobile tire or part, etc.

7. If you are interested in some phase of agriculture, draw up a sales plan for selling some agricultural product.

Chapter 31

ADVERTISING THE SMALL BUSINESS

What Is an Advertisement?

An advertisement consists of answers to the following four questions:

1. What have I to sell?
2. Why should you buy it?
3. Where can you buy it?
4. What is the price?

When writing any advertising keep these four points in mind. If your advertising answers these four questions pleasantly, forcefully, and clearly, you will have created an advertisement that will be sure to attract business.

In some places there is a rather widespread objection to including the price in an advertisement. The theory is that, if possible, the person should be induced to come in to ask about the price, thus exposing himself to personal salesmanship. However, the average man with whom the ordinary small business deals is so situated that he must consider price, and frequently it is the most important factor in determining his purchases.

Direct Advertising

Direct advertising usually refers to printed matter sent directly to the prospect. The types of direct advertising commonly used by the proprietors of small businesses are

postcards or mailing cards	booklets
letters	calendars

blotters	novelties
envelope and package inserts	stickers, coupons, etc.
folders	business cards

It is impossible to say which of these various forms is the best. Usually the form which delivers your message most effectively at the lowest possible cost is the best for your particular situation.

Writing Advertising

Various devices for advertising a small business are discussed in the rest of this chapter. Each example contains at least three of the four W's given at the beginning of the chapter; in fact, every advertisement must answer at least the first three W's and often the last. The kind of advertising used will determine how each of these questions should be answered. For example, a business card is very brief compared with a circular or an announcement, yet it may contain essentially the same information. The business card, however, is so small that it can contain no details.

The first step in writing an advertisement is to collect the information necessary to answer the four W's. After it has been secured, it must be presented so that it attracts favorable attention. An advertisement can be made to attract attention by the use of

1. A headline that is brief, interesting, definite, to the point. A headline is to an advertisement what the title is to a story or motion picture. It arrests the reader's attention and directs it to the copy. The headline usually tells the most important part of the message at a glance. Notice the following headlines copied from the advertisements of small businessmen.

> Bring in Your Car Today
> Will Your Car Start Quickly This Winter?
> For Only $1.50 We Will . . .
> Don't Push a Dull Lawn Mower
> Five Dollars Saved in Five Minutes

Last Call for Winter Protection
A New Idea

2. Type of different sizes.
3. Illustrations.
4. Different colors.
5. Borders around the advertisement.
6. Trade-marks or slogans, such as:

> No Job Too Large—None Too Small
> Automobile Painting the Right Way
> When We Do It, We Do It Right
> The One-Trip Plumber

7. Items placed in small boxes within the advertisement. Most grocery store circulars contain many examples of this.
8. Odd arrangement of the material.

Once the headline and the arrangement of the advertisement have attracted attention, what the advertisement says must hold the reader's attention and turn it into a desire for the thing advertised. This can be done by presenting the following in the advertisement:

1. Facts, figures, and evidence.
2. Information.
3. Details, test results, samples, etc.

The Core Idea

It is very important that the selling point be properly selected. Perhaps the service or article possesses five or six good selling points. How many selling points can be used in selling regular inspections for automobiles? Examine them: safety, economy, freedom from annoyance, comfort, increased life of the car. From these five points must be selected the one main idea that is to be stressed in the advertisement. This central or core idea must appeal to prospective customers as being important to them. Remember that you are not selling automobile inspections so much as you are using an inspection to sell safety, economy, comfort, increased life for the automobile, etc.

A Suggested Procedure for Developing an Advertisement

1. Gather information to answer the four W's.
2. Select the core idea or central selling point that you want to emphasize.
3. Decide upon some device to attract attention. (A headline, an odd arrangement, a slogan, or different colors in which the advertisement can be printed.)
4. Get a good advertising man or a good printer to help you arrange the material and to do the printing for you.

Have a Plan

If you use postcards, blotters, circulars, etc., develop them according to some definite plan. Write a series of cards or blotters and have each one of the series present some definite idea or advertise some specific job. Such a series of cards, blotters, or circulars sent out at intervals will keep your name before the public to much better advantage than irregular but more expensive advertising.

One automobile dealer developed a series of postcards and blotters for a fall advertising campaign for service work as follows:

    October 1–Carbon and Valve Job
    October 15–Brake Adjustment or Relining Job
    November 1–Cooling System and Lubrication
    November 15–Heater Installation or Servicing
    December 1–Final Winter Appeal on Heaters, Easy Starting, Cooling System, etc.

Postcards or Mailing Cards

Postcards are widely used because they are convenient, inexpensive, and easily read. The message is, of necessity, brief; and since the postcard receives consideration as first class mail, it is generally given a glance before it is tossed aside. The address side tells nothing whatever so that out of curiosity a person invariably turns it over to see what the other side contains.

Postcards are the same as any other advertising in that people will read about only the things that interest them. For this reason be careful to send advertising only to those who are interested in your service now, or who are likely to be interested in the future.

A mailing card is useful and convenient for informal announcements of all kinds. For example, a mechanic might use a card to announce that he is opening a garage in a certain location, a paperhanger might announce a display of new wallpapers, or a television shop might announce a new service for customers.

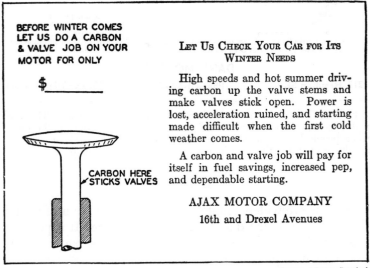

(From *Motor Service*)

FIGURE 62. A Card Mailed About October 15. This card makes its appeal on the basis of a definite job at a specific price. These cards can be either printed or mimeographed. This is card No. 2 in a series of five, mailed from October 1 to January 1.

It is a big help to the customer to be able to send return cards or envelopes without prepaying postage. Business houses often insert envelopes and cards which contain return addresses and require no postage. No stamp need be attached to these cards or envelopes under the terms of the post office permit because the company will pay the postage when it receives them.

Spring Change Over

SPRING is in the Air and it's change over time at **DAHLS.** Come in, take advantage of this special price. You save up to 25%.

ALL MAKE CARS   Offer expires April 30th

$7.80 includes all labor, grease, oil and rust inhibitor

* Complete chassis lubrication
* Check front brake lining, cylinders and retainers
* Check & tighten cylinder heads & all radiator hoses

* Change trans. & diff. gear oil
* Check & repack front wheel bearings
* Drain and fill crankcase
* Flush cooling system & install rust inhibitor
* Wash car & clean interior

DAHL MOTORS

1213 Hamilton St.   Phone 3-5231   18th & Tilghman Sts.

FIGURE 63. A Postcard for Mailing to Customers or Prospects. This card makes its appeal on the basis of definite work at a specific price in the spring when people become more interested in pleasure driving. These cards are usually printed, but they can be mimeographed. This is one of a series.

Blotters

Blotters are widely employed because they are useful, and they can be preserved and used for some time. It is possible to secure blotters having an excellent grade of paper on one side, on which printing of fine quality can be produced.

The blotter serves as a constant reminder. Although its message must be brief, the message frequently stays in front of a person and is read several times while something else finds its way to the waste-paper basket.

Some concerns issue blotters in a series just as they do postcards. Each month a new one bearing a timely message is printed and sent out. Many of these blotters have on one end a small calendar containing the dates for the next month.

Typical Blotters

(1)

Expert Welding • •

Broken Parts Made Good as New

• WE GO ANYWHERE •

Neil S. Myers

528 Emerald Street   Harrisburg, Pa.

FIGURE 64. Pictures That Illustrate Your Services Will Make Your Blotters More Interesting and Attractive

Envelope Enclosures and Package Inserts

To enclose a blotter in the same envelope containing a monthly bill or statement is common practice. Other advertising can be enclosed in a similar way.

Envelope enclosures and package inserts are the only advertising that is delivered to your clients or prospects free of charge. Most letters sent by first class mail ordinarily weigh less than an ounce. If your letter and enclosure together weigh no more than an ounce, then your advertisement requires no additional postage. One advantage of enclosures or inserts is that usually they reach present or prospective customers.

(2)

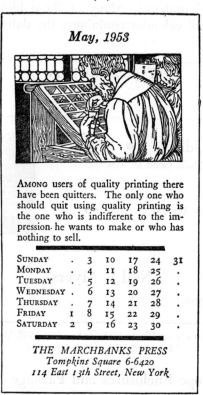

May, 1953

AMONG users of quality printing there have been quitters. The only one who should quit using quality printing is the one who is indifferent to the impression. he wants to make or who has nothing to sell.

SUNDAY	.	3	10	17	24	31
MONDAY	.	4	11	18	25	.
TUESDAY	.	5	12	19	26	.
WEDNESDAY	.	6	13	20	27	.
THURSDAY	.	7	14	21	28	.
FRIDAY	1	8	15	22	29	.
SATURDAY	2	9	16	23	30	.

THE MARCHBANKS PRESS
Tompkins Square 6-6420
114 East 13th Street, New York

FIGURE 65. This Is a Good Blotter Because It Contains an Appropriate Picture, a Brief Message That Is to the Point, and a Calendar for Reference.

Writing the Enclosure

Notice that good advertisements always use pictures, color, a large amount of white space, and only a few words of good copy. What you say must be said in as few words as possible, but it must be written so that it says something worth while to every man who reads it. Try to keep the number of words in blotters, enclosures, announcements, etc., as low as possible, perhaps twenty-five or less.

Through the insert or enclosure the attention of these people is directed to new suggestions. It is well to remember, in this connection, that regular customers are the best prospects because they already know the type and quality of the service.

Another advantage of the insert is that it goes out by first class mail. This insures its reaching the desired individual.

Since the average envelope size is 3⅝ x 6½ inches, the enclosures should be somewhat smaller to permit easy insertion. An insertion may be used for any of the following purposes:

1. To express appreciation of patronage.
2. To suggest new services or uses for the product.
3. To announce new services or articles.
4. To keep before prospects a list of your offerings.
5. To explain the services you offer.
6. To serve as a reminder.

Every business achieves permanent success only by cultivating and retaining old customers. After a business man learns this lesson, he spends more time cultivating his regular customers.

Circulars

Circulars are frequently used by both small and large concerns. They are probably most effective when they advertise a limited number of items. In many places small retailers seem to have a tendency to use too large a circular containing too many items; but Mr. Jones, who has a store on Park Avenue, uses a large circular simply because Mr. Winner, his competitor on the next street, uses a large-sized circular. Mr. Jones does not realize that many items crowded on the same large sheet are never read. The type of business will determine how many items you must advertise on a circular. However, aside from those advertising groceries or merchandise, the most effective circulars advertise one or only a few things.

Where and when circulars should be distributed must also be determined by your local situation. Before distributing circulars you should decide from what sections of your town you can expect to attract customers, and then distribute your material over that area. To circularize too large an area is always wasteful.

Announcements

When starting a new business, when moving to a new location, or when offering new services, the business man finds it necessary to inform old and prospective customers of the fact. Some men use a postcard for this purpose. Others employ a card or folder which is mailed in an envelope; still others have utilized small circulars and blotters.

GEORGE F. FETTERHOFF

2247 North Fifth Street   Oak Park, Illinois

Wishes to announce to the public that he has placed Sample Books of SUN-TESTED WALL PAPER for your convenience and inspection at

MRS. PEARL GRIFFITHS
316 West Third Street

Estimates furnished and all work guaranteed. Give us the size of your room and we will do the rest.

FIGURE 66. This Announcement Was Printed on a Good Quality Plain White Paper Slightly Smaller Than a Postcard.

The appearance of the announcement often determines in a large measure the reception and the patronage given a business enterprise.

FORREST F. CAMPBELL

FORMERLY WITH HARRISBURG BUICK CO.

ANNOUNCES THAT HE HAS OPENED AN

AUTOMOBILE REPAIR GARAGE

AT 1606 THOMPSON STREET

WHERE HE IS PREPARED TO GIVE PROMPT AND

EFFICIENT SERVICE TO AUTO OWNERS

PHONE 3-2377

FIGURE 67. This Announcement Was Printed on Plain White Card About the Size of a Postcard.

Calendars and Specialties

The argument for the use of calendars and specialties, which are widely used, is almost the same as that for blotters. Calendars, for example, may be used the entire year; and because of their good appearance, they frequently enjoy excellent positions in the home or office.

Business Cards

Ordinarily the small business man gives too little attention to the matter of business cards. They are inexpensive and they have many uses.

The business card should contain pertinent information about the name, business, address, and telephone number. In other words, it should contain all the information that a prospective customer needs in order to find a business man easily and quickly.

A cheap business card creates a "cheap" impression. Attractively printed cards are worth much more than are poorly printed and poorly arranged cards. It is advisable, therefore, that a reliable and a good printer do the printing. A business card is a sample of the thing or service sold and of the man selling it.

The examples below will give you a good idea of the type of business cards the owners of small businesses generally use.

FIGURE 68. Typical Business Cards. What differences do you notice between the four cards on the upper half of the page, and the four cards on the lower half? How do you account for those differences?

Securing the Names of Prospects

It is easy to get a list of names from a dozen different sources, but unless they are the names of persons likely to be interested in the service offered, the list is worthless.

The important thing to do at the start is to decide upon the class of people with whom you hope to do business. Are they wealthy, of moderate means, wage earners, landlords, car owners, etc.? Having decided upon this point, you are ready to start the development of a mailing list. A good mailing list possesses the following qualities:

1. It includes only actual prospects.
2. It includes all prospects that can be reached.
3. It is up to date.
4. The names and addresses are correct.
5. It includes only persons who pay their bills.
6. It includes information as to the buying habits of prospects.

At first the securing of a good prospect list seems a difficult task, but perseverance and resourcefulness will usually enable you to find a way out of the difficulty. Regardless of the source of the list, you will need to revise it constantly in order to keep it up to date. Some of the sources from which you might secure an original list of prospects are:

1. The telephone or city directory.
2. Directory publishers who make a business of selling lists of prospects classified as to address or occupation, etc.
3. Mailing lists borrowed from other business men.
4. Mailing lists bought from men going out of business.
5. Government records, such as city, county, or state voting lists, tax lists, license records, labor records.
6. Chamber of commerce bulletins.
7. Reports from salesmen, clerks, or dealers.
8. Membership lists of organizations or societies, such as lodges, granges, etc.

Applying Your Knowledge

HELPFUL QUESTIONS:

1. What four questions are answered in most good advertisements?

2. What is the chief use of a headline in an advertisement?

3. Give several methods used to attract attention in an advertisement. Which methods do you believe are the best? Why?

4. What is meant by *core idea*?

5. Why is it important that every advertisement have a core idea?

6. Does the writing of an advertisement for a post card differ in any way from the writing of an advertisement for a blotter?

7. What kinds of advertising do you believe the average small business can afford?

PROBLEMS:

1. Assume that you have started a small business of your own. If you are interested in agriculture, assume that you are operating a truck farm, poultry farm, baby-chick hatchery, a greenhouse for growing plants or flowers, etc. Develop an advertising program for your business and write up the advertising. Your program might include some or all of the following:

    a) An announcement telling about your opening the business.

    b) One or two circulars dealing with one or two special items.

    c) A short spring, summer, fall, or winter campaign using postcards or other cards.

    d) A series of blotters that you might insert in your letters when you send out your monthly statements.

    e) A business card.

When you have completed the work on all the material, place your advertising matter in a small folder or notebook.

2. Make a collection of advertising material sent out by small business or shop men in your community. Using this advertising as a nucleus, start a folder consisting of material which you consider good advertising.

3. Investigate a duplicating device such as the mimeograph or offset press as to cost, ease of operation, kinds of material that you can reproduce, how well it works. Make a report on the results of your investigation.

Chapter 32

ADVERTISING AND SALES LETTERS

After gaining sufficient experience many men start their own small business establishments. Very often these men start printing plants, upholstery shops, garages, supply houses, contracting businesses, etc. Whether or not a man can earn his living operating his own business depends upon the sales which he can make. Consequently, the better a man can plan a sales campaign and the more effectively he can carry it out, the better chance he has of succeeding.

One of the big problems of conducting a business is getting the work to do, and jobs don't just walk through the doorway, especially the doorway to a new business. Most sales must be made by personal contact, but a good sales letter is an excellent method for getting in contact with prospective customers.

Although a good sales letter is rather difficult to write, any intelligent person can learn to write one if he will keep in mind a few rules given in Chapters 30 and 31 and in this chapter. Some of these rules are:

1. Make the letter neat and correct in form and place it on a well-printed letterhead.
2. Consider the reader's viewpoint. Tell the prospect how your product or service will help him to be healthy, happy, safe, thrifty, etc.
3. Say what is most important *first*. Say it briefly.
4. "Stick" to one idea or subject.
5. Be brief. Make sentences short, paragraphs only a few lines, and the whole letter not more than two hundred words, preferably less. After it is written, take out sentences or groups of words that are not needed to develop the main idea.

December 2, 19—

(Greeting)

Dear Mr.———————.

(Contact sentences to secure interest)

It happened to me one night last Winter. Busy with my customers' cars, I neglected my own — went to bed rather early that evening and awoke to hear the North Wind whistling round my house.

And out in the cold was my own car, in danger of a costly freeze-up.

I decided then and there that it would never happen again, and this year my personal car is ready for the first cold snap, all ready to start quickly on the coldest morning and be safe through the coldest nights.

(Reason for writing and description of service)

Checking the car for winter is never costly, and may save a big repair bill if the cylinders or radiator are ruined by freezing, or bearings or pistons are burned up because of Summer oil that will not flow.

Hard starting, too, need not be tolerated if the engine is properly tuned.

(Persuasion and friendly request for action)

Why not bring your car in today; it costs nothing to talk things over. We can service your car at the lowest possible cost and relieve your mind of the worries that Winter driving usually brings.

Yours for trouble-free Winter-driving,

AJAX MOTOR COMPANY

(Reprinted from *Motor Service*)

FIGURE 69. A Personal Type of Sales Letter That the Manager or Owner of a Garage Might Send Automobile Owners When the First Cold Wave Arrives.

Note that between paragraphs of the letter on the preceding page are printed the different parts of a sales letter. Usually a good sales letter will follow this formula of about five steps. Study the letters carefully with the help of these notes, noticing in what order these steps are found.

Notice also that there is a definite request for a reply. This is an extremely important part of every letter. Make a request for action and enclose a reply card so that it is easy for the person to take the action you suggest.

Business reply cards are designed by the post office department for the especial use of mail advertisers. When they are used, postage payment is made only when the card is returned to you. You should secure a permit through your local post office and use these cards, for they save money.

On the back of your reply cards have a form printed with your name. Something like the following is suggested for enclosure with the letter shown in Figure 71:

I am interested in building a sun-room and would like to see your architect about possible plans or suggestions.

Name ....

Address...................... Telephone.........

FIGURE 70. A Reply Card.

Applying Your Knowledge

HELPFUL QUESTIONS:

1. Why is it not possible for a sales letter to take the place of a personal visit to a prospective customer? What is its real value?

2. What reasons can you give for the use of short paragraphs in sales letters?

3. Why is it so essential that you include in any sales letter a request for immediate action?

4. How can you make it easy for the person receiving your letter to take the action you request?

THE FERRISS CONSTRUCTION COMPANY
Elyria, Ohio

September 15, 19—

Mrs. James E. Pierson
42 Maple Avenue
Elyria, Ohio

eeting

Dear Mrs. Pierson:

ntact
ntence

Will you have enough warm, energizing sunshine in your home this winter? Wouldn't you like to add a small comfortable room which would be flooded with healthy rays all day?

ason for
iting

I am writing to suggest that this fall is an especially opportune time to add a sun porch to your house. With building prices way down, we can do it very inexpensively and produce such a sun-room as you have always wanted.

scription of
vice or
duct

We have a fine lot of sun porch designs—cozy, warm and healthy, bright spots even on rainy days. And on sunny days these porches enable you to make the most out of Old Sol's healthy rays.

ument or
suasion

You know how important sunlight is to health. We are now able to provide sections of glass that let all the health-giving rays through. You and your children can absorb health and energy and bask in the sunshine in warmth and comfort.

suasion &
quest for
ion

I have a crew of expert builders whom we are anxious to keep employed all winter. We are willing to make you a "thrifty" price to do so. May we discus the matter with you? Just drop the enclosed card in the mailbox. No stamp is needed.

endly
quest for
ion

If you want healthy sunshine in your home, we can give it to you, but send the card now.

Yours very truly,

Frederick A. Ferriss

THE FERRISS CONSTRUCTION CO.

ature

n Name

FIGURE 71. A Type of Sales Letter That Might Be Used by a Small Construction Company or an Expert Carpenter Seeking Fall Work.

5. Do you think it is necessary to include in a sales letter all steps given in the example?

6. In addition to the return post card is it good policy to enclose with your sales letter advertising literature of any kind?

PROBLEMS:

1. Assume that you have opened a small upholstery and furniture repair shop. Write an advertising and sales letter in an effort to locate prospective customers who might have old or broken furniture that they want re-upholstered or repaired. Make up your own letterhead. Devise some method whereby the person receiving the letter can take action easily. If you wish, you may assume that you are operating any kind of business with which you are familiar.

2. Assume that you have opened an automobile service station in some section of your town or city and you plan to specialize in greasing and washing jobs at a low cost to the automobile owner. Write a letter that can be sent to automobile owners in the community announcing your service. On a separate sheet explain how you might secure a good list of prospects to whom you might send letters announcing this service. You may substitute here any type of business you wish. (Examples: Plumbing, Television Servicing, Die-Making Shop, Contracting, etc.)

3. Assume that you have just learned that a friend of yours desires to buy an automobile such as you have for sale. Write him a letter designed to interest him in the automobile to the point where he will ask for a demonstration. You will sell only for cash in full. (You may substitute a set of tools or instruments used in your trade or business.)

Mailing Your Letters

The time you mail sales or advertising letters is important. Because there is less competition from bills, statements, and collectors between the 18th and 25th of the month, that is considered a good time for mailing. Plan to have your letters arrive on Tuesdays, Wednesdays, or Fridays.

FERRISS CONSTRUCTION COMPANY

Elyria, Ohio

November 11, 19—

Mrs. John B. Alfred
368 Green Village Road
Elyria, Ohio

Dear Mrs. Alfred:

A week ago we suggested that you look about for any odd jobs that you want done in your home. Thus far we have not heard from you, and we are wondering whether you understand that absolutely without any charge to you, we shall be glad to consult with you and to give you estimates on the work you may be considering.

Since you can have work done this winter for 25 to 35 percent less than normally, we feel sure that you will want to take advantage of present low prices.

We shall appreciate your getting in touch with us, and we shall be glad to arrange terms of payment to suit your convenience.

Very truly yours,

Frederick A. Ferriss

Frederick A. Ferriss, Pres.

THE FERRISS CONSTRUCTION CO.

FIGURE 72. A Follow-Up Letter.

Follow-Up

It is very seldom that a salesman sells his wares on his first or even his second visit. No manufacturing concern or business man expects to secure a signed order on the strength of a single sales letter. Briefly, to be effective, sales effort must be repeated and must be persistent.

A good letter is always worth following up, whether you get a reply or not. You can follow up on your letters by telephone, personal visit, or by another letter. At times, possibly all three can be used to advantage. More sales can be made or more work secured by constantly advertising your business and following up your prospects than by doing it only occasionally.

Applying Your Knowledge

PROBLEMS:

1. You have received no answer to the letter you wrote to a prospect as you were directed in Problem 1 or 2, page 330. Write a second letter to follow up on your first one, emphasizing some special service or type of work that you are specially equipped to do.

2. Assume that in answer to a letter sent out to prospects as directed in Problem 2, page 330, an automobile owner had you grease and wash his car twice, but that he hasn't stopped at your service station for about a month. Write this customer a letter asking whether he was entirely satisfied with the work, etc., and inviting him to return.

PART V

Report Writing

Chapter 33

THE INFORMAL REPORT

Why Should I Learn To Write Reports?

Here, in a few words, is one good reason why you should learn to write good reports. You will find that the preparation of a really good report is a challenging test of your skill.

How To Get To Be Boss

Few appreciate how busy a top executive is or how much patience he must exhibit to fulfil the saying, "A company is known by the men it keeps." The executive vice-president of a company told me how, twenty-five years ago, the president had taught him what management was about. Soon after his arrival, he was called on to do a market analysis. When he had finished, he brought it in, with a two-page summary of the figures. He expected a pat on the back, but the elder just grunted and asked, "What do these figures mean?"

The young man stammered and the president said, "Go back and study them."

Eventually, he came back with a written interpretation. The old man glanced at it and grunted, "What are we going to do about it?"

The junior did not know, was told to find out. Next time, he said, "Here are the figures. Here is what they mean. Here's what can be done about them."

The president leaned back in his chair and permitted himself a smile. "Sit down, son," he said. "Now we can talk business." *

---

* "How To Get To Be Boss," by J. Elliott Janney and Greer Williams. *The Saturday Evening Post*, Vol. 224, No. 35, Curtis Publishing Company, March 1, 1952. Reprinted by permission.

The Importance of Report Writing

The report is among the most important communications for a man in any position of responsibility. In general, the more important the job, the more valuable becomes the ability to write clear, accurate, and interesting reports. No matter how thoroughly a man may understand his job, or how important the information that he has collected, all this is wasted if he cannot write a report that will give this impression to others. It is not enough that a technical man, an engineer, or a foreman be able to secure the facts and to do the job; he must be able to interpret his job and to present his ideas to others in language that is clear, correct, and interesting.

Qualities of a Good Report

The qualities found in a good report are essentially the same as those found in a good business letter. Both are written to convince the reader of the advisability of doing or of not doing certain things. Neither a letter nor a report will be very convincing unless the writer can employ good English.

The technical man must be able also to describe the machines and apparatus that he sees and to explain clearly the processes that he observes. Unless the report writer can apply the fundamental principles of description, explanation, and effective business writing, he cannot hope to achieve success in report writing. He should, therefore, study the various aspects of business English and of technical English as presented in the earlier chapters of this book, so that he is better prepared to meet the special requirements of report writing.

January 15, 19___

Mr. John S. Moyer
The Cowling Agency
1341 West Fourth Street
St. Louis 5, Missouri

                    Subject: Investigation
                             Indianapolis Office

Dear Mr. Moyer:

        According to instructions, I called today at our
Indianapolis office, and I respectfully submit the following report:

        Financial status: The petty cash account showed a
                               surplus of $1.

        General conditions:

          I.   Office: On the whole the office was clean
                               and well arranged.

         II.   Records: Most entries have been carelessly
                               made; that is, figures are not
                               placed always in the proper
                               column or exactly on the lines.
                               There is some evidence that
                               entries are not always made
                               promptly each day, or the indi-
                               vidual accounts balanced each
                               month.

        Recommendations: That entries be made more care-
                               fully in the records.

                               That when an account does not
                               balance, the mistake be found at
                               once and the account properly
                               adjusted.

                               That accounts be checked more
                               carefully each day.

        Reactions of   The office manager assured me
        Office Manager: that he would follow the sug-
                               gestions made.

                                    Very truly yours,

FIGURE 73. An Informal Report Written as a Letter.

Use of the Informal Report

In a factory or other type of establishment the manager may often ask some one to furnish information on some part of the business, an account of a trip, or the way a new machine works. The information is presented as a report. It may be an oral report; but if the matter is important, it is likely that the manager will want it written out so that he can keep a copy of it for reference. Frequently the material is prepared as an informal report which is discussed in this chapter.

The informal report is written like a long letter containing official or technical information. Such a report may be written as a letter, or it may be given the customary make-up of a formal report consisting of a number of sheets of business-size letter paper protected by a cover.

How To Write the Informal Report

The informal report should be written much as you would write a personal letter, using the pronoun *I* when necessary. This type of report is often preferred when it contains the personal opinion of the writer or when the writer knows the readers.

The following suggestions will prove helpful in writing informal reports:

1. Write the informal report much as you would a letter or memorandum.
2. Give more space to important ideas than to details.
3. Rewrite the report in order to make it as clear and as easy to understand as possible.
4. Be direct and natural.
5. Be concise.

Examples. On page 337 is a short report written in the form of a letter. It is the kind of short informal report that anyone might use to report minor investigations to his superiors.

The report below describes a forced landing made by Colonel Lindbergh in November, 1926, just a few months before he flew from New York to Paris. Five years before writing this report he received a grade of B in English when he was taking an engineering course in the University of Wisconsin. This report was made to the Robertson Aircraft Corporation and post office officials. It shows a good mastery of English, and gives us an interesting and accurate picture of the conditions faced by the pilots who first flew the air mail.

Report of Northbound Mail Flight *

I took off from Lambert-St. Louis field at 4.20 p.m. November 3, arrived at Springfield, Ill., at 5.15, and after a five-minute stop for mail took the air again and headed for Peoria. The ceiling at Springfield was about 500 ft., and the weather report from Peoria, which was telephoned to St. Louis earlier in the afternoon, gave the flying conditions as entirely passable. I encountered darkness about 25 miles north of Springfield. The ceiling had lowered to around 400 ft. and a light snow was falling. At South Pekin the forward visibility of ground lights from 150-ft. altitude was less than half a mile and over Pekin the town lights were indistinct from 200 ft. above. After passing Pekin I flew at an altimeter reading of 600 ft. for about five minutes, when the lightness of the haze below indicated that I was over Peoria. Twice I could see lights on the ground and descended to less than 200 ft. before they disappeared from view. I tried to bank around one group of lights, but was unable to turn quickly enough to keep them in sight.

After circling in the vicinity of Peoria for thirty minutes, I decided to try to find better weather conditions by flying northeast toward Chicago. I had ferried a ship from Chicago to St. Louis in the early afternoon and at that time the ceiling and visibility were much better near Chicago than elsewhere along the route. Enough gasoline for about an hour and ten minutes of flying remained in the main tank and twenty minutes in the reserve. This was hardly enough to return to St. Louis, even had I been able to navigate directly to the field by dead reckoning and flying blind the greater portion of the way. The

* By Charles A. Lindbergh. Reprinted by permission of the U. S. Post Office Department and Mr. William B. Robertson.

only lights along our route at present are on the field at Peoria; consequently, unless I could pick up a beacon on the transcontinental route my only alternative would be to drop the parachute flare and land by its light together with what little assistance the wing lights would be in the snow and rain. The territory towards Chicago was much more favorable for a night landing than around St. Louis.

I flew northeast at about 2,000 ft. for thirty minutes, then dropped down to 600 ft. There were numerous breaks in the clouds this time and occasionally ground-lights could be seen from over 500 ft. I passed over the lights of a small town and a few minutes later came to a fairly clear place in the clouds. I pulled up to about 600 ft., released the parachute flare, and whipped the ship around to get into the wind and under the flare, which lit at once but, instead of floating down slowly, dropped like a rock. For an instant I saw the ground, then total darkness. My ship was in a deep bank and for a few seconds after being blinded by the intense light I had trouble righting it. I then tried to find the ground with the wing lights but their glare was worse than useless in the haze.

When about ten minutes of gas remained in the pressure-tank and I still could not see the faintest outline of any object on the ground, I decided to leave the ship rather than attempt to land blindly. I turned back southwest towards less populated country and started climbing in an attempt to get over the clouds before jumping. The main tank went dry at 7.51, and the reserve at 8.10. The altimeter then registered approximately 14,000 ft., yet the top of the clouds was apparently several thousand feet higher. I rolled the stabilizer back, cut the switches, pulled the ship up into a stall, and was about to go out over the right side of the cockpit when the right wing began to drop. In this position the plane would gather speed and spiral to the right, possibly striking my parachute after its first turn. I returned to the controls and, after righting the plane, dived over the left side of the cockpit while the air speed registered about 70 miles per hour and the altimeter 13,000 ft.

I pulled the rip-cord immediately after clearing the stabilizer. The Irving chute functioned perfectly. I had left the ship headfirst and was falling in this position when the risers whipped me around into an upright position and the chute opened. The last I saw or heard of the D.H. was as it disappeared into the clouds just after my chute opened. I placed the rip-cord in my pocket and took out my flashlight. It was snowing and very cold. For the first minute or so the parachute descended smoothly; then commenced an excessive oscillation which continued for about five minutes and which I was unable to check. The first indication that I was near the ground was a gradual darkening of the space below. The snow had turned to rain, and although my chute was thoroughly soaked, its oscillation had greatly decreased. I directed the beam of the 500-ft. spotlight downward, but the ground appeared so suddenly that I landed on top of a barbed-wire fence without seeing it.

The fence helped to break my fall and the barbs did not penetrate the heavy flying suit. The chute was blown over the fence and was held open for some time by the gusts of wind before collapsing. I rolled it up into its pack and started towards the nearest light. Soon I came to a road which I followed about a mile to the town of Covell, Ill., where I telephoned a report to St. Louis and endeavored to obtain some news of where the ship had landed. The only information that I could obtain was from a group of farmers in the general store, a Mr. Thompson, who stated that his neighbor had heard the plane crash but could only guess at its general direction. I rode with Mr. Thompson to his farm and, after leaving the parachute in his house, we canvassed the neighbors for any information concerning the plane. After searching for over an hour without result, I left instructions to place a guard over the mail in case it was found before I returned and went to Chicago for another ship.

On arriving over Covell the next morning I found the wreck, with a small crowd gathered around it, less than 500 ft. back of the house where I had left the parachute. The nose and wheels had struck the ground at about the same time and, after sliding along for about 75 ft., it had piled up in a pasture beside a hedge fence. One wheel had come off and was standing inflated against the wall on the inside of a hog-house a hundred yards farther on. It had gone through two fences and the wall of the house. The wings were badly splintered but the tubular fuselage, although badly bent in places, had held its general form even in the mailpit. The parachute from the flare was hanging on the tailskid. There were three sacks of mail in the plane. One, a full bag, from St. Louis had been split open and some of the mail oil-soaked but legible. The other two were only partly full and were undamaged. I delivered the mail to Maywood by plane to be dispatched on the next ships out.

CHECK PILOT REPORT

To: Division Chief Pilot, ATL—Idlewild Airport

Month: February

Area or routes covered by report: North Atlantic

Check pilot's name and base: F. I. Jacobs, New York

SUGGESTED ITEMS FOR COMMENT

(please check those to be covered in your report)

_____1. Navigation aids   _____10. Emergency equipment

_____2. Communications, ground _____11. Food
         air
                                 _____12. Crew scheduling
_____3. Dispatch functions
                                 _____13. New hired copilots
_____4. Maintenance
                                 _____14. Flight service per-
_____5. Meteorology   sonnel

_____6. Passenger service   __X__15. Air traffic control

_____7. Station irregularities   _____16. Route manual

_____8. Ground handling of a/c _____17. Operations manual

_____9. Line crew   __X__18. Other *

Note: Items not checked will be considered satisfactory.

   * Please indicate under "Other" any items you are reporting on that are not included in the above list.

REPORT

15. <u>OATC Clearance for pressure pattern flying</u>
    I have noticed that a number of captains hesitate to take advantage of pressure pattern and single heading crossings of the North Atlantic. This seems

Figure 74. This Type of Report Is Used by Pilots and Crew Members of the Pan American World Airways System. The example given here is an actual report made by a pilot after an Atlantic Ocean crossing.

ATL means Atlantic. OATC refers to Ocean Air Traffic Control. This is the agency that controls the flow of air traffic over the ocean.

2

to stem from a fear they will be in violation of
air traffic rules if they should drift sixty miles
or more from the route over which they were originally cleared. Accordingly they ask the navigator
to keep as close as possible to the great circle or
rhumb line track as possible. This requires heading
changes of as much as 30 degrees when crossing deep
troughs where drift suddenly shifts from one side
to the other. If the forecast longitude of the
trough is in error, the navigator may zig when he
should zag and get far off the intended track with
the chance of unnecessarily facing a very unfavorable
head-wind for the remainder of the flight.

With no wind, using an average variation of 25 degrees
applied to the rhumb line course from Gander to
Shannon, the actual track will approximate the great
circle. Most of the time the overall average drift
for the crossing will be less than three degrees,
but the actual drift over part of the route may be as
much as 10 to 15 degrees. If in these instances
the navigator takes a single heading using average
variation and average drift for the whole crossing,
the plane may drift as much as 150 miles off the
no wind track but even though it has thus traveled
a greater geographical distance it will cross the
ocean in less time than had he properly corrected for
drift in each zone.

If on a single heading the plane is apt to drift into
a region of less favorable winds, the flight can
be planned by way of any desirable point en route
with the use of two headings instead of one.

In order to encourage more pilots to use this
simplified and more efficient means of crossing the
ocean, I suggest we advise them that OATC will, on
request, reclear a plane by a pressure pattern route
over the North Atlantic. A request for reclearance
should specify one point on the expected track
where the deviation from the direct route would be
greatest. Example: "Clipper 100 requests reclear
Gander to Shannon, pressure pattern, by way of 50
north and 40 west."

18. Size of Staff at Goose Bay
    I am advised by Mr. Maugham at Goose Bay that his
    station is staffed only to handle the frequency of

FIGURE 74. (*Continued*)

3

stops which might be expected under purely emergency conditions. Apparently flights are again being dispatched through Goose Bay due to runway limitations at Gander and whenever northern route components are better. Mr. Maugham feels that this greater frequency will require more help at Goose Bay if serious transit delays are to be avoided.

18. Customs Documents — Boston
On February 28th on flight 119/27 I was confronted at Boston with customs form No. 3417 which requires the captain to swear that certain types of maintenance were not performed on the aircraft while in foreign ports. The use of this form was discontinued at New York some three years ago and should not be required at Boston, since the captain is not in a position to know the status of maintenance performed on the aircraft while out of the country.

FIGURE 74. (*Continued*)

The Progress Report

A *progress report* is a kind of informal report which tells how much of a job has been completed, and just what the situation is at the time. It may be short or long; it may be specific and in detail or quite general; it may be in the form of a memorandum, a letter, or a standard report arrangement.

The progress report answers three questions:

1. What has been done?
2. What is the present situation?
3. What are the future plans?

The following example is a rather long report on the progress made over a three-month period on an experimental school farm. It is an actual report written by the instructor in charge of operations.

SCHOOL FARM REPORT

OCTOBER - NOVEMBER - DECEMBER

This was the season of harvest; the season when many
of our projects were concluded and are now to be evaluated
in the light of their educational value. We are closing
in on the final cycle of a full year of operation, and
can now review some valuable experiences on which to base
future plans, and by which we can answer many questions as
to the success of our first phase of activity. Important,
too, is the financial aspect of the project. Adjustments
that must be made in order to decrease the financial
liability involved can now be made much more intelligently.

The following are some of the more important activities engaged in for the period:

1. Completing the poultry plant.
2. The swine program progresses.
3. Harvesting the corn crop.
4. Revamping the dairy program.
5. Construction projects.
6. Advisory committee recommendations.
7. Plans for the new year.

1. COMPLETING THE POULTRY PLANT

No sooner were the carpenters nailing the last board
on our new poultry floors in the barn on Unit I than we
were ready with our first lot of feathered tenants. The
pens built in the upper part of the barn were filled with
Leghorn birds. Here they were not so apt to be disturbed
and we haven't experienced much trouble with scaring of
birds. The New Hampshires were housed on the basement
floor, and since this breed is more docile they do not
scare so easily in the presence of strangers. We housed
about 1,100 birds of the combined breeds. No attempt was
made to do any culling before housing. We preferred to
have the students do this job under roof where we could use
it to capacity as a teaching project. Most of the students
soon developed fair skill in picking the undesirable
birds and about 150 hens were sent to market as culls.

FIGURE 75. A Progress Report Informally and Interestingly Written. Because of its length, a portion of this report is omitted. Note the construction
and arrangement of the report. The outline of the report is given in the
very beginning, then each subject is covered in detail. Notice also that the
person writing the report takes a look ahead and tells what the plans are
for the future.

Our poultry plant is constantly being improved and when finally completed, will be as modern, comfortable, and labor saving as we will be able to make it.

Improved practices that are now in use in this plant include:

    a) An adjacent, temperature-controlled egg room where all egg cleaning, grading, and packing occurs.
    b) Overhead gravity feed bins to eliminate carrying of feed. These bins are rodent proof and feed bags are no longer ruined by mice. Feed is merely tapped from a chute as desired.
    c) High pressure water floats to maintain a constant water level.
    d) Electric lights installed in all pens.

2. THE SWINE PROGRAM PROGRESSES

At this writing the stork was once again hovering over our swine farrowing pens. In fact this took on all the aspects of a mass formation of storks with two Berkshire and three Yorkshire sows preparing for familyhood about New Year's Day. This was not as scheduled, since we had hoped to breed for early spring litters in both breeds. However, our fence-jumping Yorkshire boar set up his own calendar of coming attractions and there's good news in the hog pen tonight.

Since the Berkshires were bred to a Yorkshire boar, we shall have two litters of Berk-York crosses. We had expected to effect this cross anyhow so our only hindrance will be the cold weather. These pigs will be weighed at birth and at intervals of several weeks thereafter. The gains will be compared to the rate of development of purebred litters from both parent breeds raised under similar circumstances. The results should be interesting to students and farmers, since there is much discussion in swine breeding circles at present regarding crosses of bacon and lard type hogs. . . .

We hope to increase the number of market hogs next year and also have some purebred stock for sale.

As we review our first year activities with swine we note many improvements that we might make. Among these are:

    a) Construction of a central farrowing house.
    b) Construction of concrete feed bases to prevent waste from self feeders and to keep feed clean.
    c) Feeding of legume hay to brood sows.

FIGURE 75. (*Continued*)

    d) Keeping the brood sows from becoming excessively
fat.

    e) Construction of larger and more substantial feeders
than those now in use.

3. HARVESTING THE CORN CROP

Unusually warm weather during October ripened out
our corn crop very nicely in spite of a very late start in
the spring. The very wet weather earlier in the summer
made weed control very difficult. Our cultivation
equipment was very poor too, so that some of our corn was
a lot weedier than it should have been. Accordingly our
total harvest was estimated at 3500 bushels instead of
5000 as we had estimated earlier in the season. . . .

4. REVAMPING THE DAIRY PROGRAM

With one row of stanchions installed, mangers built,
and all fixtures completed, we were ready to move our
dairy herd into the finished half and proceed with the
remainder of the construction work.

In the meantime, however, our dairy testing program
on the herd then in our stables was beginning to show
significant results. Entirely too many of our cows were
borderline and some did not even pay feed costs. As soon
as these production records and butterfat tests were
conclusive we started to sell the boarders. This procedure was an excellent demonstration by the students of
how many herds are still being kept in the country that
contain nonprofitable animals. . . .

5. CONSTRUCTION PROJECTS

The bridge to span Carpenters Run is our number one
construction problem. It was decided to build a wooden
cribbing and span the stream with either steel or wooden
beams. Work on approaches to the bridge was begun. . . .

As part of their shop training related to Poultry
Husbandry, the Sophomore group will construct two portable
brooder houses early in the spring. Each house will hold
four hundred day-old chicks. . . .

Construction expenses during the coming year should
be only a fraction of the first year's total.

6. ADVISORY COMMITTEE RECOMMENDATIONS

The annual fall meeting of the farm advisory committee met on the evening of December 12, in the superintendent's office. This committee, composed of four
outstanding farmers and other persons concerned with the

FIGURE 75. (*Continued*)

conduct of the project, met to advise on the actual managerial policies for the farm. Recommendations by this committee have proved valuable in the past and lend stability to the unseasoned judgment of your supervisor.

Here are some of the more important conclusions taken from the minutes of this meeting:

a) That we develop purebred herds of both Holstein and Guernsey cows rather than Guernsey alone. This was claimed to be a more profitable venture and would give our students firsthand experience in several breeds.

b) That we attempt to raise suitable acreages of alfalfa while eliminating our second year crop of timothy.

c) That we purchase a large tricycle-type tractor and cultivators in order to provide for a larger corn acreage. Cultivation equipment has been our weak link as mentioned elsewhere.

d) That we continue and expand our experimental program in conjunction with Pennsylvania State University.

7. PLANS FOR THE NEW YEAR

So ends the first full year of operation for the Henry G. Block Vocational Farm. Although much remains to be done to remodel this huge estate into a practical farming operation, we can gain satisfaction at least in noting that the farm is producing products at an increasing rate. Our physical plant has taken shape and the pattern of progress has been set.

On the farm proper the purebred livestock program will grow into greater prominence as our foundation stock begins to multiply. We hope to increase our swine program to about 75 head. The dairy program should receive reenforcements as income from the present herd provides the means for purchasing more stock.

Our poultry plant can be maintained at its present rate and if income warrants, another double loft set of pens should be constructed in the western part of Unit I barn. This is advisable from a management point of view. Expansion should continue until this barn has been completely remodeled into a poultry plant of most modern design. . . .

In the field-cropping plans, we shall cooperate fully with Pennsylvania State University in promoting experiments with corn and small grains. These plots have been of great value to students and farmers of the area in

FIGURE 75. (*Continued*)

selecting adapted varieties and adopting suitable cultural practices. . . .

We also expect to whip some of our better drained fields in shape for the growing of about ten acres of alfalfa next year. The second year a timothy crop on most fields will be eliminated.

One large field will be strip-cropped during the year. This is in line with our conservation program and in light of our erosion problem, strip-cropping is just plain good sense.

The present construction projects should be concluded early in the summer and all these new units will be put into immediate use.

Time does not permit going into farm plans in any more detail. The coming year is one of great promise and we hope to consolidate our gains and improve our program to the very best of our ability. Come and see us sometime. Bring your overalls.

James P. Bressler

FIGURE 75. (*Continued*)

Applying Your Knowledge

PROBLEMS:

1. Make an inspection of one of your school shops, or of the condition of some organization, and write an informal report similar to the letter shown in Figure 73.

2. After reading carefully the report by Colonel Lindbergh, write an informal report on some experience that you have had, such as a camping trip, doing an interesting job, an accident that you witnessed, a trip through a manufacturing plant, or a trip to a federal or state agricultural experiment station.

3. Assume that you are working on a job which is not yet finished. Your instructor wants a short report telling him what progress you are making with it, what you have completed, what you still need to do, when you expect to have it completed, etc.

Chapter 34

THE INFORMATION REPORT

The information report usually presents material gathered by the writer. Such material can be secured from: (1) books or magazines on the subject, (2) personal observation or experience, and (3) experiments.

The making of a careful plan or outline of what the report is to cover or include is the first step in the writing of a good report. In other words you should first determine exactly how much territory should be covered, how much material should be secured, and then develop an outline showing this.

Suppose, for example, that you want to make a report on storage batteries used in automobiles. Before you can proceed to gather information, you must determine just what type of storage battery you want to investigate and exactly what you want to find out about it. It is entirely possible to write a book on storage batteries; but since you do not wish to do that and you do not have the time, you must limit the information that you desire to secure. Notice how the following outline confines such a report to the construction and the chemical action of a lead-acid storage battery.

Outline for a Report on
The Lead-Acid Automobile Storage Battery

1. General description of a lead-acid storage battery.
2. Construction of the battery.
3. Chemical action in a lead-acid battery.

This short outline, you see, gives you three items only to investigate. It limits the amount of information that you must secure as well as the length of your report. Since this method can be used in reporting upon almost any subject, study the following complete report and pattern your reports after it.

R E P O R T   O N

THE LEAD-ACID AUTOMOBILE STORAGE BATTERY

by

ERNEST BRADBURY

Automotive Department

Allentown Technical Institute

January 5, 19—

FIGURE 76. Title Page. The title page contains the title of the report, the name of the person making the report, and the date. Other items of information such as the name of the company, the city, etc., can be added when advisable.

C O N T E N T S

FIGURE 77. Table of Contents. The table of contents follows the title page. It is actually an outline of the report, containing page references so that the reader can easily find any main topic in the report. This table of contents shows that the report is divided into four main parts, and that the second main part is subdivided into five smaller sections.

Room 205
Technical Institute
Allentown, Pennsylvania
January 5, 19__

Mr. W. A. Whitaker
English Instructor
Technical Institute
Allentown, Pennsylvania

Dear Mr. Whitaker:

For my semester report I have investigated and made
a report on the lead-acid automobile storage battery. The
report covers the construction and theory of operation of
the lead-acid, pasted-plate type of storage battery.

The material presented in the report was secured
through reading various books and manuals on storage
batteries and through personal observation in our
Automotive Department.

Very truly yours,

Ernest Bradbury
Ernest Bradbury

FIGURE 78. Letter of Transmittal. The letter of transmittal follows the
table of contents and precedes the actual report. It serves as a sort of introduction and gives the reason for the report, information as to what the report
includes, and the method of securing the information.

1

THE LEAD-ACID AUTOMOBILE STORAGE BATTERY

General
Description

The storage battery is a reservoir
for electrical energy. It is in the battery that the electrical energy from the
generator is stored while the engine is
running, or when the battery is being re-
charged in a service station.

The battery consists of a series of
hard-rubber jars, each jar containing a
number of lead plates immersed in a solution of sulphuric acid and distilled
water. This solution is known as the
electrolyte.

The plates of the battery consist of
lead grids, and chemically active materials are usually pressed into the
gridwork of the plates. In each cell the
plates are divided into two groups. The
one group or the positive plates are connected to the positive terminal, and the
other group or the negative plates are
connected to the negative terminal. The
plates and the electrolyte contain the
materials which because of electro-
chemical action produce an electric current under certain conditions.

Plates

The type of plate in general use is
known as the Faure or pasted plate. A

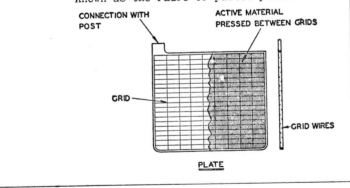

CONNECTION WITH
POST

ACTIVE MATERIAL
PRESSED BETWEEN GRIDS

GRID

GRID WIRES

PLATE

FIGURE 79. The Report Proper. Page 1 of the body of the report illustrates
one method of arranging a report such as this. Notice the subject headings
in the left margin.

2

pasted plate consists of a flat framework
or grid of lead-antimony alloy. The
active materials are pressed into this
framework in the form of a paste. The
framework of the grid holds the paste
firmly in place.

<u>Positive</u>   The positive plates are filled with a
<u>Plates</u>   paste of red lead or litharge.

<u>Negative</u>   The negative grids are filled with a
<u>Plates</u>   paste of spongy lead.

<u>Wooden</u>   The plates are generally separated
<u>Separators</u> from each other by thin sheets of wood
about the thickness of wood veneer. These
sheets of wood, known as separators or
insulators, are porous and consequently
permit electrolytic conduction, but prevent metallic conduction. Metallic conduction would short-circuit the cell. The
wooden separators are corrugated or heav-
ily grooved on one side and smooth on
the other.

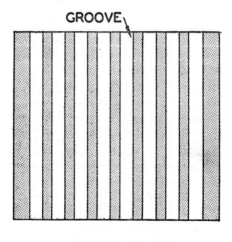

GROOVE

WOOD   SEPARATORS

FIGURE 79. (*Continued*)

3

The smooth side of wood separator is always placed next to the negative plate and the corrugated side, to the positive plate. Although the wood separators can be made from other woods, they are usually made from cedar.

Before being made into separators, the wood must be treated to remove foreign substances and acetic acid or other chemical substances. It is this treatment which makes the wood so porous and permits the electrolytic conduction by means of the electrolyte between the plates.

Rubber
Separators   Rubber separators are sometimes placed between the ribbed side of the wood separator and the positive plate. At other times the rubber separators are used alone. The hard-rubber separators are perforated with many very small holes which are usually threaded with a fine cotton thread.

Electrolyte   The electrolyte consists of distilled water (H_2O) and sulphuric acid (H_2SO_4). The solution is in the proportion of about 4 parts water to 1 part sulphuric acid.

When a battery is functioning properly, the amount of charge in it determines with a reasonable degree of accuracy the density or specific gravity of the electrolyte. The following figures will show the change in relative weight of the electrolyte as the battery is charged or discharged:

Density of water........... 1
Density of sulphuric acid... 1.84
Density of electrolyte
    fully charged..... 1.28 − 1.3 (70°F.)
Density of electrolyte
    fully discharged.......... 1.15

The figures for density given here will vary about .001 to every 3 degrees

FIGURE 79. (*Continued*)

4

of change in temperature of the electrolyte. The specific gravity of the electrolyte refers to the number of times it
is heavier than an equal volume of water.

Since acid is heavier than water,
the weight of the electrolyte increases
as the amount of acid it contains increases. As the battery is charged, the
amount of acid in the electrolyte increases because of the chemical reactions. As the battery is discharged, the
amount of acid the electrolyte contains
decreases.

Because of these changes, the condition of the battery can be measured by
determining the weight (specific gravity)
of the electrolyte with the hydrometer.
The float of this type of hydrometer is
so made that it will float in a liquid
heavier than water. The heavier the
electrolyte the higher the float of the
hydrometer will float. A graduated scale
encased in the glass tube of the hydrometer indicates the specific gravity
(weight) of the liquid.

Cell & Plate   Automobile storage batteries are
Arrangement   either 6 to 8 volts or 12 to 16 volts.
The cells may be arranged in a number of
different ways. The Society of Automo-

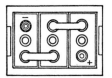 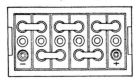

6 VOLT SIDE TO SIDE   12 VOLT SIDE TO SIDE

CELL ARRANGEMENT

tive Engineers recommends the arrangement shown in this report. Each cell
has a voltage of about 2.2 when fully
charged; consequently, it takes three
cells for the 6-volt battery and six

FIGURE 79. (*Continued*)

5

cells for the 12-volt battery. The
cells are so placed that the positive
pole of one cell is opposite the negative pole of the next cell.

Chemical   Actually a storage battery does not
Action   store or accumulate current. While the
               battery is being charged, the current
               flows in at the positive pole, passes

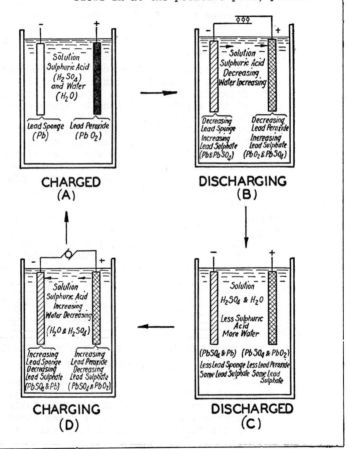

FIGURE 79. (Continued)

6

through the cells, and flows out at the
negative pole or terminal.

No electric current is left in the
battery, but as the current flows
through the electrolyte in the battery,
it produces a chemical change in the
active material of the plates. If an
electrical conductor is provided from
the positive to the negative pole after
the charging is completed, the chemical
processes set up in the plates will
begin to go in the opposite direction
(reverse themselves) and produce an
electric current in the battery. This
current, which is actually produced
within the battery, flows out the positive pole and in at the negative pole.
In other words, while the battery is
being charged, the current enters the
battery at the positive terminal; but
when the battery is being discharged,
the current also leaves the battery at
the positive pole.

The place the current leaves the
battery is always called the cathode;
the place it enters, the anode. Thus,
the positive pole during charging is the
anode, the negative pole the cathode.
While discharging through use, the
positive terminal becomes the cathode
and the negative terminal the anode.

FIGURE 79. (*Continued*)

A P P E N D I X

References

Dyke, A. L., *Dyke's* Automobile *and* Gasoline Engine
Encyclopedia, pp. 537-542, The Goodheart Wilcox
Company, Inc., Chicago.

Wright, J. C., and Smith, Fred S., *Automotive Construction*
and Operation, pp. 258-280, John Wiley & Sons, New York.

Crouse, William H., *Automotive Mechanics*, Second Edition,
pp. 198-216, McGraw-Hill Book Co., New York.

Crouse, William H., *Automotive* Electrical Equipment,
Second Edition, pp. 29-48, McGraw-Hill Book Co.,
New York.

Jaffe, Bernard, *New* World *of* Chemistry, pp. 479-480,
Silver Burdett Co., New York.

FIGURE 80. The Last Page of the Report. The books listed here were used as references for the information presented in the report.

Applying Your Knowledge

HELPFUL QUESTIONS:

1. From what sources can you secure information for a report on subjects in your trade or on other subjects in which you are interested?

2. What is the first step in the making of a report? Why is this first step essential?

3. List the different parts of a formal information report. Explain the function of each part.

4. Why is it a good plan to place the topics of the different parts of the report in the left margin?

5. Why should reference books used in securing material for the report be included as a part of the report?

PROBLEM:

With the help of your instructor select a scientific or technical subject in which you are interested and about which you would like to make a report. Make a short, definite outline on the subject, and using the outline as a guide develop a complete and carefully written report on the subject.

If this report is used as a semester project, you should do the best work possible. Use your knowledge of drafting to illustrate your report with appropriate drawings or sketches.

REPORTING ON YOUR COMMUNITY:

A good citizen should know his community. The methods used in writing technical reports can also be used in developing reports on social, economic, or community problems. The methods and the format used in the information reports are exactly the same methods which you can use in investigating and reporting on community problems.

It is suggested that each student select a phase of community life or a community problem and develop a report on it. All the reports could then be put together into a comprehensive report on the community.

The following are some of the phases of community life that can be investigated and reported: Geographical Location, Homes, Education, Recreation, Manufacturing, Employment, History, Government, Community Problems.

SUGGESTED TOPICS FOR REPORTS:

The following list of topics is merely suggestive. Some of the topics suggested are rather general and need to be made more definite.

Air and Water Pollution
Air Conditioning Small Homes
Atomic Energy
Atomic Pile
Automobile Lighting, Ignition, Braking Systems, Streamlining, etc.
Civil Air Regulations
Common Woodworking Joints
Construction of an Airplane Engine
Diesel Engine
Different Kinds of Paper and Their Uses
Electric Eye
Electric Refrigeration
Feeding Dairy Cattle
Fluorescent Lamp
Generators, A.C. or D.C.

Growing Fruit Trees
How To Estimate the Cost of a Job
Judging Poultry for Production
Management of Farm Soils
Manufacture of Aluminum
Manufacture of Glue
Mixing Colors
Offset Printing
Papermaking
Radio
Rural Electrification
Soil Conservation
Stereotyping
Telegraph
Telephone
Television
Tool Grinding
Varnish

Chapter 35

REPORTING AN ACCIDENT

At one time or another many of us either meet with an accident or witness one. After we have been connected with an accident in some way, we usually wonder exactly how everything happened. Since no two persons see exactly the same thing even when standing in the same place and watching the same event, stories as to the causes of an accident practically never agree in all details.

It is important that you learn to analyze an accident and to remember the important details as accurately as possible. If you ever drive an automobile, you may need to write or to give a report of an accident either to the police or to an insurance company, or to serve as a witness. As a workman you may at some time be asked how a fellow workman was injured; or as a foreman, you will find that very few days will pass without your having to write a report of an accident in which one of your men was involved.

Most companies regard accurate accident reports as very important because compensation cases are frequently decided on the basis of such reports. Accident reports are also used to secure information in the prevention of future accidents. When an accident occurs, follow these suggestions:

1. Secure first aid immediately.
2. Determine exactly how the accident happened and what caused it.
3. Report the accident to the proper person immediately.
4. See that a written report is made properly.
   a) Your failure to report the accident immediately and to have a written report made of it may at some time prevent you from securing compensation that is rightfully yours.

363

ACCIDENT REPORT
MOTOR VEHICLE Immediately after an accident fill out this blank and send to:

Claim Department

THE TRAVELERS INSURANCE COMPANY
THE TRAVELERS INDEMNITY COMPANY

COLONIAL TRUST BUILDING, READING 13, PA.

Give details as fully as possible, but do not delay report. If extremely serious, telephone or telegraph.

POLICYHOLDER

NAME								POLICY NUMBER
HOME ADDRESS (No. and Street)	(City or Town)	(State)	HOME PHONE NO.	BUSINESS ADDRESS (No. and Street)	(City or Town)	(State)	BUS. PHONE NO.
NAME OF AGENT				ADDRESS OF AGENT
MAKE OF AUTOMOBILE		MFR'S SERIAL NO.		MOTOR NO.		STATE LICENSE PLATE NO.
NAME OF DRIVER					AGE OF DRIVER
HOME ADDRESS			HOME PHONE NO.	BUSINESS ADDRESS		BUS. PHONE NO.
NAME OF OWNER

TIME AND PLACE OF ACCIDENT

| DATE OF ACCIDENT | HOUR OF ACCIDENT | WHERE DID ACCIDENT HAPPEN? (Street or highway) | (Town) | (State) |

PERSONS INJURED

| NAMES | ADDRESSES |

NATURE AND EXTENT OF INJURIES

| IF MEDICAL AID WAS RENDERED, GIVE NAME OF DOCTOR | WHERE WAS INJURED TAKEN? |

DAMAGE TO PROPERTY OF OTHERS

KIND OF PROPERTY AND DESCRIPTION OF DAMAGE

| IF AUTOMOBILE, MAKE OF CAR | STATE LICENSE PLATE NO. | ESTIMATED COST OF REPAIRS |
| NAME OF OWNER | | ADDRESS |

DAMAGE TO VEHICLE OF POLICYHOLDER

EXTENT OF DAMAGE TO YOUR AUTOMOBILE

| Does The Travelers insure you for Collision (damage to your car)? ☐ YES ☐ NO | WHERE MAY AUTOMOBILE BE INSPECTED? | WHEN? |
| NAME OF PARTY WHO CAUSED DAMAGE | ADDRESS | IS HE INSURED? | NAME OF COMPANY (if known) |

IMPORTANT! NAMES AND ADDRESSES OF WITNESSES

Be particular to secure the names and addresses of disinterested witnesses, bystanders, or persons in the immediate vicinity who may have seen the accident or heard any statement made by the person damaged.

NAME	ADDRESS
NAME	ADDRESS
NAME	ADDRESS

Over—Be Sure to Give Information Called for on the Other Side of this Report

C-5461 Rev. 6-50 PRINTED IN U.S.A.

FIGURE 81a. Automobile Accident Report.

(continued)

DESCRIPTION OF ACCIDENT

WEATHER AT TIME OF ACCIDENT	CONDITION OF ROAD AT PLACE OF ACCIDENT	DIRECTION YOUR VEHICLE WAS GOING	WHAT SIDE OF ST.?

RATE OF SPEED (Insured's vehicle) (Other vehicle)	IF OBJECT COLLIDED WITH WAS MOVING, IN WHAT DIRECTION WAS IT GOING?

DID POLICE MAKE REPORT OF THIS ACCIDENT?

☐ YES   ☐ NO

NAMES AND ADDRESSES OF PERSONS IN POLICYHOLDER'S VEHICLE	NAMES AND ADDRESSES OF PERSONS IN OTHER VEHICLE
(1)	(1) (Driver)
(2)	(2)
(3)	(3)
(4)	(4)
(5)	(5)

DRIVER'S STATEMENT OF HOW ACCIDENT OCCURRED

SIGNATURE OF DRIVER

SHOW HOW ACCIDENT OCCURRED BY USING ONE OF THESE DIAGRAMS:

DATE	SIGNATURE (Policyholder)

IMPORTANT!

When this report is completed at agent's office, the information called for below should be entered to facilitate processing of the claim.

POLICY NUMBER	POLICY PERIOD

CHECK COVERAGES

☐ BODILY INJURY   ☐ MEDICAL PAYM'TS.   ☐ PROPERTY DAMAGE   ☐ COLLISION $_____ DED.   ☐ COMPREHENSIVE

BRANCH OFFICE WRITING POLICY	SIGNATURE (Agent)	DATE

FIGURE 81b. Reverse Side of Automobile Accident Report.

On November 15, at about 8 to 8:15 P.M. I was driving my car, accompanied by my brother, Harold A. Robinson, of Newark, N. J., age 40 years, in the front seat with me, my brother's wife, Margaret E. Robinson, age 38, who was riding in the left rear seat, and my wife, Sarah A. Robinson, age 42, riding in the right rear seat.

We were returning from a trip to Coatesville, Pa., where I had taken my brother and sister to visit some of their friends. I was driving about 35-40 miles an hour with my headlights turned high. The pavement was concrete. To my recollection it was dry at the time near the scene of the accident. The weather was cloudy. The pavement was two-strip width, upgrade, and comparatively straight right up to the scene of the accident. The grade was probably five or six percent. I was driving north on the highway between Dauphin, Pennsylvania, and Clarks Ferry Bridge. There were no cars coming and none immediately ahead of mine. I was driving on my right half of the road when suddenly I saw a truck about 75 feet ahead which appeared to be east of northeast and facing northeast, blocking entirely my half of the road. I swerved to the left, but believe that I had time to apply my foot brakes very little. I saw no lights on the truck before the collision. Because I was knocked unconscious for a few minutes and because of the shock, I do not remember whether the truck had any lights lit on it after the collision nor what part of my car came in contact with the truck. I believe that the truck was either standing still or drifting slowly backwards because of the grade. The right front corner of my car was pushed in towards the left front corner. The other car was a Dodge with a stake body loaded with apples and owned by Samuel C. Griffith of Milton, Pennsylvania, R. D. 2, license number ER403.

Mrs. Samuel Robinson received cuts and bruises of the body and a fractured right leg which was broken in two places below the knee. Her husband, Samuel Robinson, received a dislocated and fractured right hip and severe cuts about the face. They were taken to the Harrisburg Hospital by an unknown passing motorist where they are still confined.

I have been operating cars since 1930 and have had no other accidents.

The above statement is a true and correct statement to the best of my knowledge and belief.

Witness   Signed

James C. Hill   *Carl B. Robinson*

FIGURE 82. Driver's Report.

How To Fill Out an Accident Report Blank

1. Type the report if possible. If that is not possible, print the answers to the questions on the blank.

2. Draw a diagram to help make your explanation of the accident clearer. This applies to all types of accidents.

3. Write all information on a piece of paper if no accident report blank is available at the time of the accident.

4. Make definite and accurate statements.

Permissible	*Better*
"...about 5 o'clock"	"...5:05 o'clock"
"...about 16 feet"	"...16 feet 6 inches"

5. Make all statements short, clear, and to the point. Short statements are usually clearer and more accurate than long statements.

6. Recopy your statements if you have time. This procedure tends to eliminate mistakes, helps you make a better report, and gives you an extra copy of the report for filing.

7. If you can suggest anything which would help prevent similar accidents, add it to the report or write it on a separate sheet. Suggestions and steps aimed at preventing accidents must help

a) make the person accident free, or

b) make the physical conditions surrounding the job safe.

After the printed form given on pages 364 and 365 has been filled out and sent to the company, the insurance adjuster will sometimes have you and every other person connected with the accident either write or dictate a statement concerning it. The statement on page 366 was made by the driver of an automobile which figured in an accident. The names of the individuals, the license numbers of the cars, and the names of the towns have been altered.

File No................................

FOREMAN'S ACCIDENT REPORT

Department or shop--

When did accident happen? Date--------------19---Time-----$\begin{smallmatrix} A.M. \\ P.M. \end{smallmatrix}$

Did injured employee stop work?-----Date--------19---Time-----$\begin{smallmatrix} A.M. \\ P.M. \end{smallmatrix}$

Name of injured employee----------------------Check number-------

How long employed?----------------------Occupation---------------

Was he doing his regular work?------If not, what was he doing?-------

Had you instructed him regarding hazards of his job?----------------

If not, who had?--------------------------When?------------------

What is the apparent nature of his injuries?-----------------------

Where did accident occur?---

What machine, tool, or appliance was involved?----------------------

Power or hand driven?---

Was it guarded?----------------Can it be guarded?------------------

Was accident due to defective condition of property, floors, stairs, etc.?--

----

Describe---

Describe how accident occurred-------------------------------------

----

Did you see the accident?--------Who else saw it?-------------------

1. ----------------------------- 2. -----------------------------
   (Name)   (Check No.)   (Name)   (Check No.)

3. ----------------------------- 4. -----------------------------
   (Name)   (Check No.)   (Name)   (Check No.)

What will you do to prevent a recurrence of this accident?-----------

----

When? ---

Date----------------19--- Signed by-------------------------------
                                        (Foreman)

FIGURE 83. Form Used by Foreman to Report an Accident.

Applying Your Knowledge

HELPFUL QUESTIONS:

1. Of what practical value is the ability to make an accurate report of an accident?

2. Are accident reports usually oral or written? Why?

3. Do you think the average person can better explain how an accident happened from a sketch or with a written description? Should only one method or both methods be used at the same time?

4. What items of information should you secure in order to make a correct report of an automobile accident? A study of the forms given earlier in the chapter will help you.

5. What information should you secure to make an accurate report of an accident that occurs where you work or in a factory or other place of business?

PROBLEMS:

1. Several members of the class should study and make a report to the class on the compensation laws in your state. While these boys are giving their reports, take notes on the important information they have secured. Place the notes you take in your notebook.

2. Secure an accident report blank or make up one of your own with the help of the examples in this chapter. Write up a report of some accident in your shop. Be sure that you get the details and the exact cause of the accident.

3. Assume that you are out on the highway and that an accident has just occurred. Write the information that you would need to make a complete accident report.

4. Secure a form used to report automobile accidents and with the information you accumulated in Problem 3, fill out this blank. Did you have enough information from Problem 3 to fill out the blank properly? Make a list of the things you missed so that you will remember them.

5. If you are studying aviation mechanics get from your aviation instructor or from the Air Safety Board of the Civil Aero-

nautics Board a copy of the correct form for reporting accidents involving private aircraft. Fill out properly the form for an accident with which you may be familiar or on which you can secure some information.

6. Write a report on a shop or laboratory accident with which you are familiar. Do not use a printed form. Develop the report in either paragraph or outline form. After you explain what happened, be sure to analyze why it happened.

7. Develop a short speech or paper on Accidents and Accident Prevention.

Chapter 36

MAKING AN INSPECTION REPORT

One of the most frequently used reports is based on inspection. Employees may make such reports to their superiors or to customers without consciously realizing that they are actually making a report of an inspection that has been made. For example, an auto mechanic examines an automobile engine for a customer to determine what repairs are advisable, what the condition of the motor is, whether the pistons need to be replaced, and so on. Later he makes a report to the owner informing him of what was found during the inspection of the motor. Electricians, plumbers, technicians, engineers, and other types of workers make such reports every day.

How To Make a Report of an Inspection

If no printed form is provided or other method required, you will find the following suggestions practical and helpful:

1. Arrange the report in some form of outline.
2. Place the main headings in the left margin.
3. List the findings in a series of short sentences rather than in paragraphs.
4. Make definite statements.
5. Base all statements on facts.
6. Make any recommendations after stating the facts.

Before you start out on a shop inspection, plan your trip. Determine your route through the plant and make a list of those things for which you want to look.

September 28, 19—

REPORT ON

THE

WEEKLY CLEANLINESS AND SAFETY INSPECTION

The Safety Committee appointed to examine the plant weekly during the month of September made its last inspection for the month on September 28. The following report summarizes the findings and the recommendations and gives the ratings awarded the different departments.

The committee urges the foremen to remedy as soon as possible the various situations mentioned in this report as objectionable.

5th Floor Waterproof Dept. – Good

1. Soft drink bottles on table.
2. Curtains pulled down and lights turned on unnecessarily.
3. Pink shoe stick tags all over the floor.
4. Some scrap rubber on the floor.

Recommendations: The Safety Committee recommends that waste containers be placed at more frequent intervals about the department, and that each group of workmen be held responsible for waste found on the floor in their section of the department.

Cafeteria – Good

Fitting Department – Fair

1. Rolling machine dirty.
2. Rubber cement spilled on floor around new bowser.
3. Milk bottle in sink.
4. Wood thrown in paper can instead of being taken to wood pile.
5. Old trays stored behind paper bags.

FIGURE 84. Report Made by the Safety Committee of a Large Rubber Shoe all unsatisfactory conditions, and gave each department a rating.

2.

Recommendations: The Committee urges that the foreman hold each individual operator responsible for the cleanliness of his machine. The old trays hidden behind the paper bags are an accident hazard which should be removed. If the trays are no longer needed they should be placed in storage.

3rd Floor Waterproof — Good

1. A soft drink bottle in northeast corner.
2. A broken window.

Last Room — Poor

1. Broken window.
2. Dirty aisle littered with lasts.
3. Apron on fire bucket.

Recommendations: The Committee recommends that the men working in this department keep the aisles as clean as possible. A dirty aisle such as was found during this inspection is too hazardous from the point of workers falling and injuring themselves. Nothing whatever should be placed on the fire buckets at any time.

Upper Cutting — Good

Mill Room — Good

Stitching Room — Good

Carpenter Shop — Good

1. Material stored under bridge is poorly piled.

Machine Shop — Fair

1. Untidy condition in general.

Respectfully submitted,

SAFETY COMMITTEE

J. A. Mahaffey

D. J. Brewster

E. I. Smith

Manufacturing Plant. The committee made weekly inspections, reported

TROUBLE REPORT

PENNSYLVANIA WATER & POWER CO.

File No. __209-TH-52__

Date __3-3-—__

Hydro Sta._____Steam Sta._____Substation_____Circuit_____Property_____

Apparatus: #3 Lub. Oil Pump
Worthington Turbine
2½" No. 3115

Nature of Trouble: **Middle** guide bearing runs **hot.**

Reported by __H. Stokes__
Assigned to __C. E. Boettger__
Date _____3-3-—_____
Charge No. __HH-91.77__

Instructions: Issued by ____A. Z. Shaub____

Dismantle the bearing, and make a careful investigation as to the cause of bearing failure.

Check and do the following:
1. Check oil leaks
2. Inspect oil ring to determine if anything would prevent it from revolving
3. Scrape the bearing if it is not too badly damaged
4. Polish the shaft
5. Reassemble the bearing and run the pump for test

Detailed report and complete data for Machinery Record:

Before we started to inspect and repair the bearing, we checked the oil level and found the bearing with sufficient oil. When we drained the oil from the bearing, it was dark in color. To remove the bearing it was necessary to move the motor and pull one half of the coupling from the pump shaft as this is a sleeve bearing. The damage to bearing was directly in the center or where the oil ring is located. The bearing was not damaged to the extent that it has to be rebabbitted. The bearing was scraped, oil grooves cleaned, and the bearing journal polished. The oil ring was in good condition. The bearing and motor were reassembled and the pump returned to service. After five hours of running in normal operation, we declared it satisfactory.

It is difficult to say exactly why the bearing ran hot. It may have been caused by some dirt getting through the oil ring inspection hole or the oil may have been low. Out of reach of the oil ring, no leaks were detected.

C. E. Boettger

Repairs completed by C. R. Stokes Date 3-3-—— Man hrs. 25
Inspector/s/ A. Z. Shaub

Entered in Machinery Record?——————————Noted————————————

FIGURE 85. The Type of Report Required by a Large Power Company at One of Its Hydroelectric Plants When an Inspection Is Made or any Maintenance Work Is Done.

ALLENTOWN HIGH SCHOOL ELECTRICAL SHOP
TECHNICAL INSPECTION REPORT

Subject: Lighting in the A. H. S. Cabinet Shop Finishing Room.

Object: To check the present illumination intensity and distribution in the A. H. S. Cabinet Shop Finishing Room and recommend any changes to improve this illumination.

Recommendation: It is recommended that the present four incandescent fixtures be replaced with four, three-lamp, 40 watt white, Industrial Type Fluorescent fixtures similar to the two now there. See Exhibits A and B.

This change will bring the light intensity from the present 22.8 foot-candles (within the incandescent area) to 36 foot-candles with considerably improved light distribution.

Twenty to fifty foot-candles is recommended for work of the sort being done in this room.

Substantiating Data: The data used in the calculations follow:

Room size	22' x 24'
Room height	13'
Mounting height	8'
Area per unit	88 sq. ft.
Ceiling and wall color	Gray to Buff
Room index	E
Reflection factor	50-50
Coefficient of utilization	.62
Maintenance factor	.75

Method: Present layout was made from measurements taken on the job site.

All illumination calculations were made through the "Lumens Method" equation as follows:

$$\text{Ft. C.} = \frac{\text{Lamp Lumens x Coef. of x Maintenance}}{\text{Utilization Factor}}{\text{Area per Unit}}$$

Technical factors were taken from technical information tabulated in Croft's American Electrician's Handbook.

Submitted by

Girard Brown
Ronald Stahley
Eugene Brokloff

December 11, 19__

PRESENT ILLUMINATION LAYOUT

A. H. S. CABINET SHOP FINISHING ROOM

22.8 FOOT-CANDLES (AVG.)

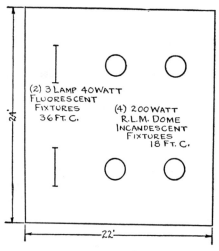

(2) 3 LAMP 40 WATT
FLUORESCENT
FIXTURES
36 FT. C.

(4) 200 WATT
R.L.M. DOME
INCANDESCENT
FIXTURES
18 FT. C.

24'

22'

Exhibit A

RECOMMENDED ILLUMINATION LAYOUT

A. H. S. CABINET SHOP FINISHING ROOM

36.4 FOOT-CANDLES

MOUNTING HEIGHT 8'

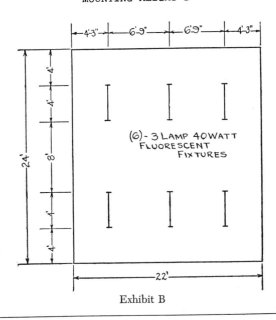

Exhibit B

FIGURE 86. This Is an Example of a Report Made by Three Students in an Electrical Course. The report was made following an inspection of a finishing room. Notice that the recommendation here is made at the beginning with supporting data given later.

Applying Your Knowledge

PROBLEMS:

1. Make a list of the situations in your trade or business where you may be able to use inspection reports.

2. Make a safety and cleanliness inspection of your school shop. Write a report of your findings and recommendations.

3. Examine very carefully some machine or piece of work related to your trade or occupation and make a report on the results of your inspection.

a) An automotive student can make a safety inspection of an automobile. Such an inspection should cover:

(1) Brakes

(2) Steering

(3) Lights

(4) Miscellaneous

(*a*) Horn

(*b*) Mirror

(*c*) Wiper

(*d*) Tires

Before proceeding with the inspection, the student should list all items to be checked under the above headings.

b) A cabinet-maker can inspect a piece of furniture such as a bureau and make a report on how well it is constructed.

c) An electrician can examine a wiring job to determine how well it has been done.

d) Students in other fields will secure problems for inspection reports from the instructor.

4. Make an inspection of some project or job that is not yet completed, but on which some one is still working. Make a report on the progress being made on the different parts of the job and on the quality of workmanship.

Chapter 37

REPORTING TRIPS

Frequently the industrial executive visits manufacturing plants other than the one in which he works in order to find out how other manufacturing concerns do things and to get new ideas which he might use in his own factory. When an executive makes such a trip, he is usually required to write a report of the trip for his fellow executives. In these reports he includes any worth-while information and makes suggestions to improve conditions in his own plant.

Many teachers arrange class trips to industrial plants, construction projects, and other places of interest. The value of these trips naturally depends upon the way they are conducted and the information the students acquire.

When you visit an industrial plant, you should try to learn something definite, something that will give you additional trade knowledge and help you to understand industrial processes better. In order to do this, you should make a list of definite questions to which you would like to find the answers while making the visit. For example, as a drafting student you might make a list containing some of the following questions before you visited a manufacturing plant:

A Suggested List of Questions for a Drafting Student Who Is Going To Take a Class Trip Through a Factory

1. What system is there in the drafting room for preventing errors getting into the shop?

2. How is the drafting department organized? (Be able to make a simple organization chart of it.)

3. At what job does a beginning draftsman start, and what are the successive steps of promotion?

4. What hours do the men work, and what wages do they receive?

5. How do the draftsmen make a pencil tracing so that a good blueprint can be secured from it?

6. What are some of the standard procedures used?

7. What are some of the machining processes in the shops?

8. What jigs and fixtures are in use on the various machines?

The kind of questions you would list for a visit depends largely upon the occupation you are studying; for example, an auto mechanic visiting an up-to-date garage might look for such things as the following:

A Suggested List of Questions for an Automotive Student When Visiting a Garage

1. In what condition do the mechanics keep their tools and tool kits?

2. What safe methods of working are in use? (For example, do the mechanics block up a car in the proper way?)

3. What is the general appearance of the garage and of the mechanics who meet the customers?

4. How is the garage laid out? Where are the different machines located? Where are the different kinds of repair work done?

5. What are some of the methods used in doing repair work?

Of course, many more questions can be listed; they will depend upon the particular department or operations in which the student is interested during that particular trip.

In general, it is best to use some plan similar to the following when making a class trip:

1. Secure from your instructor or prepare for your use a list of things that you should observe.

2. Make notes during the trip or immediately after it.

3. Ask your guide questions while you are going through the plant. You will learn more by asking a few questions than by any other device.

4. Place at the beginning of your report the things of general interest and in the second half the things pertaining to your trade.

Students in the Arthur Hill Trade School, Saginaw, Michigan, have used the following outline in writing reports of plant visits:

Outline for Written Report of Industrial Trip

I. Introduction
   A. General Information
      1. Number of students and teacher in charge
      2. Time of visit; and place of factory visited
   B. Purpose
      1. To gain some knowledge as to the kinds of work being done in the various departments of the factory visited
      2. To gain practical shop knowledge by observation of shop processes and methods

II. Description
   A. Department No. 1
      1. Describe items or shop processes of most interest
   B. Department No. 2
   C. Department No. 3

III. Conclusions
   A. Most interesting features
   B. Value of the trip

The next report was written by a junior in the Arthur Hill Trade School. Notice how the student followed the preceding outline in writing this report.

An Industrial Trip to Baker Perkins, Inc.*

A group of students of the Arthur Hill Trade School drafting classes visited the Baker Perkins plant on the afternoon of Friday, May 10. There were thirty-two students in charge of Mr. Radford, instructor of the drafting classes.

* By Raymond Kawiecki. In Stanley S. Radford, *Industrial Arts & Vocational Education Magazine*, The Bruce Publishing Co.

The purpose of the trip was to gain knowledge as to the kinds of work being done in the various departments of the factory, and also to gain practical knowledge by observation of shop processes and methods.

At the plant, the group was divided into three smaller groups, each under the direction of a guide.

The first building visited consisted of the following departments: patternmaking, engraving, confectionery machinery, gas-oven equipment, and stockroom.

Patternmaking

The pattern shop is well lighted and well ventilated. We observed a number of workmen making core boxes and patterns for the foundry, and also a number of machines in operation. A special sanding machine in which the spindle traveled up and down and also rotated was called to our attention.

Engraving

The engraving room is adjacent to the patternmaking room. We observed a workman carefully tracing a letter on a master plate, while a needle following his exact movements engraved the letter on a brass roll. This roll was to be used to make impressions on cookies.

Confectionery Machinery

In this department, machines for mixing candy are assembled. There are also machines for forming candy into different shapes.

Gas-Oven Equipment

Large gas ovens for baking bread are assembled in this department. Workmen were welding a number of small tubular burners on a long pipe. Each burner unit is . . .

Foundry

The second building visited housed the foundry department. Friday, at the foundry, was pouring day, and we observed the pouring of a number of small and large molds. The large molds are poured from a huge ladle carried by an overhead crane. Two men, one on each side of the ladle, did the pouring. The smaller molds were poured from small ladles carried by the men.

In the core department we observed a large number of cores on shelves ready to be baked. The baking, which is done in a large oven at 450 degrees Fahrenheit, takes from two to three hours depending upon the size of the core.

The centers of the large cores are filled with either coke or cinders. This is done for several reasons, namely:

1. Filling the center of the core with cinders saves molding sand.

2. Less gas collects and it is easier to remove the gas when casting, as the core is more porous.

3. The core is more compressible, allowing it to crush and take care of the shrinkage of the iron when cooling.

4. The core bakes quicker and lessens the chance of cracking, which often occurs when a solid core is baked for a long period. . . .

The third building visited consisted of the following departments: machine shop, drafting, tracing, blueprinting, and filing.

Machine Shop

Castings from the foundry are machined in the machine shop. We observed . . .

Applying Your Knowledge

HELPFUL QUESTIONS:

1. Why is it important that you plan your trip before you take it?

2. Explain how you would prepare for a trip to a factory. What definite steps would you take?

3. While you are going through the factory, should you ask the guide any questions?

4. Should you wait until you have had a class discussion about the trip before you write any notes on your observations?

PROBLEMS:

1. Assume that you are to take a trip through a place of business or an industrial plant in which your trade is carried on. Prepare a list of questions or items on which you wish to secure information during the trip. These questions should be concerned with things of interest in your trade.

May 28, 19—

A REPORT ON

A TRIP THROUGH THE KENT COMPANY

PHILADELPHIA, PENNSYLVANIA

I. Buildings and Construction

    A. All buildings are one story high, making possible
easy transportation of materials by either conveyers or trucks. Relocation of machinery in such
a building is also easily accomplished by using
motor trucks.

    B. Lighting - All buildings have sawtooth roof con-
struction with skylights facing the southwest.
This construction affords excellent daylight
illumination and also provides for proper
ventilation.

    C. Heating - It was very interesting to note that
practically all heating was accomplished by unit
heaters which not only provided good direct radiation but also served as a means of ventilation.

    D. Machine Layout — A large number of men were em-
ployed in the maintenance department in the
locating and the setting up of machinery and equipment. In order to facilitate the locating of
equipment, a layout man marks the location on the
floor in a frame. This not only speeds up the
actual work of installation, but it also allows
executives to see the actual floor plan layout.

II. Processes

    A. Conveyers - Conveyers made by Webb, Matthews, and
Lamson are used extensively throughout the plant.
None of the conveyers were of particularly novel
design or construction, being used principally for
conveying material to and through groups of
operators on the assembly line. Running on slider
boards were belts of stitched waxed canvas, which
gives the best results.

FIGURE 87. A Report by an Engineer After a Trip Through an Industrial
he has selected only those items which would be of interest or which might

2.

1. There was one conveyer of interest which was used for handling transformers as various operations were completed during their building. This conveyer consisted of two angle-iron tracks on which cams traveled, turning the clip holding the transformers in the proper position for each operation. This idea has possibilities for positioning the last holding devices on makers' teams.

2. Speed Reducers: Reeves' speed reducers were used extensively as a means of varying conveyer speeds and pacing work to operators.

Respectfully submitted,

Ralph W. Gross

Ralph W. Gross
Plant Engineer

Plant. Note that he has not written a general account of his visit. Instead, have some application in the plant in which he works.

May 9, 19—

A REPORT ON

A TRIP THROUGH THE WEST BRANCH MANUFACTURING COMPANY

SAN FRANCISCO, CALIFORNIA

Standard Instruction Boards

In the mechanical department each machine was equipped with a standard instruction board and a blueprint specification book. The standard was made of pipe and was about 4 feet high and 1½ feet wide. Hanging from the top of the standard was an instruction board. A blueprint, telling the workman how to operate the machine properly and at what speeds to run it when using various tools, was fastened to the instruction board. The blueprint was covered with shellac to protect it from grease and dirt.

Tool Racks on Machines

Each machine was fitted with a tool rack. This rack was so constructed that all tools had to be taken from the rack in proper sequence and placed back in the rack in the same way. All tools were symbolized and delivered to a tool crib where they were stored by symbol numbers on racks constructed from adjustable steel shelving. All dies and drills were kept in individual boxes to protect them from breakage.

Calender Rolls

The mechanical department makes all of its equipment except motors and highly specialized drives. The foreman of the department stated that the calender rolls which his department produced were just as good and just as cheap as the D_____ roll which we buy.

FIGURE 88. Another Report by an Engineer.

Slatted Belts

Slatted belts constructed of wood sticks 8 feet long, 1 inch wide, and ½ inch thick are driven by roller-bearing chains. The slats are fastened about 4 inches apart on chains so that the air can circulate on the under side of the stock. This device may be applicable to our outsole stock or other stocks requiring cooling or drying. The belt runs in an angle iron frame.

Ball and Jewel Grinder

This is a grinding machine which might be used for grinding rags. The stock is fed into the machine from a hopper located above the machine. The grinding device is similar to that on a Banbury mixer except that it is built on a smaller scale. Mr. Kime will write for details and sizes of machines.

Wire Trimmers

The West Branch Company uses wire trimmers on all their calenders. This seems like a very simple way of trimming stock. Very fine wire is used and is located along the burlap allowing no edges whatever.

Respectfully submitted,

George A. Pepperman

George A. Pepperman
Industrial Engineering Dept.

FIGURE 88. (*Continued*)

2. Assume that you are to take a trip through a factory or business establishment that has very little or nothing to do with your field. Prepare a list of items or questions on which you would find it worth while to secure information. Would this list be more general or more definite than the list which is chiefly concerned with things in your trade?

3. Tell the class about a visit that you have made to some place of interest. Give in your talk only the items that describe the place you visited. Do not bother telling how you reached the place, how you returned, or little things that happened, because the class is especially interested in what you saw after you arrived there.

4. Sometime during this semester or at a time designated by your instructor, make a written report on a visit that you have made to some industrial plant. This report should be made as soon as possible after you make the visit.

5. Agricultural students can make reports on visits to agricultural experiment stations, dairies, markets, livestock farms, county fairs, etc.

Chapter 38

SOLVING PROBLEMS

The Problem-Solution Report *

A problem-solution report presents facts which are necessary to the solution of a problem and a discussion of those facts in order to suggest a way out of the difficulty. The problem-solution report is one of the most valuable and helpful types of reports that you will study. This is true because problems are constantly arising in every business no matter how large or small it may be.

Even though you never write a single report after leaving school, the ability to secure facts, to organize them, to study them, and then to make some decision of your own will prove valuable to you.

Study the examples of problem-solution reports on the following pages, then carefully develop one or more reports of your own under the direction of your instructor or from the problems given in this chapter. All the problems and examples given here are typical and actual cases.

Not long ago a young man, about twenty-six years old and a graduate of a technical school, was confronted with the following problem. Read the problem that he had to solve, and then see how he proceeded to find a solution to his difficulty.

William Carson's Problem: Whether or Not To Buy a Small Printing Business

William Carson had been out of school about seven years. In school he had taken the Printing Course. After leaving school, he worked for two years in a printing plant in his

* These reports are commonly called recommendation reports.

home town. Work became slack and he was laid off. After this he secured a job in a small printing plant in another city. He had worked at this small plant for about four years when he learned that the owner wanted to sell it. Bill wanted to buy the business, but he had not saved enough money to make the initial payment. His father-in-law, realizing that it is easier to lose money in business than it is to make it, wanted to know more about the situation before lending Bill any money.

What would you do in a situation of this kind? Let us see just what Bill did.

What Bill Did

1. First, Bill made a list of things that he wanted to know about the business and about his chances of running the plant successfully. He listed these items, worded in the form of questions.

2. Bill next tried to find the answers to these questions he asked himself. To do this he investigated thoroughly the business of the shop, the books the owner had kept, he talked to other business men about the future prospects of the community in which the shop was located, he made an inventory of the equipment in the shop and tried to determine its value, etc.

3. After securing all possible information, Bill used this information to write a complete report concerning the business and the advisability of buying it.

4. Finally, Bill used the report to convince his father-in-law that this particular printing plant was worth buying and that he also knew something about the problems involved in buying a business.

Read every word of Bill's work because you may have a similar business problem to decide some day.

Bill's list of questions to which he wanted answers:

1. If I should buy the business how many of the old and regular customers will continue to bring their business to me? How many will I lose?

2. Can I get enough new business to make up for the business that I might lose through old customers leaving?

3. Will the other printing plants in the neighborhood help or hurt this business?

4. Do the other shops in the neighborhood cut prices or do they charge reasonable prices so that it will be possible for me to earn a fair wage and to make a legitimate profit?

5. Will this neighborhood remain a good location for a printing plant?

6. Do I have enough experience to run the business successfully?

7. What is the lowest price the owner will accept?

8. How much equipment is considered a part of the shop and how much is it worth on the market; that is, for how much could I buy the same equipment from a secondhand printing machinery dealer?

9. If business continues much as it is at present, how long will it take me to pay for the plant?

A REPORT

on

THE ADVISABILITY OF PURCHASING

THE HARRISON PRESS

in

LANSING, MICHIGAN

By

WILLIAM CARSON

October 1, 19—

FIGURE 89. Title Page. The title page of the report that Bill wrote to assemble his facts after he had secured all the information possible about the business. Read Bill's report carefully. You may need to do the same thing some day.

A REPORT

on

THE ADVISABILITY OF PURCHASING

THE HARRISON PRESS

in

LANSING, MICHIGAN

I. Description of the Problem

A. For the last one and one-half years I have been
working at the Harrison Press, a small printing
plant in Lansing, Michigan. This business and the
shop equipment is now for sale for $9500. Since
I have been working here, I have learned to know
most of the customers and I have gained in all-
round knowledge of the business. However, the
problem is whether or not the business is desirable
and whether it is a good investment.

This report presents briefly the facts that I have
been able to secure about the business, and the
decision reached after a study of these facts.

II. The General Situation

A. In order to discuss in a business-like way the
items that determine whether or not it would be
advisable to purchase the Harrison Press, I have
listed the questions that one might ask before
buying such a shop. Immediately after each
question is the answer to that particular
question.

1. Where is the business located?

a. The Harrison Press is located at 531 Sixth
Street, Lansing, Michigan.
b. The shop occupies a one-story concrete
block building, 35 by 50 feet.

FIGURE 90. Bill's Report.

II. The General Situation

    A. Facts pertaining to the situation.

        2. How large is the business?

            a. The Harrison Press is practically a one-man business; that is, one man can conduct it with a helper.

            b. The gross amount of business averages about $250 a week.

        3. How many of the present customers would continue to bring their work to me as the owner of the shop?

            a. I have become well acquainted with all the regular customers with whom I have dealt directly. Because of this, I believe that nine out of every ten customers would continue to bring their work to me.

        4. Can enough new business be secured to make up for any business that might be lost by customers leaving?

            a. This, of course, remains to be seen. Since I have been dealing personally with most of the present customers, I have acquired some valuable experience in selling printing which should help considerably.

            b. I am quite well known in my church and lodge. These contacts should help me secure additional business.

        5. Will the presence of other printing plants nearby hurt this business?

            a. The six printing plants located within a radius of five blocks of the Sixth Street Press tend to attract printing customers to this section of the city; therefore, the presence of several other shops seems to help business.

FIGURE 90. (*Continued*)

II. The General Situation

  A. Facts pertaining to the situation.

    6. Do the other shops located nearby cut prices?

      a. Probably only one of the plants indulges in price cutting. In general the rest of the shops ask a reasonable price for their work

    7. Will this particular community remain a good location for a printing plant?

      a. The older business men with whom I have talked believe that this particular neighborhood will continue to be a small business district.

    8. Do I have enough experience to run the business?

      a. This can be answered partly from answers to preceding questions. My present employer seems to believe that I can do it. At any rate, because of the poor health of the proprietor, I have been running this shop without his help for almost two months.

    9. What is the lowest price the owner will accept?

      a. $9,500.

      b. He will accept $5000 cash and judgment notes against the business for the balance.

    10. Is the plant worth the price asked?

      a. In the opinion of several printers and a representative of R. R. Hartnett & Company, dealers in printing machinery, the plant is worth the price asked.

    11. What equipment is condsidered a part of the plant and for how much could it be duplicated?

      a. A condensed inventory of the equipment is attached to this report.

      b. It would cost about $14,000 to duplicate the plant with used machinery that has been rebuilt.

FIGURE 90. (*Continued*)

II. The General Situation

  A. Facts pertaining to the situation.

    12. Is the business sound from a financial point
      of view so that the buyer could pay for it
      within a reasonable length of time?

      a. The following figures present a fairly
        accurate picture of the financial side of
        the business during the last twelve months:

Wages	$ 2,400
Taxes	500
Depreciation & maintenance	1,000
Materials as paper, ink, etc.	2,905
Overhead—power, insurance, bad accounts, etc.	449
Total cost of operation	$ 7,254
Gross receipts	$13,000
Cost of operation	7,254
Balance	$ 5,746

      b. A careful study of the above figures indi-
        cates that the buyer of this business might
        expect to pay off the indebtedness on the
        plant within a reasonable period of time.

III. Conclusion:

  A. The business seems to be a good investment at the
  price asked.

FIGURE 90. (*Continued*)

Suggested Directions for Writing Problem-Solution Reports

1. Write out a statement of the problem.
2. Make a list of the items you want to find out.
3. Secure the necessary facts and information with which to answer the list of things you want to know.
4. Make up a balance sheet to help determine what recommendation you wish to make.
5. Write the report. Keep the report as short as possible and follow some sort of outline.
6. Reduce all facts to money wherever possible; that is, tell how much it would cost, how much money would be saved, etc. In other words, if a new method will save five hours of work each day on the part of a man who receives $1.50 an hour, then it will save $7.50 a day. If the man works 200 days a year, the company will save 200 × $7.50 or $1500 a year.

The Problem-Solution Report in Industry

The next example of a problem-solution report is presented here for advanced students. It illustrates the type of report used in the industrial engineering departments of a plant manufacturing a nationally advertised product.

Notice that the entire report is in outline form. This is done to keep the report as brief and as clear as possible. Like many others, this company also requires that all savings in time or materials be expressed in terms of money.

Reports are often numbered to make indexing easier. Notice the number on the title page of the following one.

REPORT No. 137

THE CONSTRUCTION

of

A COVERED GRAVITY CHUTE

on

THE WEST SIDE OF THE UPPER WAREHOUSE

By

JOHN C. CAMP

November 27, 19—

FIGURE 91. Title Page. This is the title page of an actual report written by an employee in the industrial engineering office of a large manufacturing concern.

November 27, 19—

REPORT No. 137

THE CONSTRUCTION
of
A COVERED GRAVITY CHUTE
on
THE WEST SIDE OF THE UPPER WAREHOUSE

I. Description of the Problem

  A. Present Method of Shipping

    1. A five-man crew is used for shipping from
    the Upper Warehouse. The division of labor
    among the crew is as follows:

      a. 1 man - numbers the cases to be shipped.
      b. 1 " - pulls the cases from the piles.
      c. 1 " - stencils the address of the cus-
             tomer, etc., on the cases and hauls
             them to the first floor.
      d. 2 men - haul the cases from the elevator
             on the first floor to the freight car
             and load the freight car.

  B. Proposed Method of Shipping

    1. Erect a covered chute on the west side of the
    warehouse. Instead of trucking the cases to
    the freight car, place the cases on the chute
    and allow them to slide by gravity right into
    the car which is being loaded. This method
    requires a four-man crew for the same length
    of time as a five-men crew is now needed. The
    division of labor among the crew is as follows:

      a. 1 man - numbers the cases to be shipped.
      b. 1 " - pulls the cases from the piles and
             places them on a truck.

FIGURE 92. Body of the Report. Notice that the report is written in outline form and that all explanations are as brief and as clear as possible.

2

    c. 1 man - stencils the cases, hauls them to a
           window, and places them on chute.
    d. 1 " - stands at the end of the chute in
           the freight car, takes the cases off
           the end of the chute, and piles
           them in the car.

II. Comments

  A. Advantages of the Proposed Method

    1. Permits all shipments to be made on schedule.
      a. At the present time shipments are often
         delayed because the cases cannot be trucked
         through the yard in inclement weather.

    2. The men will be better protected from the
      weather.
      a. It will no longer be necessary for two men to
         go back and forth from a warm building to
         the cold weather outdoors.

  B. Disadvantages of the Proposed Method

    1. Unless reasonable care is exercised by the
      shipping crew there may be some danger of the
      corners of the shipping cases being crushed
      when they are sent down the chute.

III. Comparison of Shipping Costs for the Two Methods

  A. Labor Cost per Carload

    1. Present Method-Loading time
      5 men 22.5 hrs. @ $1.25 $28.12
    2. Proposed Method-Loading time
      4 men 18 hrs. @ $1.25   22.50

      Difference in Cost per Carload $ 5.62

FIGURE 93. Page 2 of the Report. In writing any report it is important
that you state the advantages and the disadvantages of the situation. In
other words, it is necessary that you consider both sides of the question.

IV. Cost of Chute
  A. Labor $128.00
  B. Materials   113.50

         Total $241.50

V. Savings
  A. Savings in labor and shipping cost per
     carload $ 5.62
  B. 43 carloads of shoes must be shipped
     to pay for the chute. This will require
     approximately three months.
  C. Net savings for the first year at the
     present rate of shipping, about $685.80
     (annual estimate 165 cars)

VI. Recommendation
  If the management plans to continue the use of the
  upper warehouse as at present, it is recommended that
  a chute be constructed on the west side of the
  warehouse in such a way that cases placed on it from
  windows on the second and third floors will slide
  directly into the car being loaded.

APPROVED   FM   WRG   CLH   DJG

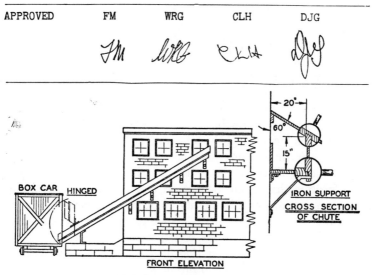

FRONT ELEVATION

LAYOUT OF COVERED GRAVITY CHUTE

FIGURE 94. Page 3 of the Report. Whenever possible, savings should be stated in terms of money as above. In this particular company the executives would sign their initials at the end of the report to indicate approval.

Applying Your Knowledge

Under the supervision of your instructor select a problem, find
a solution, and develop a problem-solution report on it.

You might develop such a report on the location of a small business, or on a problem in the operation of one of your school shops
or laboratories.

SOME SUGGESTED PROBLEMS:

The problems given here are merely suggestions. They are,
however, typical problems that many men both young and old
have had to solve. If you prefer, develop your own problem or
take a problem which some friend of yours has had to solve,
investigate it thoroughly, and make a report upon it.

1. *A Problem for the Machinist.* Investigate and report on the
advisability of opening a machine shop in some section of the
city in which you live.

2. *A Problem for the Welder.* In any city there are usually
very few shops that make a specialty of welding. If you are interested in welding, you might find it worth your time and effort to
investigate the advisability of opening a welding shop somewhere. Perhaps a shop employing oxyacetylene might be easier
to establish than one doing electric welding.

3. *A Problem in Garage Location.* Bill Smith is an auto mechanic. He has been unable to find work, and to help him out
a relative has agreed to help him start or buy a service station.
Bill, however, must assure his relative that there is enough business available to make the investment reasonably safe. Select
some location that would be a good place for a service station.
Make a report on the advisability of placing a service station at
this point. In your report include such things as population and
number of automobiles, traffic, a proposed layout, etc.

4. *A Problem in the Operation of a Small Business.* Assume
that you are operating a small business of some type with which
you are familiar and that you already have certain machines and
equipment in your shop. There is another machine which you
need to meet competition. Make out a report showing whether

it would be advisable for you to purchase the machine that you have in mind. Be sure to state the situation clearly before proceeding with the report.

5. Assume that your school either does not have a team in one of the minor sports such as tennis, or that there is not enough interest in it. Develop a report on a problem of this kind to indicate a solution, the cost, etc.

6. You cannot learn certain processes or perform certain important experiments because of lack of equipment in your school laboratory. Show the problem, the need for such instruction, the cost, etc., in your report.

INDEX